Introducing Christianity

Also by James C. Howell from Westminster John Knox Press

The Beatitudes for Today
The Will of God: Answering the Hard Questions

Introducing Christianity
Exploring the Bible, Faith, and Life

James C. Howell

WESTMINSTER
JOHN KNOX PRESS
LOUISVILLE · KENTUCKY

Originally published as *Exploring Christianity: The Bible, Faith, and Life*
Harrisburg, PA: Trinity Press International, 2001

1st edition
Published by Westminster John Knox Press
Louisville, Kentucky

09 10 11 12 13 14 15 16 17 18—10 9 8 7 6 5 4 3 2 1

Book design by Drew Stevens
Cover design by designpointinc.com
Cover illustration:© iStockphoto.com

Library of Congress Cataloging-in-Publication Data

Howell, James C.
    Introducing Christianity : exploring the Bible, faith, and life / James C. Howell.
        p. cm.
    Includes index.
    ISBN 978-0-664-23297-9 (alk. paper)
    1. Christianity. I. Title.

BR121.3.H69 2009
230—dc22

2009001914

Contents

Introduction

This book began as a class I offered, called "Christianity 101." I pitched it as "Most of what you might remember if you went to seminary or got a Masters degree in religion." I was stunned when more than 500 registered, and excerpts appeared weekly in *The Charlotte Observer*. Church members, college students, and even unchurched people came, and have come to sessions I have led over the years since—which tells me that both inside and outside the Church, people are hungry to know about God, to know about the Bible, and to explore things spiritual. Yet they also crave a faith that is intellectually substantial, not just frivolous, a faith that is not superficial or merely presumed, but weighed thoroughly, shaken, and fully owned in real life.

SPIRITUAL PEOPLE

Once upon a time, religious people made a lot of assumptions that nowadays we would regard as embarrassingly naive. It was assumed that the average person in Western civilization was a Christian, that Christianity was this self-evident body of truth with which people were familiar, that questions were out of order. But if those days ever truly existed, they are long gone, never to return—which is not to say that people are no longer interested in God. On the contrary: we are keenly interested in God and in the spiritual life, and we would like to learn more, to experience in a real way what the life of faith is all about. We need more, deep inside. Merely to have a pulse and function in the world of business and play cannot begin to satisfy us. But what exactly is this yearning we always feel for *more?*

Polls suggest that 98 percent of Americans believe in God. But aren't a lot of them fudging a bit? Shouldn't there be a gray box, between "Yes I believe" and "No I don't," indicating "Well yes, but deep inside, on some dark nights, I kind of wonder." Or we believe in God, but we struggle to find meaningful connections between traditional Christianity and our own personal sense of who God is. Perhaps we aren't all that clear on what Christianity is all about in the first place. We may have napped through Sunday school. There's a Bible someplace in the house, gathering dust. Perhaps we have walked in and out of various churches with differing angles on faith, and we feel a bit perplexed, or we have decided that theology is only a matter of personal opinion. The Internet, television, and shifting demographics have exposed us to women and men of other faiths. And then, if we manage to get a tidy theological system constructed, some surprise, some tragedy, crashes down on top of what we thought we believed, and we are left standing in the ruins, dazed.

This book is an exploration of Christianity designed for thinking, questioning people, a simplified version of the curriculum, if you will. I think you will find three kinds of things in its pages. First, I'll make a case for the Bible without denying the messiness of its formation and transmission. And I'll weed through some of the craziness in the history of the Church to notice the good in what the church has taught and believed over two thousand years. Fortunately, we do not have to start from scratch to figure out what God is about. Although we may be puzzled by many things that are ancient or medieval, it still is a virtue that Christianity is something old, something we receive, something not all that private. There is a sadness, a tragedy, in reducing the things of God to nothing more than my opinions, my warm, fuzzy (or dark) pious feelings. How unlikely that one person's private ruminations are in fact the truth about anything rightly called God! And worse, how lonely! I don't want to believe by myself; I want to believe with others, in community.

There are some very basic things that have always been true for Christians. At times there are disagreements in interpretation, but they are not as monstrous as we imagine. John Wesley suggested that we "keep close to the grand scriptural doctrines."

> There are many doctrines of a less essential nature, with regard to which even sincere children of God (such is the present weakness of human understanding) are and have been divided for many ages. In these we may think and let think; we may "agree to disagree." But, meantime, let us hold fast the essentials of "the faith which was once delivered unto the saints" . . . strongly insisted on, at all times, and in all places.[1]

Second, we will explore material that is simply fascinating. Admittedly I will include stories and quotations and issues that I personally think are interesting, and I trust you will too. If the Bible, or life in the

Church, or theology has ever seemed boring to you, then either you haven't been paying attention, or somebody else is hiding the full story from you. We will look at people and conversations and books and great turning points in history. Some of the story is funny. Some is shocking. Some will move you to tears.

Third, we will explore some very hard questions about God, faith, the Bible, the Church. God knows we have good questions. Could Hindus and Buddhists and Muslims all be wrong for all these centuries? We pick up on rumblings about archaeological excavations and scrolls unearthed and research undertaken that calls into question those seemingly obvious truths in the Bible. We've really wondered all along about Adam and Eve, an ark, walking on water, the blind suddenly given sight, not to mention an empty tomb.

THE QUESTION ASKED

Questions unaddressed lead to cynicism. We are a cynical people. We are cynical about our culture, about our institutions, and certainly about Christianity. In the name of God, preachers have bilked noncynical believers out of hard-earned money. Christians have gone to war in God's name, slaughtering foreigners. Christians line up on issues like homosexuality or abortion and spew venom at one another. The Church has majored in triviality and minored in irrelevance. Many churches are nothing more than nice places for nice people to do nice things with other nice people. Religious leaders let themselves be used by politicians. Despite its rhetoric, the Church is our most segregated institution. Hypocrites are perched on every pew. No wonder we're cynical about religion.

Our great hope rests in thinking through our questions, and this book wrestles with quite a few. Meaning unfurls itself, not merely in the answer that is given, but in the question asked, at least in the drama of our lives. We are eager to explore any and every kind of knowledge that bears on the religious life. Sadly, in our culture, we often segregate faith from knowledge, as if knowledge is anti-faith, as if faith deals with those zones that are irrational or merely mysterious. But faith and knowledge are like sisters. The title of Jean LeClercq's book on medieval monasticism, *The Love of Learning and the Desire for God,* captures what has traditionally been a single endeavor for God's people searching for meaning.

As Christians, we need fear nothing that is true. In fact, we welcome, we pursue truth wherever it may be found, knowing that God is truth, and that truth sets us free. I take personal comfort in one of Simone Weil's shrewd thoughts from her autobiography. She ironically suggests that "one can never wrestle enough with God if one does so out of pure regard for the truth."

> Christ likes us to prefer truth to him because, before being Christ, he is truth. If one turns aside from him to go toward the truth, one will not go far before falling into his arms.[2]

Theologians should be, above all people, finally and utterly humble. If we see our subject at all, we see through a glass darkly. To talk of God most assuredly tangles us up in logical inconsistencies. And instead of rallying with Churchill's bon mot, "I would rather be right than consistent," we admit that we are attempting the impossible, to talk of God. If we think we are able to do so with great accuracy we fool no one. Once we reflect on our inability to understand God with masterful comprehension, or to speak of God with crystal clarity, we notice in our inability a curious testimony to the greatness and wonder of God. If God is God, we would expect to be puzzled, awestruck, mystified, and then dizzied with delight; we brush the mere hem of God's garment, and yet the garment is splendid enough. Certainties are there, yet we always test those with questions, and knowledge from every quarter.

ILLUSION AND REALITY

Hard questions—challenging what we really mean by faith, who Jesus really was, and what reality is all about—can be threatening. But like an athlete shedding a few pounds and mastering some moves, the theological thinker must let sweet theological illusions be swept aside and arrive at a harder-won but more substantial belief that is honest, profound, and certainly humble. As we listen in on what the great spiritual masters have taught and prayed and done, we sense that our bland, tame version of Christianity must be chopped up like firewood, as we hope for some spark to set us on fire. For in Christianity there is no thinking or learning for merely intellectual purposes. We learn and know so we might understand and believe, and thereby find our lives irrevocably altered. Christianity isn't a head game, and it isn't just a "feeling." Jesus did not come so that we could *feel* different, but so that we could *be* different.

This business of "being different" is my primary interest here. Like a lot of people, I had a spotty upbringing when it came to church. Generally the Christianity I heard about was a curious blend of the harsh and judgmental with the emotional, and it just turned me off. A faith vital and yet intellectually coherent seemed impossible. My education was in science, and then philosophy. I have had and continue to have constant questions and doubts about the Bible, about God, about the Church, about the life of faith. But now I know that questions and doubts are not the twin pillars at the shrine of atheism and evil, but rather are the path more and more people cannot help but take if they are to move toward or be found by God. As a minister, I spend time daily with people who are cynical about things religious, and as counsel I sometimes refer to these wise words from Mark Helprin: "All great discoveries are products as much of doubt as of certainty, and the two in opposition clear the air for marvelous accidents."[3] I want to share my certainty, some marvelous accidents that I see.

We need a marvel or two in our titillating but hollow world. Imagine you are among those sailors of mythological times, laboring hard in rough seas, drifting off course. In the wind you hear seductive songs, those sirens luring you and your mates on, yet you suspect the destination is nothing but shipwreck. But then there is one on board, Orpheus, who picks up his lyre and begins playing a tune, a sweet melody, one so beautiful that you no longer notice the sirens. And you follow that song, and manage to row to safety.

The Church forgets the beauty of its song. Fearing the incursions of the culture, preachers and theologians assert dogmatic truths, such as "The Bible is the Word of God!" However true, such declarations fall on deaf ears, and the ship continues to list toward the rocks of destruction. I believe that if we really listen to the song, to what Christianity is about, and if we deal with our questions, and continue to listen, we will be enthralled by the song and not be lured away from God. We can live and even thrive.

WHERE WE'RE GOING

So this book is an introduction, an exploration of Christianity. Perhaps the material is new to you, and you have never thought a lot about the

Bible and theology and life. Perhaps all this is familiar, but I think the approach and the questions raised will keep it fresh. We will ask three basic questions: What is the Bible about? What is Christianity about? What is the Christian life about?

When we think about the Bible, we will ask how we go at reading the Bible and what we may expect to find and what we will never find. We'll see what the Old Testament has to say and try to make some sense out of all those commandments, sacrifices, kings, and wars. Then we'll turn to what the New Testament can tell us, probing closely into the identity and significance of Jesus. When we consider what Christianity is about, we will look at the history of the Church, its triumphs, its foibles; we will study how theologians over twenty centuries have reasoned out our beliefs; and then we will attempt a basic sketch of what Christians believe. When we explore the Christian life, we will survey how faith is put into practice; we will dare to analyze the unique places we stand on moral, ethical issues; and we will paint a picture of what life is like in community, together in the Church and world with other people.

And at the end, we will talk about "the end," our future, God's future. Perhaps the most significant accomplishment of Christianity throughout its history is its persistent lifting up of a substantial hope to people who previously believed there was no hope. Frederick Buechner put it beautifully: "Hope is the driving power and outermost edge of faith. Hope stands up to its knees in the past, and keeps its eyes on the future."[4]

PART I

The Bible

1

Scripture

Scrolls in Old Jars

The Bible is the swaddling clothes and manger in which Christ is laid.
—Martin Luther

One day, back in 1947, a young bedouin shepherd named Jum'a Muhammad Khalil was passing the time by tossing stones into cave openings in the cliff. One stone, cast into the dark, made a surprising clattering sound. Climbing into the cave, he and a friend found several old clay jars. Inside those crusty, reddish pottery jars were stunningly preserved rolls of parchment that we now know as the celebrated Dead Sea Scrolls. More jars were found, more scrolls unfurled, one a full manuscript of the book of Isaiah that is on display now in a museum in Jerusalem. With some imagination you can picture the young man Jesus opening just such a scroll to read in the synagogue of Nazareth. Another scroll turned out to be the Psalms, which must have functioned like a hymnal or prayer book for the Jews who lived and prayed out in that desert. More jars, more scrolls: Genesis, 1 Samuel, Jeremiah.

WHAT IS THE BIBLE?

The Bible is like a bunch of scrolls rolled up and preserved in old jars. We are mistaken to conceive of the Bible as a fully finished book, bound in leather with goldleaf, dropped down out of heaven onto our coffee tables or into our pulpits. Before the Bible was a book, it was a little library of books, written over many centuries, copied, unrolled, stored, treasured, altered, improved, checked, stored, studied, memorized, kissed, lived.

The language is strange. The New Testament was written in Greek, a kind of Greek so old that scholars who can read the Bible in Greek struggle with road signs and menus in Athens. The Old Testament, like those Dead Sea Scrolls, was written in Hebrew, a language that to us seems backwards, reading right to left, with the front of the book at the back, which turns out to be the real front. Reading it may persuade us that we are living our lives backwards, that we should do things differently.

The books in that library are not all alike. Some are big, some little. Some are dramatic, some dull. Some tell stories, some repeat ancient rules. Some bear sweeping narratives, some collect poetry and songs. Too many Christians handle the Bible as if it were a Ouija board, or an answer book, chock-full of orders and commands from on high. But as you read the Bible, you find stories: earthy, humorous, even bizarre. There are love poems and plenty of songs; there are pithy little sayings and some longer sermons. We see people trying to figure God out and struggling to get along with their neighbors. God didn't dictate every word or drop it down from a cloud. The process was more elusive, and more real. The results are imperfect, yet more than good enough. The pictures, colors, and shapes of the Bible, if we look carefully enough, are the greatest images we have in our exploration of God.

Somehow it all comes together in something like a great mural. Up close, you see various details. At a distance, you see the big picture, and what is portrayed is an alluring adventure, life in the world with God. This is why it is misleading to zoom in or hang very much on a single verse. The Bible wasn't written a verse at a time; no one slivered off segmented verses until modern times. To look at a single verse is akin to thinking a single brush stroke is a painting, when that stroke is merely one of thousands deftly arranged in the artist's genius for a grander total effect.

CORRECTIVE LENSES

Let us shift the image a little. Many theologians have thought of the Bible as a good pair of corrective lenses. We have this astigmatism, spiritually speaking, and the Bible corrects our vision, focusing our eyes. The Bible, then, is not something we look *at*. The Bible is something we look *through*.[1]

Or we might think of it like this: the Bible portrays a different paradigm for how to view reality. When Nicolaus Copernicus first suggested that the earth was not located at the center of the universe, critics scoffed. But he had done a lot of looking up—at the stars, the planets, the moon—and he had figured out the earth was circling the sun. Once other watchers began looking at the skies from that perspective, more of what they saw made sense. Previously unexplained phenomena now fit neatly into the Copernican scheme.

Perhaps the Bible is like this discovery of Copernicus. Some people did a lot of looking up, or looking within. They contemplated what they had seen and heard in such depth that they began to understand the underlying order of things. And they couldn't keep it to themselves. They wrote it down, so we too could look up, and look within, and understand a deeper dimension of reality than is obvious to our normal senses. Previously unexplained phenomena in our lives now make sense as part of God's larger purpose.

So we sit up and take note of what the Bible is up to. Erich Auerbach compared the Bible and its mission with other classics in literature and noticed the Bible's tyrannical claim to truth: "Far from seeking, like Homer, merely to make us forget our own reality for a few hours, it seeks to overcome our reality: we are to fit our own life into its world, feel ourselves to be elements in its structure of universal history."[2] We may ask, "How is the Bible relevant to my world? How do I fit the Bible into my life?" But the Bible counters with a very different line of questioning: "How will you fit your life into the Bible? How can we make the world relevant to the one true world portrayed in the Bible?"

THE ORIGIN OF TRUTH

The very thought of this bold, almost arrogant claim is remarkable. We prefer to see ourselves as the adjudicators of truth. We decide for ourselves what is true, what matters. But we will never understand the Bible at all from this perspective. Truth is not something you figure out today for yourself. Truth precedes all of us, and claims us. Truth perseveres; it has some antiquity about it.

In our trendy, autonomous culture, such talk of truth may seem ridiculous. But as John Updike put it, "Laugh at ministers all you want, they have the words we need to hear, the ones the dead have spoken."[3] Laugh if you will, but we highly educated modern people may prove to be the real laughingstock. My grandparents could be perfectly described by these words from Allan Bloom:

My grandparents were ignorant people by our standards, and my grandfather held only lowly jobs. But their home was spiritually rich because all the things done in it . . . found their origin in the Bible's commandments, and their explanations in the Bible's stories. I do not believe that my generation, my cousins who have been educated in the American way, all of whom are M.D.s or Ph.D.s, have any comparable learning. When they talk about heaven and earth, the relations between men and women, parents and children, the human condition, I hear nothing but clichés, superficialities, the material of satire.[4]

Bible reading itself can be superficial. One egregious error is when we begin to think that the Bible is literally divine, as if it were somehow more than a book. We do not worship the Bible. In one of his heated controversies with some religious folks who waved their Bibles at him, Jesus said:

> You search the scriptures,
>   because you think that in them you have eternal life;
> But they bear witness to me;
>   yet you refuse to come to me that you may have life.
>   (John 5:39–40, au. trans.)

The Bible is not God, but tells us about God, or rather is the literary residue of people who knew God intimately. No better description of what we may expect to find in the Bible can be articulated than the introduction to one of its letters:

> We declare to you what was from the beginning, what we have heard, what we have seen with our eyes, what we have looked at and touched with our hands, concerning the word of life—this life was revealed, and we have seen it and testify to it, and declare to you the eternal life that was with the Father and was revealed to us—we declare to you what we have seen and heard so that you also may have fellowship with us; and truly our fellowship is with the Father and with his Son Jesus Christ. We are writing these things so that our joy may be complete.
>   (1 John 1:1–4)

If we poke around in those jars, unroll those scrolls, and explore the stories, poetry, prayers, and letters, we hear the plaintive voices of people mustering their best to tell what they had experienced of God. Their lives had been changed by God, and they wanted us to know about it, so that our lives too might be changed.

IMPERFECTION IN THE BIBLE

For this book, this collection of many books, to fulfill this function, must it be flawless? Again, this book was not etched in gold above the clouds, but began as stories passed on, by word of mouth, for centuries, and finally committed to parchment, copied, recopied—and we would be surprised if such a library were utterly consistent in every factual detail, if the memories of storytellers were photographic, if copyists and translators never erred. We would not mind, and a flawless book would certainly be interesting, unique among all books ever assembled. But perhaps in God's wisdom a human book is of greater usefulness than something superhuman. For we are human, and we understand our lives and God more clearly, more personally, more tangibly, through words and stories that are real, human, mundane, and even a little flawed, like ourselves. Jesus, after all, told us about God, embodied what God was about, by what he did with his body—a body that was not miraculously shielded from hunger or pain, a body not made of shimmering platinum, a body that no onlookers admired as perfect, a body capable of destruction. And it was precisely in his humanity that Christ revealed the purposes of God, whose Word to us is always hidden and simultaneously revealed in human words about God.

Karl Barth expresses this eloquently:

> The promise of this Word is this: Emmanuel, God with us who have brought ourselves, and continually bring ourselves again, into the dire straits of not being able to be with God. Holy Scripture is the word of people who yearned, waited and hoped for this Emmanuel, and who finally saw, heard and handled it in Jesus Christ. . . . And this grasping and accepting of the promise: Emmanuel with us sinners, in the words of the prophets and apostles, this is the faith of the church.[5]

Indeed, this was why Luther could call the Bible "the swaddling clothes and manger in which Christ is laid."

The Church has claimed that the Bible is "inspired." And so it is. But it is important to understand exactly what we mean by inspired. The Bible is not inspired in the sense that God whispered the text into a scribe's ear who wrote it all down before it could be somehow tainted by humanity. Rather, the Bible is inspired because people responded to God's grace and left a witness so that others might learn about this God. And God called this witness good. God providentially guided this process, in much the same way that God nurtures the entire created order, ensuring that it all finally serves God's own good ends. Generation after generation, for centuries, the Bible has led people back to God. It is uniquely through this witness that we may come to know God and have our lives changed. We have real, flesh-and-blood witnesses, whose lives were changed, and that is our hope, for we too are flesh and blood. If they were transformed, then we may be as well.

Now many worry about the admission that there may be even a single sentence in the entire Bible that is not factually correct. The fear is of the proverbial "slippery slope": if some statement in the Bible, however trivial it may seem, is construed as not historically exact, then we lose all trust in the Bible's most central declarations, such as the resurrection of Christ. But let us consider just one example. Luke is negotiating his way through the advent of Jesus and includes the detail that "this was . . . while Quirinius was governor of Syria." Herod clearly was the king, and we know from contemporary records that Herod died before Quirinius became governor. So do we throw out all of Scripture because of this error? Hardly.

One day I drove a couple of hours and took my father to lunch at a very fine restaurant. After the meal he asked why, and I replied "It's your seventieth birthday!" He chuckled and corrected me: it was only his sixty-ninth. A factual error! But did this mean I did not love my father, or that our relationship was bogus? If anything, the factual error became endearing. Love is like that. Absolutely nothing important depends on whether or not Quirinius was really the governor when Herod was king. Luke is writing a long lifetime later, with no Internet to research the matter, and the memories upon which he relied were off just a bit. Yet nothing in the substance of Christianity stands or falls on the matter. The error is itself endearing; God enters into the mortal stuff of our reality. But we need not conclude Jesus wasn't even born. Wasn't he born, even if Luke did not remember correctly whether Quirinius was governor then? Everything hinges upon the fact of birth, and no one could doubt that he was born. Did Jesus rise from the dead? We have no contemporary records to check, but clearly everything hinges on the truthfulness of the resurrection, and clearly all the biblical writers believed it. Indeed, they staked their lives on it.

TAKING THE BIBLE LITERALLY

Almost all factual confusion falls into the category of "Nothing of substance depends on it." Lots of other material in the Bible is clearly intended *not* to be taken as literally "factual." Jesus made up stories that were not "true." Rather, his stories were true in the way only a fictional story can be true. "A man had two sons." Jesus was not talking about a specific man with a name and address, whose sons had provable birth-dates. When the Bible says that God is a rock, the writer would be stunned if we asked how many tons this rock weighs.

When my daughters were young, I realized they could easily distinguish between historical fact and metaphor. One night I was reading aloud to them from C. S. Lewis's *The Lion, the Witch and the Wardrobe*—and I told them that Aslan, the wise lion, had died. Wasn't it sad? The next day, I told them that their great-grandmother Stevens died—and they fully understood we'd be attending a funeral because her death was something fundamentally different from the mythic death of Aslan. Why can't we read the Bible and grasp the vast gulf between "Jesus was tried and crucified by the Romans," something obviously intended as a factual report, and "Jonah (whose name means 'silly') was swallowed by a fish (of which there are none large enough in the vicinity), lived for three days in its belly, was vomited onto the shore, walked to Nineveh (the Assyrian capital), preached and converted the whole city (although by what the rest of the Bible, as well as Assyrian records, tells us, the Ninevites persisted in lopping off heads and worshiping their moon god)"?

But even when the Bible reports what actually happened with Jesus' trial and crucifixion, we bump into confusion. Jesus most certainly invaded the temple precincts one day and with physical zeal threw the money changers out. Matthew, Mark, and Luke place this dramatic event during the last week of Jesus' life, but John remarkably situates it at the very outset of Jesus' career. We will say more about Jesus research, and what Jesus really said and did, in chapter 3. For now all we can and must say is that the Bible can be messy, just as life is messy. The narrative of the Bible just eludes our need to get it all managed and ordered. If God wanted it to be all straight and non-messy, there would be only one Gospel, instead of four, and there would be a tidy fit between the Bible story and what we know from contemporary sources. But God did not intend it to be so easy. The presentation of the story is human, just as we are human, just as Jesus was human. And how thankful we may be that God is revealed to us flawed people through such a book.

This view of inspiration is "functional" more than "ontological." To say that the Bible is inspired does not mean it has some strange property, intrinsic to its pattern of ink on the page. Rather, its authority has more of the force of a constitution,[6] something that defines how a community of people will act, where the fences should be put up, how we approach reality in order to continue to be who we have been and must be. The epitome of what it means to be Scripture is described in 2 Timothy 3:16–17:

> All scripture is inspired by God
> and is useful for teaching,
>   for reproof, for correction,
>   and for training in righteousness,
>   so that everyone who belongs to God may be proficient,
>   equipped for every good work.

Profitable, training, equipped—words that speak not of some property intrinsic to the book itself, but words that characterize a function, and a vital one in real life. The Bible is "inspired," a word implying that God breathes life into it, invigorating it, deploying it, with no intent to boast of its own grandeur, caring only that you and I get reproved, corrected, trained, equipped.

Christians have therefore always clung to the sufficiency of Scripture. Not always to the exclusivity of Scripture, but to its sufficiency, as declared in the *Westminster Confession*: "The whole counsel of God, concerning all things necessary for his own glory, man's salvation, faith and life, is either expressly set down in Scripture, or by good and necessary consequence may be deduced from Scripture; to which nothing at any time is to be added, whether by new revelations of the Spirit, or traditions of men." We might hear this last point, "nothing is to be added," as narrow, limiting. But there is something liberating about the fact that whatever is necessary is already in Scripture, that it functions like a "constitution," surely in need of interpretation, but not to be superseded or invalidated. For otherwise we are subjected to every trend and whim of culture, every novel theological thought, floating directionless with no mooring.

MIRROR OF THE SOUL

You can know a lot about the Bible, yet not be changed by it. Just over a century ago, Charles Marson wrote a humorous book entitled *Huppim, Muppim, and Ard*. Even the most devoted fundamentalist might have difficulty recognizing this trio as the three sons of Benjamin. Marson attacked the kind of religious education that focuses children on the minutiae of Scripture:

> These children can tell you who Huppim and Muppim and Ard were; they know the latitude of Beersheba, Kerioth and Beth-gamal; they can tell you who slew a lion in a pit on a snowy day; they have ripe views upon the identity of Nathanael and St. Bartholomew; they can name the destructive miracles, the parables peculiar to St. Luke, and, above all, they have a masterly knowledge of St. Paul's second missionary journey. They are well loaded and ballasted with chronicles of Baasha and Zimri, Methuselah and Alexander the Coppersmith. . . . Therefore while our clergy are . . . instant in season and out of season . . . to proclaim the glories of Huppim and Muppim, the people are destroyed for lack of knowledge. . . . They know all about Abraham except the way to his bosom, all about David except his sure mercies, and all about St. Paul except the faith which he preached and which justified him.[7]

It is at this point of usefulness that we might draw back. The Bible's world seems strange, an impossible fit for the mundane realities of life in our world. Cardinal John Henry Newman recognized this feeling of being alienated from the world of the Bible when he wrote: "I consider . . . that it is not reason that is against us, but imagination. The mind, after having lived to the utter neglect of the Gospels, in science, on coming back to Scripture, encounters an utter strangeness in what it reads."[8] The unreasonableness of the Bible is an affront to us. It challenges the way that we think about the world.

On the other hand, we can choose to have our lives grasped by the Bible. Stanley Fish put it this way: "In our postures as seekers, after meaning or after Christ (they are, of course, the same), we place ourselves outside a system to make sense of it, to fit its parts together; what we find is that the parts are already together and that we are one of them, living in the meaning we seek—'in Him, we live and move and have our being.'"[9] Maybe if we would stop trying to step out of the story of the Bible and stand at a distance from it, and rather try to make its world our world, some of the utter strangeness of the Bible might disappear. And we might begin to look a little strange to our neighbors, and to ourselves.

For in the Bible we learn not only about God, but about ourselves. Back in the fourth century, St. Athanasius suggested that the Bible is like a mirror in which we learn the truth about ourselves, in the light of the God who made us, calls us, and destines us for life. John Calvin called the Psalter "an anatomy of all the parts of the soul," for "there is not an emotion of which any one can be conscious that is not here represented as in a mirror. Or rather, the Holy Spirit has here drawn to the life all the griefs, sorrows, fears, doubts, hopes, cares, perplexities, in short, all the distracting emotions with which the minds of men are wont to be agitated."[10] We need not expect to find mere confirmation of what we think we already know about ourselves. Like a surgeon, probing deep into the marrow of who I am, the Bible exposes the deepest truth about me: that I am a child of God, made in God's image, a sinner, one who needs not what Madison Avenue dictates that I shall need (and buy), one desperate for the grace and mercy of God—and that my handicap in receiving that grace is precisely my sense of achievement and merit, which I cherish so deeply. We assume we know what we need, and hope the Bible bears something to satisfy that need. To our surprise, the Bible mercifully informs us that what we thought we needed we did not need at all, and that we have more profound, stranger needs, which lure us toward an unanticipated adventure with God.

THE STRANGER ASKING QUESTIONS

And so how do we read the Bible? We need not hunt for ammunition to fight the battles in which we are already engaged. Charles Schulz, of *Peanuts* fame, sketched a cartoon where a young man, engrossed in his Bible, says to a friend, "Don't bother me: I'm looking for a verse of Scripture to back up one of my preconceived notions." It's such a pleasure to wrap a Bible verse around *my* bias, or to fire off a verse like a bullet at some foe. God did not oversee the development of the Bible so that we would have a stash of ammunition to fire at somebody. Rather, its target seems to be me.

When I was in seminary, on the first day of Old Testament theology, my professor, Roland Murphy, thundered a question my way: "James, is the Bible inspired?" I nervously squeaked, "Yes, sir." He probed further: "Why?" Lacking a well-conceived reply, I resorted to humor: "Well, I find that very often the Bible agrees with what I think." A few in the class chuckled, except for a woman sitting next to me. Annoyed, she reproached me: "I disagree! I find that the Bible is inspired at precisely those points where it disagrees with what I think." The class was silenced—but my friend from the back of the room bailed me out by asking her, "Oh yeah? What about those passages that say women shouldn't speak in church?"

Our method in this book is to ask questions, and when we read the Bible, we need to be full of questions. There are no bad questions, none to be hushed up. But we know that when we inquire into the Bible, the hardest questions will not be our own, but rather those coming back at us, as we sense what T. S. Eliot meant when he said, "Beware the Stranger who comes asking questions." The woman in my class was right: we look for God's Word at precisely those points where the Bible disagrees with us, challenges us, questions us.

Mark Twain once said that he was most bothered, not by the parts of the Bible he couldn't understand, but by the parts he could understand. There is nothing easy about doing what clearly and frequently recurs in the Bible. Jim Wallis tells about an exercise some seminary students did a few years ago. They took scissors to a Bible and physically excised every passage that speaks about the poor. Major portions of the prophets, the Psalms, laws in Leviticus, the teachings of Jesus, and the epistles were snipped and clipped until the Bible was in shreds. Wallis called it the "holey Bible"![11] Unwittingly we all snip away at portions we might prefer not to deal with and delight in those that bolster our preconceptions. But when we pick and choose passages we are fond of, isn't this really an evasion of God's claim on us, yet at the same time a superficial stab at pretending we are in sync with God's ways?

So how do we read the Bible? One of the most remarkable moments in the history of Scripture being read had to be when Dietrich Bonhoeffer, armed at age twenty-five with both a doctorate in theology and wide acclaim, was surprisingly converted. He later wrote a letter to his girlfriend, Maria von Wedemeyer:

> I plunged into work in a very unchristian way. An . . . ambition that many noticed in me made my life difficult. . . . Then something happened, something that has changed and transformed my life to the present day. For the first time I discovered the Bible. . . . I had often preached, I had seen a great deal of the church, spoken and preached about it—but I had not yet become a Christian. I know that at that time I turned the doctrine of Jesus Christ into something of personal advantage for myself. . . . I pray to God that will never happen again. Also I had never prayed, or prayed very little. For all my loneliness, I was quite pleased with myself. Then the Bible, and in particular the

Sermon on the Mount, freed me from that. Since then everything has changed. I have felt this plainly, and so have other people about me.[12]

It is not that Bonhoeffer had not read the Bible before. His conversion came, rather, when he stopped reading the Bible *for* himself, and began to absorb what it had to say *against* himself, to let the words do their inexorable work of judging, altering, even demolishing, reshaping, perfecting, flowering.

LEARNING TO READ

Reading the Bible requires time, repetition, practice. While we may not be able to decipher Hebrew or Greek, the thought and worldview of the Bible seem strange, alien to our own. When we learn a foreign language, our first attempts at reading are awkward, excruciating, confused; but over time we begin to get it, to make sense of it, even to delight in the flow of the language. We need not expect the Bible to divulge its mysteries through a quick glance at a verse or passage. We read, and read more, and immerse ourselves in the rhythm of the Bible's life. We begin to think the way the Bible thinks, that is, to see our lives and all of reality from God's perspective. We notice, understand, and begin to mimic the movements and speeches of the characters in the stories of the Bible. We learn to pray its prayers and yearn for its hope.

Scholarship may be of help to us; and then again, scholarship may do us no good at all. Beyond question, educated people have rifled through ancient manuscripts, learned of the oddities of ancient cultures, dug up ancient cities, sifted information, and asked exceedingly hard questions about the texts that make up the Bible. As far as possible we need to learn all we can from those fine scholars who have done such yeoman detective work for us all. Robert Jenson has wisely said that "discovery and exploration of the oral and literary processes that eventuated in the Gospels beneficently *complicate* our involvement with the Gospel texts."[13] We tend to romanticize and oversimplify the Bible, and scholars can debunk some of our foolish notions and banish a lot of nonsense we would unwittingly read into the text.

And yet the very enterprise of studying may put us in a mood that inhibits us from getting out of the Bible what is intended for us. We distance ourselves and objectify the text, treating the Bible as a fascinating object to be debated and analyzed, but perhaps never actually lived out.

The Danish philosopher Søren Kierkegaard sarcastically declared that "Christian scholarship is the human race's prodigious invention to defend itself against the New Testament, to ensure that one can continue to be a Christian without letting the New Testament come too close."[14]

For the spirit required is one of humility, not intellectual mastery, an attitude Calvin called *docilitas*, a meek, "teachable" spirit. Describing his own conversion, Calvin said:

> At first, since I was too obstinately devoted to the superstitions of Popery to be easily extricated from so profound an abyss of mire, God by a sudden conversion, subdued and brought my mind to a teachable frame, which was more hardened in such matters than might have been expected from one at my early period of life. Having thus received some taste and knowledge of true godliness, I was immediately inflamed with so intense a desire to make progress therein, that although I did not altogether leave off other studies, I yet pursued them with less ardour.[15]

Reading the Bible is all about desire—desire for God, desire to make progress, desire to be different, desire to act differently.

THE LIVING OF IT

Acting differently. We have misconstrued religion as something "spiritual," something merely in the mind, God being something like an idea. But God is far more than an idea, and religion confined to the mind is not the religion portrayed in the Bible. The Bible is all about real life, and until we begin to embody what the Bible is talking about, curiously enough we will never understand it. St. Athanasius put it well:

> For the searching and right understanding of the Scriptures there is need of a good life and a pure soul, and for Christian virtue to guide the mind to grasp, so far as human nature can, the truth concerning God the Word. One cannot possibly understand the teaching of the saints unless one has a pure mind and is trying to imitate their life. Anyone who wishes to understand the mind of the sacred writers must . . . approach the saints by copying their deeds.[16]

This doesn't mean you have to be totally holy before you can understand anything in the Bible. But it does mean that the Bible, when properly comprehended, issues in altered patterns of behavior. The most solid

Bible interpretation is found on no printed page, but rather in the real lives of Christians. Scripture is holy, and we know it is genuinely understood when its readers become holy.[17]

For if faith has any truth to it, then faith must be lived, embodied, practiced. To do theology in this way requires that we speak of exemplars, heroes, saints, and we will say more about them in chapter 4. But for now, let us begin at the beginning, and unroll and examine the contents of those jars discovered by the bedouin shepherd, the first cluster of books in the library called the Bible: the Old Testament.

QUESTIONS FOR DISCUSSION

1. What terms would you use to describe the Bible? What does the Bible mean to you?
2. Why is it important to recognize that the Bible has come to us through the writings of humans and is not a book "etched in gold above the clouds"?
3. In what ways does reading the Bible alter your patterns of thinking? Of living?

2

The Old Testament

The Chosen People

> My thoughts and feelings seem to be getting more and more like those
> of the Old Testament. It is only when one knows the unutterability of
> the name of God that one can utter the name of Jesus Christ; it is only
> when one loves life and this earth so much that without them everything
> seems to be over that one may believe in the resurrection; it is only when
> one submits to God's law that one may speak of grace. It is not Chris-
> tian to want to take our thoughts and feelings too directly from the New
> Testament.
>
> —Dietrich Bonhoeffer[1]

The Old Testament is "old" in terms of when it came to be. But for
Christians it is most surely part of the Bible, with its glories and its
embarrassments, with its clarities and its oddities. To immerse ourselves
in its manner of thought requires considerable imagination. For
instance, the "unutterability" of God's name: it is an odd religion indeed
that thinks of God as having a personal name, but then hushes those
who know the name, not because it is secret, but because it is just too
wondrous.

HOW MANY GODS ARE THERE?

A name of a god is needed only when there is a crowd of gods in the
heavens and behind every bush. If we could go back in time and ask the
average Israelite on the street, "How many gods are there?" the answer
would be "Plenty—but I serve only one." Intellectually we know that,
by definition, there can be only one God. But in the swirl of our culture, many gods compete for our loyalty. When Bonhoeffer and other
Christians protested Nazi arrogance by asserting, "There is only one
God," they were not pressing people toward the mental deduction that,
by definition, there can only be one god. Rather, the stakes involved passion and allegiance, and demanded courage, hard decisions, even civil
disobedience. Israel's "monolatry" (the insistence on serving a single

God among many) is a reminder that we must stand and say, "Money, pleasure, glory—I will reject those gods and serve just one, no matter the cost."

The Israelites themselves found the lure of multiple gods hard to resist. The seductiveness of other gods can never be underestimated. Think of it this way: the Israelites settle in Palestine, after spending literally a generation roaming about in the wilderness. They know how to camp out and herd livestock, but they know nothing of farming. So they go to their Canaanite neighbors for counsel, which is happily given: "At the third new moon, you plow up the ground, throw away the big rocks, and then make furrows in long rows. Get some seed—and we'll help you with that—and plant the seed a little beneath the surface. Use some fertilizer now and then, and you'll find that animal dung works wonders. Watch out for nuisances like bugs and birds. And then you hope it rains."

But it doesn't rain. A little bit desperate, you go to your Canaanite neighbor and ask, "Does it ever rain around here?" And your friend says, "Well, we pray to Baal, the god of rain, over in the valley at our sanctuary." Indignant, you declare, "We will never do such a thing! We are worshipers of Yahweh, the God of Israel!" Your neighbor shrugs, and says, "Have it your way. I and my ancestors have trusted Baal for centuries to raise a storm and deliver the rain. But it's your choice." Days pass. No rain. Your meager leafy produce is withering, dust puffing around your feet. Quietly one night, you sneak off when nobody is looking, down into the valley, and say a prayer at that sanctuary to Baal, half hoping it won't work, but half hoping it will. All it takes, then, is just one shower, and you're hooked. The more gods the better. Cover your bets, get some insurance, draw on all the help available.

This kind of promiscuity (and that is how prophets like Hosea and Jeremiah regarded it) was heartbreaking to God, who knew why the rains fell, who grasped the disaster inherent in dallying with other gods who are mere pretenders. Israel's God had a name, just as Egypt's divinities were named Horus, Re, and Osiris, and Babylon's were named Marduk, Ishtar, and Ea. That name, rendered "Lord" in most English Bibles, was Yahweh. What did the name mean? "Yahweh" seems to be a verbal form, coming from a root meaning "to be," and something in the name suggests that this God "is." This God exists, is alive, vital, moving around like a verb. But that first *a* vowel, which in Hebrew denotes a causative verb, may be a hint that this God Yahweh causes things to happen, is an actor on the stage of history.

Then there is that *y* at the very beginning of this verbally named God, which gives this verb a future connotation, a sure declaration that this God "will be," that Yahweh isn't just a relic of the past—here today, gone tomorrow—but that above all we know this God "will be" there. Notice there is no guarantee in this God's name that everything will come up roses. The Israelites, who were not as glib as are we, who so trivially toss about the divine name in expectation of comfort and ease, knew from bitter experience that this God, for inexplicable reasons, did not shelter them, and didn't seem to shower them with prosperity. Their life was hard to bear, with much suffering. The one thing they knew was hidden in the name of their unique God: "I will be with you always, no matter what happens, no matter where you go." Why did they believe that about Yahweh?

THE SEA OF REEDS

Egyptian records took no notice of a large mass of Hebrew slaves during the reign of Rameses the Great. Neither pyramid nor tablet laments the day they exited the country. But Israel remembered. After an intense period of upheaval in the Nile Valley, the people, led by Moses, fled as far as the sea. The King James and other versions have translated "Red" Sea. But the Red Sea, which isn't red at all, is further east than the itinerary suggests. And the Hebrew original does not indicate the "Red" Sea at all. The body of water was the *yam sûf*, the sea of "reeds," and in the backwaters crawling across the Nile delta, many bodies of water along the Israelite route fit that description. The Israelites witnessed what for them was indeed a miracle, as the sea was parted and they crossed on dry land. Since they were not at the Red Sea, we may scrap the Cecil B. De Mille fantasy of Charlton Heston parting massive towers of water in the classic film *The Ten Commandments*. But the escape would never have happened without some piece of seeming luck, some astonishing good fortune, something construed by those present as an act of God, as a watery, impassable, unguarded region at the boundary of Egypt became surprisingly passable. They did in fact leave, and gave glory to God for their freedom.

Retelling this story, Elie Wiesel imagined the people panicking, dashing headlong away from the Pharaoh in terror. Moses raised his hand and ordered a halt: "Wait a moment. Think, take a moment to reassess what it is you are doing. Enter the sea not as frightened fugitives but as

free men!"[2] To witness a walk to freedom is liberating. Nelson Mandela
walked out of a prison in South Africa into the history books. John
Lewis, who became a congressional representative from Georgia,
pointed to a photograph of himself as a young seminarian being released
from prison in Nashville. His face glowed with a dignity, a confidence:
"I had never had that much dignity before. It was exhilarating—it was
something I had earned, the sense of the independence that comes to a
free person."[3]

That day by the Sea of Reeds revealed the powerful heart of this God,
Yahweh, and defined this people, chosen by God, set free from the cru-
elest bondage. But God did not set them free to do as they pleased, or
to blend happily into the culture—for that would be to submit to a new
bondage. God led them to Mount Sinai and gave them the Law, the
Torah. We may chafe under the notion of God's law imposed from
above. But for Israel, divine directives were "more to be desired . . .
[than] much fine gold" (Ps. 19:10). God set the people free, then told
them clearly how to stay free.[4] Sadly, in America we've been fooled into
thinking freedom is doing whatever I want to do. But the Old Testament subverts such a vapid freedom, which is no freedom at all. Israel
knew that freedom was exercised only in commitment. We are free only
to the degree that we are in sync with the God who made the universe
and showed up by the Sea of Reeds. The Torah, God's precious gift, was
Israel's charter of freedom, utterly practical, detailing God's way in
diverse zones of life, implying that God cares about how and when you
have sex, how you prepare dinner, how you treat somebody you've never
seen before. Every corner of life is pervaded with the presence of God
and with the loving, compassionate demand of God that the chosen
people live freely.

THE FINDINGS OF ARCHAEOLOGISTS

Eventually, after a whole generation of meandering through the wilderness, the people came into the "promised land," and to this day there is
no real estate on our globe more contested than Palestine. For just as the
establishment of the modern state of Israel in 1948 ousted inhabitants
who had lived there for centuries, so the people led by Moses entered
an occupied land. A huge issue raised by the Old Testament is the relationship of God to war and violence, and we will return to this problem
in chapter 7. But for now, a good map and the most elementary book

on the archaeology of the Holy Land will reveal that the so-called "conquest" was not so dramatic as a superifical skimming of the story might imply. Out of hundreds of cities, the book of Joshua reports that only a handful are taken, and they were situated in the relatively less settled hill country. As we know now after years of excavations, towns like Jericho were basically ruined, abandoned sites when Israel showed up, populated with the disgruntled poor who may well have welcomed the invasion of these adherents of a God named Yahweh, a God with a countercultural bias toward the disadvantaged.[5]

Archaeologists have been scouring over the Palestinian countryside for more than a century now. We may swoon over the notion of romantic archaeologists (like Indiana Jones) nabbing treasures (like the ark of the covenant). And how many adventurers have scaled what they believe to be Mount Ararat, hauling down scraps of petrified wood allegedly from Noah's ark? Again, we lose track of what the Bible is about and its intended effects. If a bona fide boat, with something akin to "S.S. Noah" etched in some paleographic script on the bow, were discovered and verified, would everyone suddenly become holy? The tabloids would rejoice, some Indiana Jones look-alike would bask in fame and fortune, talk-show appearances, and a mountain of money. But would the churches overflow? Would poverty and injustice be eradicated?

Real-life archaeologists proceed more soberly, digging long trenches into the mounds that are the debris of ancient Israelite villages, sorting through broken pieces of pottery, generally learning much about daily life in Bible times. And that daily life was grinding. Every able-bodied person struggled valiantly from sunup to sundown against weather, birds, brigands, and erosion, to eke out a meager subsistence of barley, a little wheat, olive oil, lentils, and chickpeas. Rocky terraces, temperamental rainfall, and untreatable disease conspired to make life precarious. Clothing was of goat hair. Few people wore shoes. Plows, tools, jars, and lamps were made in the home. Houses were thatched and susceptible to wind and rain, and there was little furniture. If you had livestock, they slept in the room with you, and water had to be toted uphill in dripping buckets. Your roommates included fleas, lice, rats. The slightest infection could kill.

We need to hold these hardships in mind before we conclude too much about topics like "love life and marriage in the Bible." If you were a young man in a village of thirty or forty residents, there might be one, or two, young women of marriageable age. And you would marry her—or the other one. No honeymoon, no nights out on the town, nothing but backbreaking labor just to survive. Children were a necessity, for they were additional workers and the only social security for your old age. And yet they were the gravest risk, as women died in childbirth as often as they survived. Affluent Americans nowadays love to turn to passages in the Old Testament that speak of God "blessing" God's people with the produce of the land. By "blessing" we often mean a big house, nice clothes and cars, a sumptuous retirement. But for real biblical people, the blessing for which they gave thanks was simply that it actually rained and they scraped together a meal of bread and soup so they could get some sleep before another grueling day.

CHOSEN TO BE A BLESSING

And yet they sang, knew joy, danced, told stories. Brutal as was their lot, they stunningly cradled profound meaning that illumined it all, these strange people who knew themselves to be "chosen" by God. God chose Israel, not to the exclusion of others, but because they were charged with a special mission, to be the ones God would use to demonstrate God's truth to everybody else. When God spoke with Abraham, the challenge was clear. Israel was blessed, so that through them all other people could be blessed (Gen. 12:1–4). Israel was to be a "light to the nations" (Isa. 49:6), the people whose mission would always be to embody what God was about, to mirror the glory of God to others, to serve foreigners and strangers.

The sort of example Israel set is fascinating. Politically, Israel was never a heavyweight. The economy always struggled. But as God's chosen people, Israel functioned like some prism, refracting the pure light of God's love into beautiful, surprising colors. Consider prayer. Far from polite and regimented, Hebrew prayers are bold, impertinent, making demands of a God they knew well enough to wrestle with gamely, trusting that God's grappling arms never rest until they embrace us. With his dying gasp, Jesus prayed the beginning of Psalm 22: "My God, my God, why have you forsaken me?"—not exactly the epitome of pious trust. And yet to cry out and rage against the darkness, and to do so to the God you assume is still listening, is a more profound kind of faith than the sweet, platitudinous kind.

Old Testament prayers never say "thanks," a mere word being too cheap.[6] When the wheat finally ripened, instead of rushing in to bake the loaf for which your family was desperately hungry, you took that first grain, spread it on a stone altar, and burned it, the smoke curling heavenward, the scent a sensory expression of thanks to the one who sent the rain and made the soil yield something beneficial. If your flock of sheep prospered, you expressed gratitude by killing and burning the most stalwart male (not the runt), the one that if you're smart you know you need for next year's breeding. Yet if you trust God, this is the sheep that you give up—proving you know the sheep and your future belong to God in the first place.

Crying out, and giving thanks. These two primal modes of prayer, this pair of gut responses, have been what people do, and have done since the dawn of time. Do we mean since Adam and Eve? Aren't the Bible's first "couple" representative of every person? The very name Adam, never used again as a proper name in Hebrew, simply means "man"—a clue that Genesis 2 and 3 dramatically and poetically portray not just two but all real people doing what all real people do. As Mark Twain mused, "I don't know why Adam and Eve get so much credit. I could have done just as well as they did."

SCIENCE AND CREATION

Of course, Genesis immediately provokes controversy regarding the relationship between faith and science. The notorious "Scopes monkey trial" featured William Jennings Bryan prosecuting a part-time teacher named John Scopes in rural Dayton, Tennessee, back in 1925. Piously, Bryan trumpeted that he was "more interested in the Rock of Ages than in the age of rocks." His foe, Clarence Darrow, withstood all the bombast and succeeded in his stated intention, "to show that Bryan is an ignoramus." Five days after the court sided with the "ignoramus," Bryan died suddenly, prompting H. L. Mencken, the satirist who had covered the trial, to remark, "God aimed at Darrow, missed, and hit Bryan instead."[7] Many argue that the jury is still out today. School boards are warned about the evils of evolution and are lobbied to consider teaching the Bible as if it were a textbook of physics, geology, and biology.

How can we resolve this seeming conflict? Can we see science and religion as complementary instead of conflicting? Albert Einstein, skeptical about the uncertainties of quantum mechanics, famously remarked, "God does not play dice"—to which Niels Bohr replied, "Albert, don't tell God what he can do!"[8] When it comes to science, religion frequently is guilty of hysterically boxing God in, of lamely twisting or denying some wonderful facts: there just *is* a fossil record (humans 2 million years old from Tanzania, dinosaurs from the Gobi). There just *are* genetic facts (our humorous kinship to chimpanzees). The universe just *is* expanding. Once upon a time, Copernicus and Galileo were scolded by the Church for telling what they saw in the skies. According to his ever growing legend, Galileo was dressed down by religious authorities for suggesting the earth is not the center of things but circles the sun, leading him to mutter (under his breath so they could not hear), *E pur si muove* ("But it does move").[9] Faith never involves shutting our eyes, fleeing in fear from any fact.

God's grandeur has not been diminished, but rather heightened by what we now know as the immensity of the universe, the complexity of life here on earth. The earth, and therefore humanity on the earth, is not the center of the universe. Fifteen billion years ago, something extraordinary happened that sent energy and light rocketing outward. Against astronomical odds, it all settled, cooled, cells divided and redivided. Life began, with a fraction of the profligate life forms standing up on two legs, only to kneel down and lift eyes and hearts to heaven seeking something that transcends it all.

Yes, the Bible neatly fits it all into a mere six days. But in the sixth century BCE, would a proper quantum mechanics explanation, the adaptations of organisms and their mutations, have made the slightest sense? John Calvin, back in the sixteenth century, understood biblical speech about creation as an "accommodation" on God's part to the minds and hearts of people. And don't exclusively scientific explanations miss out on the hidden meaning of it all? Genesis is preaching, speaking more profoundly than science, that God is responsible, involved, sharing in it all, out of nothing but the sheer expression of love.

The mind-boggling expanse of time involved is as we might expect. John Polkinghorne wrote that the world's "many-billion-year history of evolving fruitfulness will discourage any thought of a Creator who works by magic. The Creator is not a God in a hurry; rather God is patient and subtle in relation to a world that its Creator has allowed largely to 'make itself.' Theologians may well reflect that there is unlikely to be any other way in which love would choose to work."[10] Like a lover, or a wise parent, God takes the long view and has a gentle touch, leaving space for the life and dignity of the beloved.

Indeed, one invader that destroys love, shoving it aside, is control. I wonder if many Christians are uncomfortable with the long, slow, crazed march of evolution because chance is involved, preferring to think that God is in absolute control. But love requires risk, and there are theological ways to deal with chance and vulnerability; we will return to this subject in chapter 6, when we will grapple with the problem of evil. Austin Farrer once was asked about God's will in the Lisbon earthquake, which killed 50,000, in 1755; he suggested the hard truth that God's will was that the elements of the earth's crust should behave in accordance with their nature. God allows the universe to go its own way, for life to have its own existence, for God is interested in love, not control. Polkinghorne was right: "God's action will always be hidden. It will be contained within the cloudy unpredictabilities of what is going on. It may be discernible by faith, but it will not be exhibitable by experiments. It will more readily have the character of benign coincidence than that of a naked act of power."[11]

We are not the center of the universe, but we do not live in a random universe either. I certainly feel fortunate that there is all this remarkable fine-tuning in our universe: if the force of gravity or the charge of an electron were just a tiny fraction higher or lower, life as we know it could never have come to exist. Nothing random here. While we cannot prove (or disprove) it, we can make sense of the idea that God is the author of the laws of physics, the process of evolution, creator and preserver of a world crammed with wonders for God and us to enjoy. The Christian theologian might even dare to ask us to consider this: perhaps all the fine-tuning was intended not primarily for me and my benefit, but rather to fashion the arena in which Christ could be born. For it is the incarnation of God, in this person Jesus, that seems to be the apogee of history.

THE SECRET OF LIFE

We all ask, "Who made me?" One cold evening, in March of 1953, at the Eagle Pub in Cambridge, Francis Crick, having just unscrambled the secret of DNA with James Watson, raised the following toast: "Gentlemen, today we have discovered the secret of life." I am largely defined by the occurrence and arrangement of minuscule genes and nucleic acids, all elaborately coded. We cannot prove that God is the master engineer or nursemaid of the millennia-long process that culminates in "me." But we cannot dismiss God, and our inclination to believe in God need not be diminished; faith may be stretched and our awe for God magnified because of the curious fact that such complex creatures have always yearned for something beyond ourselves, beyond this life.

When did human life begin to sense some connection with God? About 50,000 years ago, close to the epoch when our ancestors' brain size began to expand dramatically, painted art began to appear on caves, abstract, but hinting at some primal religious groping. Alan McGlashan wrote, "There is strong archaeological evidence to show that with the birth of human consciousness there was born, like a twin, the impulse to transcend it."[12]

Admittedly Darwin, whose studies at first reinforced his belief in God and the soul's immortality, conceded later in life that even "the grandest scenes would not cause any such convictions and feelings to rise in my mind. It may be truly said that I am like a man who has become colour-blind."[13] This inability to see God in the grandeur of nature is always a possibility; books that mock the very idea of God on the basis of science sell well, and can make for superb reading.[14] And yet the surprise is that people still (and most likely always will) believe in, yearn for, and stake their lives on the colors, on the transcendent. We resist the thesis of Francis Crick: "You, your joys and sorrows, your memories and your ambitions, your sense of personal identity and free will, are in fact no more than the behavior of a vast assembly of nerve cells and their associated molecules."[15]

No theologian can disprove Crick's hypothesis, but we acknowledge that it is just that, a hypothesis, one that seekers rightly resist. The theologian's only recourse is to say out loud what we believe about life, and how everything hinges on God—or better, to sing the song, as did Orpheus, trusting in its beauty. The failure of many Darwinists to account for all that is human is summed up by Loren Eiseley:

> They ignore all man's finer qualities—generosity, self-sacrifice, universe-searching wisdom—in the attempt to enclose him in the small capsule that contained the brain of proto-man. Such writers often fail to explore man's growing sense of beauty, the language that has opened and defined his world, the little gifts he came to lay beside his dead. There is no definition of man possible by reducing him to ape or tree shrew. Once, it is true, the shrew contained him, but he is gone. He has broken from the opened seed pod of the prehominid brain, a thistledown now drifting toward the empty spaces of the universe. He is full of the lights and visions—yes, and the fearful darknesses—of the next age of man.[16]

BROTHER SUN, SISTER MOON

Who are we in our age? and who is God? God is Lord of all: the brilliant who may prefer not to find a god, hypocritical churchgoers, the mentally handicapped, dogs, whippoorwills, wildebeests, centipedes, things that blossom and shed leaves each fall, rocks, rivers, galaxies. Our larger brains are simply our privilege to contemplate the wonder of it all. Our job is to show up, to notice the wonder of how hummingbirds fly, fish leap, bats echolocate, bees pollenate. Maybe science's divinely ordained task is to help us notice, to widen our perspective on what God can do. A strain of Christian tradition has held the created world in contempt—but that is not of the Old Testament! Francis of Assisi embodied an affectionate attitude to creation in his life and in his famous canticle praising God for "brother sun and sister moon," praising the kinship of all creatures great and small. Psalm 19 sings, "The heavens are telling the glory of God; and the firmament proclaims his handiwork." And God made a startling speech to Job (chaps. 38–39): God laid the foundation of the earth, and the morning stars sang for joy; God fashioned the clouds as garments for the sea; God is present at the calving of hinds, in the nests of the ostrich, where the hawk soars, where sea creatures frolic. All creation is good; all things by their being praise their maker.

Science can help us sift through the kind of thinking we often hear about "blessing." "I am blessed with excellent health, with a keen mind, with muscle and speed." But are these so directly from God's hand? Somebody is always trying to figure out why God doled out cancer or heart disease to some individual. In Old Testament times, people with great faith but limited knowledge chalked up infertility and disease to God. But science teaches that bodies develop and grow unevenly, unpredictably. Aberrations just exist, wanted or not. The Gospel, after all, is about God's sharing in our physical life, bearing our tangible pain and agony.

Science *has* damaged our faith, though, not in what has been discovered, but in what we have devised. My children cannot see the 100,000-light-year expanse of the Milky Way as I could when I was a boy, for we have strung lights all over my city. The sky has grown darker, as has our ability to look up in wonder and awe at God's creation. We have come to believe we can solve our own problems, and Christianity's basic premise is that we have a problem that we cannot solve. That problem is articulated in the lives of biblical characters, their missteps, the strangeness and inexplicability of their behavior, something mirrored in the very texts that narrate their lives.

STORIES AND MANUSCRIPTS

Dealing with errors, strangeness, the inexplicable—the strangeness of the Old Testament is its challenge and its delight. We can only shake our heads and guess at how its oldest stories traversed from whatever happened to the earliest Hebrew manuscripts now housed in museums and libraries. Story after story, wise sayings, commandments, prayers, and songs, all like quirky but beautiful pearls, strung together over the centuries, passed along by word of mouth, told around the campfire, whispered to children nodding off to sleep, argued and debated, dreamed, dared.

Writing it down was at the end of a very long, vital, mysterious process that only a God with a sense of humor—and dead seriousness— could have nurtured. Poor copyists. Somebody had to get it down in writing to preserve it for posterity. They made errors. Sometimes in weariness they just skipped a few lines. Sometimes they had their own agenda. Sometimes a scribe just had too much zeal for his subject, or for God. Depending unwittingly on Hebrew manuscripts centuries newer than the Dead Sea Scrolls, children have always learned of Goliath's prodigious height: "six cubits and a span" (1 Sam. 17:4), or roughly nine and a half feet. But among the Dead Sea Scrolls was found the oldest known copy (by many centuries) of the story of David and Goliath, and the text clearly measures Goliath at "four cubits and a span," or six feet, six inches (which certainly qualified as a giant in biblical times, when the average man ranged barely to five feet).[17] Like a fisherman, the storyteller may have stretched it just a bit, making David's feat all the more astonishing.

But not all the confusion grew at the end of the copyist's quill. The very "original" material being copied simply grates on our sensibilities of order. Genesis 1 tells how God created the world, and then Genesis 2 starts right over, as if nothing has happened yet. God seems to despise the idea of the Israelites having a king, but then God turns right around and anoints and blesses a king of God's own choosing. God says, "You shalt not murder," but then God orders up executions.

Whoever patched all these disparate stories together, as if they would conspire to form a coherent book, must have been crazy. Or perhaps that editor was wiser than we would be. We want everything to be neat, organized, with a smoothly flowing plot toward a pleasant ending. The editor of the Old Testament allowed contradictory stuff into the final copy, with not even a feeble effort to satisfy our wish to have it all harmonized. The dissonance is left standing out in the open. The wisdom in this is elusive, but crucial.[18] When people put into words what they know, what they believe, what they hope about God, messiness is inevitable. It is as if the community knew that no one picture of God was adequate. Put two or three very different pictures of God on the board, and while they don't fit together neatly like pieces of a jigsaw puzzle, if you keep studying all of them and don't settle on just one, your grasp of what God really must be like is enhanced. Put two or three contradictory stories about how this experience of God is lived out on the board, and you shake your head. But in that very shaking of the head your illusions are debunked, and you are surprisingly drawn into a richer sense of what living with God is like.

THE PERSPECTIVE OF GOD'S HEART

Not only are the stories messy, with competing versions blatantly exposed side by side. In God's own heart there is a deep complexity, with moments of seeming contradiction. We recognize that Israel's neighbors had multiple gods, who rarely got along well. The Babylonian epic called *Enuma Elish* imagines a host of deities having a party. Tiamat's rest is disturbed; a fight between Marduk and Tiamat ensues, with wise old Ea intervening in mercy to keep the peace. A parallel to the flood story we know from the Bible is found on tablet XI of the Epic of Gilgamesh. The hero Gilgamesh recognizes his mortality and sets out to find Utnapishtim, who had survived a great deluge and was rumored to possess the secret of eternal life. Again, it was Ea the compassionate who shielded Utnapishtim from the angrier gods, who were none too happy that their wrathful intentions were thwarted.

Ancient Near Eastern gods were like that: capricious, moody, winning, losing. How odd of Israel to have only a single God! Some have suggested that Israel's God has no rivals; forces of nature are not gods, but subordinates doing the one God's bidding. An argument among the gods? A more intriguing way to think of this scenario is this: it is as if Israel's God internalized the debate. While we may think of God as immutable, omniscient, infinite, beyond emotion or change, we never understand the Old Testament God until we perceive an ongoing, passionate combat being waged within God's own heart—at one moment lashing out in exasperation over people behaving worse than the beasts, at the next moment recoiling into tender compassion. This God seems to have all the problems of the loving parent trying to deal with recalcitrant children, with a fierce love winning the day: "The LORD [is] merciful and gracious, slow to anger, abounding in steadfast love and faithfulness, keeping steadfast love, . . . forgiving iniquity" (Exod. 34:6–7).

Such a God is elusive, and theology gets messy, clarity and simplicity being very hard to come by. Yet there is a perspective—just as countless brush strokes combine into a mural—that pervades the whole. Consider how rudely the annals of monarchy were assessed. In 886 BCE, Omri ascended the throne in Israel and built an entirely new capital city, Samaria. The economy and the military flexed their muscles; a restoration of national pride pulsated through the land. So great were his exploits that he was noted in glowing terms by one King Mesha on the so-called Moabite Stone, which is on display today in the Louvre. Rarely were Israelite kings mentioned by foreign potentates. But Omri is summarily denounced as wicked by the theologians who wrote 1 Kings: "Omri did what was evil in the sight of the LORD" (16:25), for his policy was to respect the deities of all his subjects, and so he built a sanctuary to Baal right in the capital city. An admirable political move in our world, but theologically disastrous in biblical times. Hezekiah, on the other hand, late in the eighth century, was mentioned by a competitor on the world stage. On the Taylor Prism, Sennacherib, the bloodthirsty ruler of Assyria, boasts that "I made Hezekiah a prisoner in Jerusalem, shut up like a bird in a cage." During Hezekiah's rule, the economy was troubled, and the military cowered in fear. The Bible's verdict on Hezekiah? "He did what was right in the sight of the LORD" (2 Kgs. 18:3), by removing altars to foreign gods, praying in the teeth of danger, listening to God's prophet, ignoring the practical consequences.

The Old Testament wads up our measures of success and greatness and tosses them in the garbage, caring for nothing but loyalty to God and God's law, fidelity to a way of life at odds with other cultures, one seemingly doomed to worldly failure. And just because Omri and Hezekiah were politicians, they enjoyed no immunity from the harsh glare of the Word of God. On the contrary, the Old Testament seems particularly determined to bring God's law to bear on leaders and on public policy, because God is the creator of everything, and because leadership and policies affect all of God's children. Amos, Hosea, Isaiah, Jeremiah—all these great prophets, spokespersons for God—invaded the corridors of power and spoke strong words of judgment.

Interestingly, these prophets were not themselves oppressed, but were numbered among the affluent. Therefore they were independent, and could not be intimidated or railroaded by the powerful. Their contacts gave them insights into the goings-on in the corridors of power. Yet their passionate faith prevented them from caving in to their very own vested interests, so profound was their commitment to speak for God.[19] And their words reverberate through the centuries, continuing even today to denounce injustice in the public arena, to thunder judgment upon political maneuvering, to plead with us for faith and action in the mundane realities of society. So much for those Bible readers who want to keep everything on some "spiritual" plane, who insist that religion and politics just don't mix. Gustavo Gutiérrez was right: "Any claim to non-involvement in politics . . . is nothing but a subterfuge to keep things as they are,"[20] a subterfuge employed by the beneficiaries of the status quo, those utterly uninterested in God's claim on all of life, and especially God's requirement that change be made in their lives.

The characters God deals with are not sweet, pious, pastel saints, but grimy, flawed, and foolish; we may take heart that those ancient story-tellers refused to whitewash Abraham, Jacob, Moses, and David. Families are dysfunctional, kings make foolish decisions, lovers run afoul, faith and courage fail. No pastel saints, but people, and we may be grateful. For they are like us, we like them. And so there is hope for me, for us.

EVIL AND SUFFERING

We may wish God had made people immortal, high functioning and impeccably behaved, free of evil and suffering. But when God put Adam and Eve in their paradise, God included that one dangerous tree, over which they stumbled (Gen. 3). Why create room for error? Because the Old Testament God is not interested in control. Sure, in the big picture, ultimately, God has the universe well in hand. But day to day, in real life, God is interested not in control, but in love—and so God became vulnerable and allowed people space to love, but also to rebel and hide.[21] And space to question: the books of Job and Ecclesiastes feel thoroughly modern in their expressions of cynicism, thundering after God with questions that are anything but pious. Job's chilling screams at the

Almighty are shouted, not out of a lack of faith, but out of a more pro-found kind of faith. However remote the Almighty seems in the begin-ning, Job discovers in the end a God who is far from aloof. God has long arms around the grandeur and wildness of all created beings, the good and the bad, all encompassed by God's care.[22] This engagement of God in suffering, which takes center stage in the story of Jesus, is already pres-ent and full of anticipation in the cries of Job—or, rather, in God's unex-pected patience with Job, who rebuffs God so rudely.

Curious thing about this God. Popular thinking notwithstanding, the Old Testament is not about the wrath of God. There are embarrass-ing passages depicting God as a warmonger, ready to toss down a thun-derbolt of judgment on sinners. But to read the thirty-nine books in this little library is to come to know a God who is amazingly patient, unfailingly merciful, bearing our raging, always creatively seeking some means to get back into relationship. "Can a woman forget her nursing child?" (Isa. 49:15)—so great is this God's love for people, for those chosen, for us.

Mercy is actually what much of the bloodshed is about. Christian hymnody has bloody, gory stanzas among its favorites. Just watch well-scrubbed, finely dressed, intelligent churchgoers singing "My hope is built on nothing less than Jesus' blood," "To thee whose blood can cleanse each spot," "With his own blood he bought her," "There's power in the blood," and "There is a fountain filled with blood . . . and sin-ners washed beneath that flood lose all their guilty stains."

To us, all the blood may seem ghastly. A bigger problem may be the portrait of God implied. What sort of God is this, virtually bloodthirsty, gruffly satisfied only when innocent blood flows? Is Yahweh really such a sadistic despot? If we feel for the pulse of this God, for the broader plot to the long story of Israel, we see that the God of the Bible simply isn't a power-hungry autocrat whose game is power, guilt, punishment, and who values his honor above human life. If the Old Testament teaches us anything, and if Jesus echoed that teaching in any way, it is that God is humble, compassionate—not the tit-for-tat type at all. When Jesus was killed, the Jews who were the first Christians wrapped their minds around it and made sense of it in the light of their age-old practice of blood sacrifice. At Passover, the day Jesus died, perhaps as many as half a million lambs were slaughtered in a veritable bloodbath. All this killing was no doubt something like a lesson in living. God wanted us not to be so materialistic—and so God required that we vol-untarily give up a lamb, a ram, not just to be burned for our own good, but given to the needy who had no lamb at all. And if you know it will cost you your best ram or goat, you'll think twice before hurting your neighbor.

Ancients believed the healing power of God was hidden in the blood of livestock. When our relationships are broken, no matter how hard we try, we can never fully repair the damage. Some residue of guilt lingers. My soul, our marriage, a fractured community—the mythical bleeding never quite stops. The Old Testament understood and believed that only God's power, God's healing energy, released by the sacrifice of something precious, could bridge that gap and finish the healing.[23]

GOOD OUT OF EVIL

For Yahweh is not a God who merely gives people a "second chance." Anne Tyler's wonderful novel *Saint Maybe* tells of the winter evening Ian Bedloe stumbled into the Church of the Second Chance. Usually he would have fled such a ridiculous church, but in his desperation he stayed and prayed. After the service closed with "Leaning on the Everlasting Arms," Ian confessed his sins to Reverend Emmett, and then asked, "Don't you think I'm forgiven?" Reverend Emmett briskly responded, "Goodness, no!" A stunned Ian then heard the pastor say, "You can't just say, 'I'm sorry, God.' Why, anyone could do that much! You have to offer reparation—concrete, practical reparation."[24] An Old Testament sentiment, to be sure: reparation had to be made. But this Yahweh does not merely wait for us to get it right on a "second chance," a truth illustrated in the very finest, most profound story in the entire Old Testament, the little short story about Joseph and his brothers.

Once upon a time, in the Middle Bronze age, in the hills of the Middle East, there was a dysfunctional family. Sound familiar? As Tolstoy wrote at the beginning of *Anna Karenina*, "Happy families are all alike. Every unhappy family is unhappy in its own way."

Joseph's family is unhappy in many ways. The dad, Jacob, has a dozen boys, but Joseph is his favorite. Jacob honors Joseph with what Andrew Lloyd Webber called the "amazing technicolor dreamcoat." Probably it wasn't colorful so much as it was long-sleeved. If you know the difference between blue collar and white collar, you can guess the significance of the longer sleeves: long sleeves were reserved for leisure pursuits. Laborers would get too hot, their dangling sleeves would be caught in briars and would drag in the mud. Those long sleeves were just one more reason for the brothers to resent this pampered little brownnoser. Joseph makes things worse by telling the brothers about one of his many dreams. He couldn't help having dreams. But a wise brother would have kept it to himself if he dreamed his brothers would bow down and worship him! No surprise then when the brothers hatch a cruel plot to get rid of Joseph. They sell him as a slave to the Ishmaelites (who make him wear short sleeves), tear his garment, bloody it, and plunge the ultimate dagger into their father's heart: Joseph, your favored son, is dead.

But against all the odds, Joseph survives, gets in and out of jail in Egypt, and emerges as a power broker in the courts of Pharaoh. He's got brains, courage, a big boost from God, and even some luck—which the brothers back home don't have. The skies get stingy; the parched ground cracks, and there is no food. No choice but to go down to Egypt, the breadbasket of the world, where crops depend not on some whim in the weather, but on the clockwork flooding of the Nile. A crazy twist of fate: the person they must ask for bread is their own brother, Joseph. But of course, they don't recognize him: years have passed, and poor Hebrews are not exactly on the lookout for one of their own to command such authority in the august courts of the Pharaoh. He recognizes them, though. After dallying with them a bit, he finally banishes his entourage from the room, lets loose a long-pent-up cascade of emotion, gathers himself, dries his tears, and reveals the secret: "I am your brother, Joseph" (Gen. 45:4).

It takes no imagination at all to guess what the brothers felt: shock, then terror, guilt, trepidation, doom, their heads spinning in panic and remorse. But it would take an unusually creative imagination to guess how Joseph in fact deals with his brothers. His words must have taken light years to sink in: "Do not be distressed, or angry with yourselves, because you sold me here; for God sent me before you to preserve life" (Gen. 45:5). Even after the glorious reunion with his father, even after Jacob's death, Joseph says the most remarkable thing: "Do not be afraid. . . . Even though you intended to do harm to me, God intended it for good, in order to preserve a numerous people" (Gen. 50:19–20). Joseph forgives in the most awesome sense of the word. He doesn't say what they did was okay, or that it didn't matter. Joseph is tender; he casts their common life into the hands of God's intent.

How can anyone know what God intends? Joseph managed to climb out of his two-dimensional world and look at his life from God's sweeping vantage point. Martin Luther King Jr., in his last Sunday morning sermon, said, "The arc of a moral universe is long, but it bends toward justice."[25] The center of gravity of God's great arc is plotted in those words of Joseph: "Even though you intended to do harm to me, God intended it for good, in order to preserve a numerous people."

It's not all up to us. It's not that God gives Joseph's brothers a second chance, another crack at getting it right. God actually embraces them in his broader plan that is bigger than what they have done. We trudge around like Atlas, feeling the weight of the world on our shoulders. No wonder we're exhausted. Our lives are littered with the debris of our mistakes, the carnage of our guilt. But our hope is that God can overcome all that is evil—and that God can even use our mistakes, and somehow in the long run bring us and our world to his own good end, which just cannot be thwarted. Maybe our lives can turn out like a beautiful Persian rug. This spot or that spot on the rug is just some dark, ugly thread. But woven around and through are surprising, recurring threads of beauty, with the finished work a fascinating thing of joy. God doesn't cause evil; but God can manage it, reshape it, and bring good out of it all.

GOD'S SURPRISE

In *A Farewell to Arms,* Hemingway wrote, "The world breaks everyone, and then some become strong in the broken places." God does not cause evil! But we may look at our lives and into the place where we have been wounded and find our giftedness. Evil never has final say. Evil is not left unaddressed. God is holy, far from indulgent or lackadaisical. Prophets were raised up to denounce corruption, to plead for a return to God. Priests received sacrifices and reparations for wrongs done. And from an embarrassing lineage of bumbling kings, a descendant emerged—Jesus, who came not to abolish the Old Testament, but to call people to its fulfillment.

Surprisingly, in the Old Testament there is no life after death. You are some stuff, a body, into which God breathes the breath of life. When you die, you're dust. But if this were so, would we all lead decadent lives? A college student once told me he wanted to become a Christian—but wondered if you could do so and not believe in life after death. His concern was that he didn't want to become a Christian because there was some grand payoff after death, or out of fear of what might happen later if he didn't believe. Rather, he wanted to do all this because it is true, and good—and I told this very Old-Testamentish young man, "Yes, you can be a Christian." But I added, "When you die, if God surprises you with the gift of eternal life, would that be okay with you?" And so we turn now to the New Testament, all of which points toward and explicates precisely that surprise.

QUESTIONS FOR DISCUSSION

1. What are some implications of the Old Testament insistence that there is one unique "God" and not "many gods"?
2. How do you view the relationship between "science" and "faith"? Are they enemies? Friends?
3. In what ways have you seen or experienced God bringing good out of evil?

3

The New Testament

The Historical Jesus

For the New Testament writers the place where Israel's God had acted decisively for the salvation of the world was not in their taking pen and ink to write gospels, but in their God's taking flesh and blood to die on a cross.

—N. T. Wright[1]

Disembarking from a boat, Paul walked up the Egnatian Way, began preaching in a town called Philippi, full of Roman war veterans, and was thrown in jail for "disturbing our city" (Acts 16:20). In Thessalonica he was blasted for "turning the world upside down" (Acts 17:6). Then in Ephesus a riot broke out, instigated by the silversmiths, whose profit margins in their cozy business crafting figurines of the goddess Artemis were getting squeezed (Acts 19). What is it about Paul that touched off this firestorm?

"We proclaim Christ crucified" (1 Cor. 1:23). The New Testament is a little library of twenty-seven writings, varied but with a single focus: the life, death, and resurrection of a man named Jesus. An astonishing feat, the way a handful of people—socially marginal, not the movers and shakers—conceived of what they had experienced with Jesus as worldwide in scope, and got busy passing the contagious word swiftly along Roman roads and shipping routes. At rest stops along those roads, and in the course of conversations at hundreds of outdoor shops, the story of Jesus was told and retold, finally issuing in the volume we call the New Testament.

At a distance of two millennia, an encounter with this Jesus is possible, life changing, elusive, controversial: Possible and life changing because, like that first handful of followers, thousands continue to experience and believe in Jesus. Elusive and controversial because there are so many competing versions and images of who Jesus really was or is.

37

Lecturing to his Bible students in Strasbourg in 1905, Albert Schweitzer unmasked how we ascribe to Jesus "our own thoughts and ideas," resulting in "the Jesus of our own making": "Each successive epoch of theology found its own thoughts in Jesus. . . . But it was not only each epoch that found its reflection in Jesus; each individual created Him in accordance with his own character. There is no historical task which so reveals a man's true self as the writing of a Life of Jesus."[2]

We try to modernize Jesus and recreate him as a capitalist, a family-values guy, a feminist, a fundamentalist. Instead of patterning ourselves after his image, we refabricate him into our own image. Intriguingly, Schweitzer was right when he went on to say that the real Jesus will not be popular or universally intelligible, but rather "to our time a stranger."

> He comes to us as One unknown, without a name, as of old, by the lake-side, He came to those men who knew him not. He speaks to us the same word: "Follow thou me!" and sets us to the tasks which He has to fulfill for our time. He commands. And to those who obey Him, whether they be wise or simple, He will reveal Himself in the toils, the conflicts, the sufferings which they shall pass through in His fellowship, and, as an ineffable mystery, they shall learn in their own experience Who He is.[3]

How can we sort through all that has been written, said, and believed, and meet up with this stranger? And how will we follow and fulfill his tasks for our time?

STONES AND PAPYRI

Archaeologists have poked around for tantalizing glimpses into Jesus' time by the lakeside. A boat fifty feet long, datable to the first century, has been found near Bethsaida, where Jesus fished with Peter and John on the Sea of Galilee. In Capernaum, a network of small stone houses has been dug up; most of them, as expected, had fishing hooks and broken pottery on the floor, but the walls of just one house, within a generation of Jesus' death, were plastered and decorated with religious graffiti, leading us to surmise this may well have been the house where Jesus taught and healed.

In Jerusalem we can see the massive stones fronting the temple mount, cut in the distinctive style of Herod's masons; down one tunnel you can see a single stone forty-five feet long, weighing 570 tons.

No wonder, when they saw the temple, Jesus' disciples gasped, "Look at those stones!" (Mark 13:1). On the south side we can stand on a broad staircase that led to the double and triple gates in Jesus' day, the steps across which he no doubt drove the money changers out of the temple. Strikingly, scratched on the outside of a limestone ossuary bearing the bones of a sixty-year-old man is the name of the priest who connived to have Jesus killed, Caiaphas. Sensationally, other ossuaries have been studied, spawning ferocious controversy over whether these ossuaries could possibly have borne the remains of Jesus' family—and Jesus himself.[4]

Then we have some old manuscripts. The jury is still out on a little shred of papyrus that may actually contain fragments of a couple of sayings from Matthew; Carsten Peter Thiede, a German papyrologist, dates it to within a generation of the death of Jesus.[5] The oldest papyri of any substance are the Bodmer Papyrus stored in Geneva, from the early third century, and the Chester Beatty Papyrus in Dublin, two decades newer.[6] So we see that the oldest copies of the original Gospels are about as long after the fact than the United States is old. We do not have the original Gospels (just as we don't have the original *Gallic Wars* of Julius Caesar or Livy's poetry or anything else from antiquity). Even if we had the original manuscript of, let's say, Matthew, we would still be fifty or more years removed from the events described. Jesus lived and taught, and stories were passed along by word of mouth for decades.

Not surprisingly, once various writers put what they knew onto parchment, inconsistencies were evident. Did Jesus clear the temple the week he died, as in Mark? or early in his ministry, as in John? The sayings are in all kinds of order, or disorder. Then we can detect errors made by those who copied the texts by hand, and like detectives we have to examine the oldest texts we have, compare others that are different, and try to deduce what the original might have been. And beyond this kind of literary confusion, the Gospels relate plenty that to the modern mind is just incredible: storms quelled by mere words, blindness cured by mere touch, corpses resuscitated by a mere mortal.

SCHOLARLY SENSATIONALISM

The nature of the material opens up some gaping holes, into which critics eagerly step. Occasionally some would-be scholar makes a splash in the newspaper claiming some "scholarly evidence" about Jesus. In 1992

alone, three curious books made headlines.[7] Barbara Thiering claimed
that Jesus was married, divorced, and remarried; was the the father of
three; and that he did not die on a cross but was drugged. Simon Magus
(mentioned in Acts) administered an antidote, and gullible disciples
believed he had been raised. The novelist A. N. Wilson claimed Jesus
was executed by the Romans, but then the disciples saw James, his look-
alike brother, and mistook him for a risen Jesus. John Shelby Spong, the
famous Episcopal bishop, asserted that Mary was probably raped, and
that Jesus was married to Mary Magdalene.[8] Then, with much glitzy
publicity, a squadron of scholars collectively known as the Jesus Seminar voted with colored beads (red, pink, gray, and black) and proclaimed their results: Jesus "really" said only about eighteen percent of
what the Gospels say he said. And in a companion volume they declared
that Jesus "really" *did* no more than sixteen percent of what the Gospels
say he did.[9] For them, the Gospels are little more than the church's
superimposition of divinity upon an itinerant Jewish teacher. While
grabbing headlines, these assertions are mere guesses and are not sup-
ported by the majority of scholars.

In the early twenty-first century, bookstores and online sellers reaped
large profits on books declaring that the Jesus traditionally believed in
is an easily exposed fake. The immensely popular novel by Dan Brown,
The DaVinci Code, and the subsequent film with Tom Hanks ingrained
in the public mind the notion that the Church has hidden the truth
from us—and readers were eager to snap up books that revealed the
truth. In Brown's novel, a character portrayed as immensely learned, Sir
Leigh Teabing, exposes a massive Church cover-up of the truth about
Jesus, who was merely human, married Mary Magdalene, and didn't rise
from the dead. Dan Brown's "research" hangs on a single book: *Holy
Blood, Holy Grail*, by Michael Baigent, Richard Leigh, and Henry Lincoln, a book that sold extremely well but was met with a sound thrashing from all scholars who are knowledgeable. Baigent, parenthetically,
also wrote a book (also the subject of scholarly denunciation) declaring
the Vatican was suppressing damaging truths hidden in the Dead Sea
Scrolls;[10] but this is absurd, as the Dead Sea Scrolls have been widely
published and available for many years, full of fascinating information
about Judaism in the time of Jesus, but without one word about Jesus
or any viewpoint, positive or negative, about Christianity.

What we learn from the mind-boggling sales of *The DaVinci Code*
and the long train of books that were published to capitalize on its popularity is twofold. First, we modern readers have a taste for the sensa-

tional, the unheard of. Jesus was odd, indeed, but not in the ways that titillate our modern media fantasies. Jesus was odd, in fact, in ways that offend modern sensibilities.

Second, Jesus just won't go away! Weathering an onslaught of attempted debunkings, Jesus is still intriguing. Despite the foibles of Jesus' critics, the attention is welcome. Marcus Borg has championed such work as "a way for people to be both thoughtful and Christian, rather than having to choose between the two."[11] A vigorous scrutiny of the text, the asking of critical questions, is never fatally wrong. We dig into the text, and we realize that the Gospels are not literal transcriptions of Jesus' words and life, but are heavily edited documents with their own biases—about which we will say more later.

PARTISAN PORTRAYALS

Waving off trifling misconstruals of Jesus (like those of Thiering, Wilson, Spong, and Brown) does not mean that getting back to the real Jesus is easy. The quest to lift the real Jesus out of the later Gospel portraits of Jesus is nothing new. While he was president of the United States, Thomas Jefferson began writing what he called a "wee book" on the life and morals of Jesus, a book now buried under the cornerstone of the Jefferson Memorial in Washington. Voracious student of diverse subjects as he was, Jefferson in this case was on the defensive. Clergy were uncertain that a despiser of the church should lead the country, and so he countered by staking out his support for Jesus. But as he explained to Benjamin Rush, he "rejected the corruptions of Christianity," but accepted the "genuine precepts of Jesus himself."[12] As he wrote to John Adams, those precepts formed "the most sublime and benevolent code of morals which has ever been offered to man." To discern this code, the president strove to separate "what is really his from the rubbish in which it is buried."[13] The "rubbish" included the miraculous, anything "divine." Not surprisingly, Jefferson's biography of Jesus ends with the sealing of the tomb.

Clearly Jefferson was doing what Schweitzer warned us about. But today's scholars, while pursuing the task far more intelligently than Jefferson, share many of his concerns. How can we sift through and make sense of the varied wordings and orderings of Jesus' teaching? What are the "corruptions" in which the historical Jesus is embedded? Methodologically, can modern people make the "miraculous" intelligible? To ask the question "Did this really happen?" seems out of bounds, or the question is winked at, as if to say, "Of course such events cannot really happen." What of the rubbish in which Jesus seems to be buried?

Even a cursory reading of the Gospels uncovers genuine disorder, as wordings vary between Matthew and Luke, expansions pop up over against Mark, and the entirety of John's longer discourses cannot be made to "fit" with the other three. As we will see, the writers were not asking about clinical accuracy, but marshalling any and everything they could round up about Jesus to convert listeners. And they witnessed such conversion going on regularly wherever they lived and preached. They saw Jesus not as a character out of the past, but living still, very much present, continuing to speak and work in the missionary endeavors of Christianity. We may well distinguish between a historical statement ("Jesus was crucified outside Jerusalem") and a theological statement ("Jesus died for our sins"); Martin Kähler famously distinguished "the Jesus of history" from "the Christ of faith."[14] But the Gospel writers conceived of no gulf, and seamlessly wove together history and theology; modern believers resist the idea that the Christ in whom they believe is different somehow from the Jesus who lived in Palestine.

In part, the problem emerges in that we have no single, unbiased documentary of his life. Instead, we have four Gospels, four theological portraits of Jesus, with positively no pretension to dispassionate accuracy. This is not to say the Gospels are false. Rather, they have a life-and-death agenda rippling through every sentence; they are passionate not about objectivity but about persuading readers to abandon their known world and risk everything for their subject. Just before he was put to death for his agenda, Socrates wryly confessed that "we ourselves are still intellectual invalids": "You know how, in an argument, people who have no real education care nothing for the facts of the case, and are only anxious to get their point of view accepted by the audience? Well, I feel that at this moment I am as bad as they are."[15] John 20:31 can speak for all the Gospels: "These are written so that you may come to believe that Jesus is the Messiah, the Son of God, and that through believing you may have life in his name."

WHAT WAS CALLED FOR

So, if here and there we have an expansion or two that emerged from the writer's pen instead of from Jesus' lips, then is that a loss or a gain?

In the ancient world, no one expected otherwise. The great Greek historian Thucydides recounts the speeches of Cleon, Diodotus, and others during the Peloponnesian War, some of which he had heard himself and others of which he had not: "I have found it difficult to remember the precise words used in the speeches which I listened to myself and my various informants have experienced the same difficulty; so my method has been, while keeping as closely as possible to the general sense of the words that were actually used, to make the speakers say what, in my opinion, was called for by each situation."[16]

Although skeptics are not so sure, many Christian scholars believe that God did not leave the early Christians to their own devices, but continued to guide them in their preaching, to speak to them through the Spirit, drawing their minds to the fuller, truthful implications of what Jesus had said. New situations called for new words, fresh understandings of Jesus that were timely, consistent with the man himself, inspired by God, and lived out among those following Christianity in changing times. The truth about Jesus, then, is not less than the Gospels, but more than the Gospels.

John, among the Gospels, is either the most suspicious on historical grounds or the richest theological construal of the historical Jesus. Obviously the author had taken time and prayer to reflect on the words, deeds, and significance of Jesus. John selected and arranged exactly seven signs, seven "I am" sayings, seven discourses, all intended for persuasive, rhetorical effect, which is powerful indeed. John could simply have listed sayings and events: Jesus did this, then he said this, then he went over there. But the drama, the rhetorical presentation, the literary craft mattered, because lives were at stake. No wooden documentary would be sufficient, so consumed was John with the wonder of this Jesus, so eager was he that all might believe. Ben Witherington has said it well: "I think in the case of the Fourth Gospel we are talking about a document that reflects the fact that the Beloved Disciple did meditate on, and preach and teach, the Jesus traditions for a long period of time, at some point casting the material into his own style and idiom, likely before writing it down."[17] John, guided by the Spirit promised by Jesus in his own Gospel (14:26), truthfully and profoundly drew out the depths of what Jesus talked about, and yet always tied his story to real events, even with remarkably earthy details.

Recognizing the bristling difficulties, I sense a general reliability in what the Gospels report. The tenacity of memory was impressive in the first century; students could recall verbatim long speeches of orators years after the fact. The Gospels vary in the location and wording of various sayings, but surely Jesus told his prize stories more than once and performed them in varied styles for varied audiences. Like all good Jewish teachers, Jesus used formulas and devices that were memorable; and the disciples would have been eager to recall his words. Far from hiding the real Jesus from us, the four Gospels pass along to us the testimony of eyewitnesses (as Richard Bauckham has argued quite persuasively).[18] We cannot miss the basic thrust of Jesus' message and actions. And we must somehow account for the intensity of his followers, who did not merely muse over his interesting thoughts, but risked (and sometimes lost) life and limb to alter the course of history in his name.

THE RUBBISH IN WHICH HE IS BURIED

Think once again about the seemingly unwelcome complication that we do have four Gospels, not just one. Other "gospels" were written— and interestingly, the four we have in the Bible are the least sensational of all. Contrary to Sir Leigh Teabing in *The DaVinci Code*, it is misleading to say there were many gospels and Church authorities squashed those that didn't suit their purposes. Church leaders weren't covering anything up; on the contrary, they were doing everything possible to get the word out. Other gospels were eventually written, but only after many decades had passed since the first four, those we know from the Bible, were written, circulated, and with total unanimity accepted by all Christians. Other gospels were not suppressed so much as they simply were not recognized as having any validity.

Sir Teabing implies that the other gospels reveal a more human Jesus. But the truth is the opposite. For instance, one gospel tells of Jesus in the crib playing with clay, fashioning little birds that he then miraculously causes to fly away. Or his father is in the carpentry shop, and one board is too short, so the toddler Jesus magically lengthens it. One day little Jesus turns his playmates into goats. These stories are clearly legendary, written by people who were not at all comfortable with a human Jesus and wanted him to appear to be as divine as possible. Just as the biblical Jesus hushed those impressed by his wizardry, the Church did not select the most fantastic writings available, but stuck with the oldest Gospels, the ones we know, which portray a very human Jesus who was born, hungered, wept, bled, and died.

Interestingly, the Church kept four Gospels instead of just one. In fact, they refused to choose just one Gospel or even a digest of all the Gospels. Such a harmony of the Gospels, called the *Diatessaron*, was widely available and quite popular. But bishops, like Theodoret in 423, denounced such harmonies and had them burned. We might have preferred the church to settle on a single, coherent narrative that would minimize questions and confusion. But William Placher has discerned something vital about these four Gospels: "Perhaps their very diversity and ambiguity represent part of the meaning of these texts, one of the ways in which they function for readers by raising questions about the varied voices within the world they narrate and the relation of that world to history and to the reality of their readers."[19]

We cannot burrow "behind" the Gospels, and this seems to be God's design. John Calvin said that we do not have to deal with a naked Christ, but with Christ "as he is offered by the Father: namely, clothed with his gospel."[20] Jefferson spoke more shrewdly than he imagined of the "rubbish" in which Jesus is buried. In the first chapter I spoke of the inspiration of the Bible as incarnational; God uses not flawless, supernatural means to reach us mortals, but what is mundane, suspect in the world's eyes, a form that can best be described by the centuries-old prophecy in Isaiah about the servant who suffers and yet redeems:

> Many . . . were astonished at him—
>   so marred was his appearance.
> . . . .
> He had no form or majesty that we should look at him,
>   and nothing in his appearance that we should desire him.
> He was despised and rejected by others.
>   (Isa. 52:14, 53:2–3)

In places, the four Gospels are marred; they were not lauded for their literary beauty; they were and still are despised and rejected. In the third century, Origen, whose learning exceeded the philosophers of his day, wrote:

> In the apostles there was no power of speaking or of giving an ordered narrative by the standards of Greek dialectical or rhetorical arts which convinced their hearers. It seems to me that if Jesus had chosen men who were wise in the eyes of the multitude, and who were capable of thinking and speaking acceptably to crowds, and if he had used them as the means of propagating his teaching, he might on very good grounds have been suspected of making use of a method similar to that of philosophers. . . . The truth of the claim that his teaching is divine would no longer have been self-evident.[21]

We need not despair that Jesus comes clothed in such Gospels, just as we need not despair at Christmas that Jesus came to a poor peasant woman in a lowly stable for cattle in a backwater village. God would have it this way. And it is precisely what Jefferson would dismiss as the "rubbish" that is the Gospel, the story that lures us toward the God who crazily but surely comes to us hidden beneath the contrary appearance of the rubbish of flesh and blood, mortal, woundable. The real Jesus is not extractable from the Gospels but always lives through and beyond them. The Gospels are surely vulnerable to criticism, but then so was Jesus. In his own lifetime he opened himself up to misunderstanding and ridicule, to the point that they quit studying his life and words and decided to get rid of him.

THE TEACHINGS OF JESUS

So let us turn to the Gospels, listening to what Jesus said, what he did, and even who he was. Jesus taught, but not merely in pithy little sayings to be cross-stitched or applied like a bandage to a wound. He redrew the mental map of the universe, turning our perspective on everything inside out. Matthew's first major block of transmitted teaching, called the Sermon on the Mount, begins with a memorable section called the Beatitudes (Matt. 5:1–12).[22] "Blessed are the meek—and blessed are the poor in spirit." Notice Jesus didn't say, "Blessed are those who work hard, for they shall have a comfortable retirement." Jesus did not relax the admittedly tough requirements from his Bible, the Old Testament. You haven't had an affair? Well, if you have felt lust for another, you're just as guilty. Haven't murdered anybody? But if you even get angry, at the heart of things it's the same.

Jesus never let up. Tearing down barns to build bigger barns? You fool! Today your life is required of you (Luke 12:16–21). Haven't fed the hungry or visited in prisons? Then you are a goat, not a sheep, utterly lost in the final judgment (Matt. 25:31–46). Having a dinner party? Don't invite those who can return the favor, but go out into the streets and compel the blind, lame, and maimed to sit at your table (Luke 14:7–24). Anyone who says, "I take the Bible literally," ought to shudder over this business about dinner invitations, so very do-able, so consistently ignored.

The signature pieces of Jesus' teaching are the stories he made up. Jesus was not a systematic theologian, and you get the sense from him that tightly organized thought somehow misconstrues what the kingdom of God is about. Jesus never said, "There are five logical propositions to which you must give assent," or "There are five keys to the spiritual life." Instead he held up a seed in his hand, told about some barns being torn down, bridemaids running out of oil, sewing a patch onto clothing. Life isn't like propositions. Life is like the food you taste, the hand you touch, the house you build.

TROJAN HORSES

Deftly deploying everyday images from the fields, family, and business, the parables reveal what God is up to with this raconteur, while simultaneously throwing a cloak over the head of the confused student. When the disciples ask Jesus why he tells these fascinating but open-ended tales, he responds by explaining how the parables tell the truth for those who ponder slowly, who let the stories infiltrate and do their work on bared souls. Yet the same stories bury the truth for the intelligent who are in a hurry for clarity and simplicity, who wish to master the material and to remain masters of their lives. Explaining a parable is like explaining a joke, the explanation itself never being funny at all. Clarence Jordan said a parable is like a Trojan horse; at first it looks harmless, so you let it in, and then—Bam! It's got you.

Jesus' stories don't have a "point," something easily summarized, mastered, and shelved. They speak freshly on each hearing. Consider the well-known Good Samaritan parable (Luke 10:29–37), which seems to admonish us to be like the Samaritan, to stop and help those in need, and to avoid the haste of the priest, who was too busy being holy to have compassion on the wounded. But use some imagination and try on other characters for size. Maybe I have been one of the robbers who has hurt someone and left them out on the road. Maybe I am the one who has been beaten and left for dead, and no one but no one stops to help. St. Augustine and many preachers have read the story this way, and perceived in the foreign traveler—the stranger who spares no expense to help—none other than Jesus himself, the teller of the story.

The first parable in Matthew, Mark, and Luke is about a sower throwing seed on the road, among thorns, on the rocks, and on fertile soil. We leap to moralize and ask, "What kind of soil am I?" The lesson thereby must lean toward "Be fertile soil!" But maybe Jesus wanted us to delve into the mind of the sower. No sower in his right mind would waste seed on thorny, rocky places. But this crazed sower is imprudent, profligate, flinging seed anywhere and everywhere. Jesus was certainly like that, doling out love on any and all people in every corner of Palestine. God is like that, and the story embodies the truth better than the proposition "God's love is for everyone."

Consider the famed parable of the Prodigal Son (Luke 15:11–32), superficially a story of the morally bankrupt individual repenting and being forgiven. Francis Thompson, after his conversion, looked back on the years he frittered his talent away in carousing: "I fled him down nights and down the days, down arches of years, through a mist of tears, and under running laughter I hid from him." James Weldon Johnson preached it:

> Every young man, everywhere, is one of these two sons—there comes a time when every young man looks out from his father's house, longing for that far off country. The young man said to himself as he traveled along. This sure is an easy road. Nothing like the rough furrows behind my father's plow. Young man, young man, smooth and easy is the road that leads to hell and destruction. Down grade all the way, the further you travel, the faster you go. Just slip and slide, slip and slide till you bang up against hell's iron gate.[23]

John Newton, slave trader and scoundrel, sang it: "Amazing grace, how sweet the sound, that saved a wretch like me. I once was lost, but now am found, was blind, but now I see." Here's the good news: we can return. There is forgiveness! And we need, of course, to rap the knuckles of modern Pharisees, those self-righteous churchgoers, who don't dance in the aisles just because somebody claims to have found God.

But these parables of Jesus are sneaky.[24] Of the lad in the pigsty, Jesus says, "He came to himself." Did the boy repent? Did he have some religious experience in the pigsty? We tend to overrate the young man. He may simply have been hungry, thinking of one person only: himself. If so, he hatched a rather cynical plan to go home and use his father again. If there was any change in the boy—any real change—it came not in the pigsty, but when he found himself surprisingly swept off his feet by his father. He barely got a chance to repent; he could hardly get a word in before his father swept him up into the party.

It was not unheard of for sons, younger sons especially, to try to make it big in the burgeoning mercantile economy of the Greco-Roman world. But a son was supposed to invest, to save. The money this boy squandered was his father's, his family's social security. By wasting his inheritance, the son in effect said to his father, "You don't matter," or even, "I wish you were dead." Common wisdom said you don't tempt your son this way; he'll only take advantage of you. This father let himself be taken advantage of. George Balanchine got it wrong in his ballet (which debuted in 1929 in Paris) when he portrayed the son as groveling and the father as austere. No, Jesus says, the father ran. In Jesus' day, men didn't run; to run was a sure sign you had lost all dignity. But this father, who let himself be taken advantage of, cares more for the boy than for his own dignity. He could have given the boy a thrashing, required heavy penance, sackcloth, fasting, ashes. But he ran. Dignity matters nothing to this father—only the reclamation of the son. No more poignant image of the God Jesus taught, followed, and embodied is imaginable.

Then there is the older brother. Lincoln was once asked what he would do with the Confederates once the Civil War was over. He said, "I will treat them as if they had never gone away." Of course, there's always some carpetbagger, some spoilsport, who relishes a brother's ruin. Jesus gave us a vital clue at the beginning of the story, one we usually miss. The father divided his living between *them*. It's not that he gave the younger son some cash and hung on to the rest. He gave it all up to his two sons. What that means is that when the father kills the fatted calf and gives the boy sandals, a ring, the best robe, he is giving away what belongs to the older son! Calf, sandals, ring, robe—all earned and well deserved by the older brother—are cavalierly bestowed on the younger, lost brother. The principle seems to be that this lost brother cannot be restored until some of the stuff that rightly belongs to the older brother is spent. Most of us have worked hard; we've earned what we have. We have a lot of good stuff, and we deserve it. It is ours! But we need to let go of what is rightly ours in order to restore that lost brother, that lost sister. We need to part with what is ours, not just for them, but for our own joy!

Jesus' stories coyly refrain from telling the feeling or motivations of characters. We have events and words only. And Jesus left most of his stories hanging, open ended. Did the older son ever come into the party? Or did he forever stay outside? The listener is invited to complete the story, to ask, "How do I step into this narrative and become part of the denouement?"

But then perhaps "invitation" is too gentle a conception. For there is offense in Jesus' words, and plenty was taken. Times were perilous for all Jews, with botched revolts and ironfisted retaliation from the Roman overlords, debates about the true nature of the faith. Into such an explosive era Jesus stepped and spoke, daring to redraw precious boundary lines, the very markers that identified the faithful. To consort with prostitutes, to pick grain on the Sabbath, to dine with tax collectors—all were perceived not so much as gross neglect of God's law but as sheer danger for a people whose existence hung by a mere thread. Yet we dare not think of Jesus as lax about holiness.[25] Rather, he redrew the lines and cut to the heart of why there were lines in the first place, daring to include those ostracized by a religiosity aimed at goodness. He dared to offend the righteous, whose goodness could become for them a barrier to God, not to mention an instrument of prejudice. Clearly the Sermon on the Mount (Matt. 5–7) relaxes no commandments, but turns up the intensity, denying us any legalistic wiggle room, probing our souls like a psychologist, cutting to the heart of anger and lust, exposing the rigorous challenge, the profound adventure of living in the light of Christ's coming.

What Christians might miss, if we are not careful, is how Jewish Jesus was. Along with his audience, Jesus was deeply immersed in the Scriptures and teachings of Judaism. Recently scholars such as E. P. Sanders and N. T. Wright[26] have helped us to grasp how Jesus presumed a complex of notions about Israel, its history and destiny, God's gift of the Torah, the law, and the radically hopeful preaching of the prophets and apocalyptic writers, who fully expected the inbreaking of God's kingdom, the ultimate irruption of God's rule into the arena of history. What all Jews, Jesus included, understood well was that the expectation of the dawning of God's kingdom motivates not just altered thinking, but also altered behavior.

THE DEEDS OF JESUS

Jesus didn't just talk. He lived an extraordinary life, yet in thoroughly mundane circumstances. We know precious little about his childhood, youth, and early adulthood. Raised in Nazareth, an inconspicuous village whose population may have been as few as a hundred, Jesus was apprenticed by his father in carpentry—or it could be they were more generally "builders," a term that included stonework. We may well imagine that much of the wood- and stone-working business came out of Sepphoris, a neighboring city of some affluence. Archaeologists have discovered a sumptuous villa there featuring a stunning mosaic of a woman dubbed "the Mona Lisa of Galilee"[27]—slightly later than Jesus' day, but indicative of the expensive construction going on. Jesus left work and home behind in response to a sense of mission, first encountering John the Baptist, then moving around the shores of the Sea of Galilee, where he assembled a band of followers.

As Jesus ventured from place to place teaching, he touched the untouchables, fed the hungry, prayed, and served—and perhaps we will never understand him until we do the same. Some of what he did strikes us as impossible, not only for us to do, but for anybody ever to have done. Many stories about Jesus fall into the category of what we call "miraculous." Some care is required to contemplate what is miraculous. Sadly, modern people feel they must choose between two options: either the miracles are sheer fiction, devised for the gullible and simpletons, sensible only to a prescientific mindset; or the miracles are true, they really happened, with God abrogating the normal rules of how things work, dipping into the usual run of cause and effect, so that the sun actually stands still, the blind regain their sight, the dead live again. And the wire with which some bind up their assertions is barbed, for if you even wonder if Jesus "really" walked on water, then you are not a believer at all. Even if you believe the miracles "really" happened, perhaps that was a unique moment in God's history, a proof of who Jesus was, not something we expect to see today. But others are certain that same power is operative and accessible today.

Certainly God, if there is a god worthy of that name, can do anything. We may scratch our heads and contemplate what would ensue if the sun actually stood still (as in Josh. 10:13), which would mean the earth abruptly halting its rotation, and the inevitable cataclysms geologists and meteorologists could explain. For the moment, though, we may explore a third option, something between the miracles as silly fiction and the miracles as interruptions of natural law.

Philosophically we may question the very category "miraculous." Centuries ago we chalked up much of what transpired—a clap of thunder, sickness, victory in battle—to direct, divine intervention. As knowledge grows, the category "miraculous" seems to shrink. But should it? Maurice Blondel wrote, "There is nothing more in the miracle than in the least of ordinary facts. But also there is nothing less in the ordinary fact than in the miracle." From God's perspective, either everything is a miracle, or nothing is a miracle. The world and all that transpires within it is of God, and that grand fact stirs in us what Martin Buber called "an abiding astonishment,"[28] a sense of wonder. Onlookers were astonished by what Jesus did, whether he calmed a storm or touched a leper, whether he multiplied five loaves into food for thousands or let a sinful woman wash his feet with her hair. An excited frenzy rifled through the crowds that saw Jesus, a frenzy he sought to quiet.

Why was Jesus so hush-hush with his miracles? Why was he hesitant to dazzle the throngs with his power? Jesus perhaps sensed that the sheer exercise of miraculous power would be misconstrued, that people would pin their fantasies on him, that the unscrupulous would devise plans to capitalize on his wizardry. There were other miracle workers from Jesus' own era and region, Hanina ben Dosa and Honi the Circledrawer being the best known. More to the point, Jesus evidently performed whatever "miracles" he performed, not to impress anybody with his power, but to teach a lesson. During Jesus' lifetime, plenty of people still got sick, and limped, and suffered, and died. He did not heal everyone. And, at least as far as we know, he rarely healed in private. He healed in front of a crowd, and he always attached a sermon, a point to the miracle.

The blind were his favorites. Blindness as a metaphor for not being able to comprehend truth, as an image for a failure of the imagination, was not unique to the Bible. Plenty of thinkers used blindness, which was far more prevalent in ancient times than our own, as an illustration of intellectual or spiritual confusion. Sophocles' drama *Oedipus Rex* is a riveting exploration of how and what and why we see and don't see. In the royal house of Thebes, Oedipus boasts, "I would be blind to misery not to pity my people." It is Tiresias, the blind prophet, who accurately assesses the situation. Ridiculed by Oedipus, he responds: "You mock my blindness? You with your precious eyes, you're blind to the corruption in your life." Just so, as the blind were healed, Jesus turned to the mortified Pharisees, the great see-ers and visionaries, and rudely suggested that they were the blind who needed healing.

The ultimate agenda in this ministry of healing was not health and physical well-being, but rather salvation itself. Jürgen Moltmann put it well:

> In the context of the new creation, these "miracles" are not miracles at all. They are merely the fore-tokens of the all-comprehensive salvation, the unscathed world, and the glory of God. They point to the bodily character of salvation and to the God who loves earthly life. . . . There is a difference between salvation and healing: *Healing* vanquishes illness and creates health. Yet it does not vanquish the power of death. But *salvation* in its full and completed form is the annihilation of the

power of death and the raising of men and women to eternal life. In this wider sense of salvation . . . people are healed not through Jesus' miracles, but through Jesus' wounds; that is, they are gathered into the indestructible love of God.[29]

Yet, as we attend to the point of a miracle, we need not infer that nothing of wonder happened. Marcus Borg suggests that "the *purpose* of the narrative may be symbolic rather than historical. Moreover, it is no less *true* for being symbolic; indeed, its truth is verified in the experience of Christians ever since."[30] Purpose is all that matters. Evil and suffering were being resisted, and signs were appearing that the rule of God was dawning. Something extraordinary happened with Jesus, the greatest evidence being the changed lives of those who knew and followed him.

THE CLIMAX OF THE DRAMA

That change was accomplished not by the spectacular deeds or even the provocative words of Jesus. Karl Barth took note that Jesus healed no one during Holy Week. For he was engaged in another kind of battle: "In Jerusalem He performed no such healings. For the Galilean healings and those on the way to Jerusalem were only preliminary skirmishes. In Jerusalem He Himself died—paradoxically enough. . . . Yet the dying of Jesus is the decisive event, the climax of the whole drama, of which the miracles are only a preliminary announcement."[31]

At the heart of the Gospel narratives is a protracted battle against evil and, therefore, for God. At Jesus' birth, a paranoid Herod slaughtered innocent children, sounding the harsh note that would recur in skirmish after skirmish. Jesus went into the wilderness, willingly enduring not only hunger and exposure, but severe temptation, a harrowing test. Andrew Canale pictured it: "So he sat on the rocks under the hot sun and walked the barren desert listening to the silence. Slowly, painfully, his Nazareth life melted away; he shed that old skin like a snake of the desert. Then came that infinite time between what was lost and what is to be found."[32] Public controversy surrounding modern productions such as Martin Scorsese's film *The Last Temptation of Christ* or even Andrew Lloyd Webber's *Jesus Christ Superstar* hints that we are not comfortable with Jesus' humanity; many Christians adore the notion that he was "without sin" more than his being "in every respect . . . tested as we are" (Heb. 4:15).

His sorest temptation had to be to steer clear of Jerusalem. Jesus needed no supernatural gift to foretell the future to recognize the deadly danger he would face. Frequently we ask, "Why did Jesus die?"—and the answer seems to be, "For our sins." But if we shift the question just a little and inquire, "Why did they kill him?"—the answer is no longer, "For our sins." They killed him for complex and very understandable reasons. At Passover the city was engulfed with hundreds of thousands of pilgrims; security measures were more intense than usual. Jewish religious leaders had good reason to feel threatened by this itinerant healer whose Trojan-horse stories challenged their authority. The Roman authorities, under the brutal Pontius Pilate, were more than skittish about the potential for armed revolution. Jesus' every action—his choice of those he befriended, his failure to bow to the powers that be, and his startlingly bold and offensive act of driving the money changers from the temple precincts—led precipitously to a contrived "trial" and execution, an untimely and gruesome end for a thirty-year-old teacher.

In a cemetery in Jerusalem called Givat ha-Mivtar, archaeologists found the skeleton of a thirty-year-old male from the first century—with a six-inch iron nail driven through his ankle, a gruesome relic from the capital punishment called crucifixion. In chapter 6 we will say more about the remarkable shift in Jesus' ministry from dizzying activity to a taciturn passivity, from conquering every foe to being conquered, from breathing life into a deceased child to breathing his last. Jesus acts, but then Jesus doesn't act; he is acted upon, but is no less himself when he is arrested, bound, suffering, and dying. In fact, it is in the dramatic moments when Jesus becomes helpless that we discover the startling nature of his power and therefore the shape of our salvation.[33]

All four Gospels devote themselves at great length to the details of the crucifixion of Jesus, so much so that some scholars regard the Gospels as basically narratives about the trial and death, to which some stories from Jesus' earlier life were attached. And of course, we also find stories from his brief, subsequent life: the first Christians believed that Jesus was raised from the dead, that he was no longer in that grave, and they were transformed from fearful, unlettered fishermen into giants who changed the world. This is no afterthought; all of Christianity hinges on the resurrection of Jesus, as the truth of the faith is enveloped in the discovery that "he is not here; he is risen!"

Given the centrality of the resurrection, we may pause and scratch our heads over what we in fact find in the Gospels about the resurrection. For there is no sign whatsoever that this story has been "managed" or even told carefully at all. Who really got to the tomb first? And to whom did Jesus appear? Did he appear just outside the tomb? or was it up in Galilee? The four narratives of the resurrection are impossible to fit together into a coherent "harmony."

Charles Colson once argued that the story of the resurrection must be true, since even a smaller number of Watergate crooks couldn't keep their stories straight and wound up exposing Nixon as a liar; had the resurrection been fabricated, some bumbling disciple would have leaked the information. The issue actually is different. Surprisingly, almost embarrassingly, several stories—seemingly self-contradictory, mutually exclusive, somewhat incoherent, and not at all "kept straight"—were allowed to stand. The contradictions shout out in the open, as if begging for critics to scoff. Almost as if the fact of the matter were so contradictory to life as we know it that the feeble efforts to put it into words had to seem crazed, just as Luke characterizes the reaction to the women's breathless report of the empty tomb: "These words seemed to them an idle tale, and they did not believe them" (Luke 24:11). The philosopher Ludwig Wittgenstein once asked why these texts were so unclear.[34] He compared the situation to someone wanting to warn someone of a terrible danger, but telling them a riddle. "Isn't it possible that it was essential in this case to tell a riddle?" Wittgenstein wisely asked, as if a riddle were the clearest way to convey this particular kind of truth. An empty tomb. Conflicting accounts. Rumors of meetings. Doubts, surprises, but a powerful message. This Jesus—reared in Nazareth, itinerant preacher, quiet healer, offense to the pious, scandalously executed—could not be contained by the grave.

THE APOSTLE PAUL

And it was Paul who grasped the meaning of it all. One tantalizing portrait, penned a century after his death, stated that he was "a man small of stature, with a bald head and crooked legs, in a good state of body, with eyebrows meeting and nose somewhat hooked, full of friendliness; for now he appeared like a man, and now he had the face of an angel."[35] There is nothing angelic, though, about the Paul revealed in his own letters. Fierce and combative, Paul could boast of Roman citizenship and was well schooled in (and diligent about obedience to) Jewish law. As his drama opens, he is harassing the first Christians, for they believed in a man who had suffered the holy law's worst curse. Customs stretching back to Moses himself were threatened by this new movement.

But on the road to Damascus he was jolted by a blinding experience that not only brought about his conversion but also served as his calling, his vocation to serve this Jesus he had fought against. The shock of his transformation was multiplied as other Jews converted, but even more dramatically as Gentiles were included, with Paul making absolutely no requirement that they embrace the ethos and lifestyle of Judaism. The early church valiantly struggled with hard issues: Must Judaism be embraced by all Christians? And if not, must Judaism be dispensed with by Christian Jews—of which there were many in viable communities like the church in Jerusalem? Paul forever altered the Christian movement from something within Judaism to something international in scope, eclipsing essential aspects of its Jewish heritage.

The eventual severe split between Judaism and Christianity (which meant Christians could no longer be Jewish!) was sad and was not exclusively about whether Jesus was the Messiah or not, and certainly not over belief in resurrection. Plenty of Jews believed in the resurrection, and many went so far as to name a messianic leader. The controversies were over more mundane matters like diet, circumcision, the observance of the calendar of festivals. No small firestorm erupted over this, as Paul was vehemently opposed, not merely by the Jews, but even more so by Christians who clung to Judaism with tenacity. Paul took some ironic pleasure in his sufferings, boasting of his beatings, jailings, stonings, lashings, hunger, exposure, deducing that he thereby bore God's authority, his own tribulations proof that God's power is made perfect in weakness (2 Cor. 12:9).

We have a handful of personal letters Paul wrote to people he knew personally. We call them "books" of the New Testament. They are not compendiums of doctrine, but his passionate advice to real people about how to live out the news they had heard about this crucified but risen Jesus. The ad hoc character of Paul's letters tells us something about the nature of Scripture, how to read it, how to live it. Theology is not something rarified and timeless, but rather mundane and timely.[36] Paul writes one thing to the Galatians, and another to the Corinthians, and something else to the Christians at Philippi, for each had peculiar crises, unique situations, specialized backgrounds. Certainly a consistent, coherent message underlies all the letters, a message Paul was incapable of bending. Life was no longer about striking a business deal, no longer about piling up a mountain of good behavior. Life was all about grace, the generous, outlandish love of the God of the universe enveloping you and setting you free—not to do as you wish, but for a radically different kind of life, one of profligate service and exuberant joy. The application, the embodiment of this message, is an art, hanging on the proclivities and peculiarities of place, personality, history.

THE LIVING WORD

If we read Paul closely, we either chuckle or squirm over how utterly nosy his meddling gets. We overhear Paul talking about whether to eat vegetables or meat, and what sorts of meat, how much to eat, court procedures, the avoidance of marriage, conjugal rights, which gender may speak and which may be silent, what to wear on one's head, the payment of taxes—as if for Paul everything, every corner and moment of life, has theological implications. His uneasiness about marriage casts a shadow over our glorification of that blessed estate, and C. S. Lewis is probably right when he says that Paul feared not sex so much as "preoccupation,"

> the need of constantly "pleasing"—that is, considering—one's partner, the multiple distractions of domesticity. It is marriage itself, not the marriage bed, that will be likely to hinder us from waiting uninterruptedly on God. And surely St. Paul is right? If I may trust my own experience, it is (within marriage as without) the practical and prudential cares of this world, and even the smallest and most prosaic of those cares, that are the great distraction. The gnat-like cloud of petty anxieties and decisions about the conduct of the next hour have interfered with my prayers more often than any passion or appetite whatever.[37]

In fact, all the letters that have become books of the New Testament are amazingly obsessed with the basics of daily behavior and how Christianity alters everything we think and do. Consider the letter of James: some scholars believe this James to be the younger brother of Jesus himself.[38] As a young brother myself, and now as a parent coping with sibling rivalry among my children, I can think of no more persuasive proof of the truth of Christianity than that this James became a believer and leader in the Church that worshiped his brother! Martin Luther found James abhorrent, mocking it as an "epistle of straw," so zealously did Luther uphold that salvation is by grace, not works. But once faith catches hold, it necessarily leads to doing. James is the necessary corrective to the sorry tendency of Christians who hear that we are saved by faith and not works, and nestle back into our easy chairs, relieved, and grow complacent about holiness and charity. James reminds us of what Paul assumed, that we are called to be "doers of the word, and not just hearers." Indeed, Paul's message and James's are complementary, and Richard Bauckham has even surmised that "between James and Paul there would be much nodding of heads and smiling agreement, as well as some knitting of brows and some exclamations of surprise."[39]

We know of a heated exchange between Paul and Peter, and all such conversations remind us that there is something flawed about having written texts, as indispensable as they are. For the New Testament portrays something oral, something vibrant, real people believing, debating, living, suffering. The very texts we now read were originally intended to be read aloud, and not alone, but in a community of people. Paul sent personal representatives like Timothy to interpret the words of the page, knowing that verbal nuance, inflection, emphasis, the raised eyebrow, mean everything. A warm body can respond to questions, notice who leans forward, who shakes his head, who stomps out of the room. In Colossians 4:7–9 we see Paul coupling his written letter with the assurance that the letter carriers, Tychicus and Onesimus, will go more deeply into things.

For the ancients, there is nothing peculiar about this anxiety over what is committed to paper. Plato, a prolific author, felt squeamish about the written word:

> Once a thing is put in writing, the composition, whatever it may be, drifts all over the place, getting into the hands not only of those who understand it, but equally of those who have no business with it; it doesn't know how to address the right people, and not address the wrong. And when it is ill-treated and unfairly abused it always needs its parent to come to its help, being unable to defend or help itself.[40]

As we move now to consider how this material and people who adhered to it drifted all over the place, we may reflect that the beginning of Christianity was not that books were written, but rather that there was a person, Jesus, who lived and lives, never fully captured by the books. By the Sheep Gate in Jerusalem, Jesus spoke to people who knew their Bibles: "You search the scriptures because you think that in them you have eternal life. But they bear witness to me, yet you refuse to come to me that you may have life" (John 5:39–40, au. trans.). The history of the Church is precisely the history of this refusal and Jesus' ill-treatment, and yet also the history of understanding and Jesus' Parent coming to his help.

QUESTIONS FOR DISCUSSION

1. Is it important to try to recover the "historical Jesus"? Why or why not?
2. What is the significance of Jesus' teachings being drawn from everyday life instead of being put into a series of logical propositions?
3. In what ways do you experience Jesus Christ through the pages of the New Testament?

PART II

Christianity

4

Church History

Saints and Crusaders

Christian history is a constant process of struggle and rebirth—a succession of crises, often accompanied by horror, bloodshed, bigotry and unreason, but evidence too of growth, vitality and increased understanding.
—Paul Johnson[1]

The story of Jesus Christ is not exclusively encased within the pages of the four Gospels. His history continues with a series of stories that fall under the academic category "Church history." The first sequel in this adventure is the New Testament book of Acts, which is really volume 2 of the third Gospel. The connection with the gospel of Luke and the dramatic plot of the history of the Church is declared in the first verse of Acts: "In the first book, O Theophilus, I have dealt with all that Jesus *began* to do and teach" (Acts 1:1 RSV, emphasis added). Jesus began to do things, to teach things, and the Church, which Paul aptly portrayed as "the body of Christ," continues what Jesus began.

There are several ways to think about Church history. We may consider the spread of Christianity across continents and through the ages, the Church's buildings and programs, its power and influence. Some of that story is heroic, some of it embarrassing. Many of its sordid episodes we may prefer to sweep away into some dark closet and throw away the key. But as we will see, therein lies the hopefulness of the story, the sure sign that the history of the Church is not entirely in the hands of mere mortals and their foibles but is, in spite of everything, most certainly the work of God. Charles Williams understood this when he sketched out his history of the Church and entitled it *The Descent of the Dove*.

The Church did continue what Jesus began, and with superhuman energy. With the unshakable conviction that their story was *the* story, that the Christ they served was the good news of hope for everyone

everywhere, a small band of unsophisticated believers, with no financial
backing or experience, fanned out across the Mediterranean, first to the
big cities along major trade routes, then into the surrounding countryside, telling of a teacher who was gruesomely executed but raised out of
the grave. People were fascinated, and many believed. Jesus had com-
missioned them to "be my witnesses in Jerusalem, in all Judea and
Samaria, and to the ends of the earth" (Acts 1:8)—and they were. Christian communities appeared throughout Palestine, across Asia Minor,
throughout Greece and in the very capital of the empire, Rome. The
eruption of Vesuvius destroyed Pompeii in 79; in the ashes a Christian
inscription was found. The faith spread southward to Egypt and northern Africa, and to the east, to Persia, as far as India.

In cities where the congestion and crowding would seem mind-
boggling to us, Christianity spread by word of mouth, in the market-
place, and in a culture far more diverse than any in modern times; the
average city featured temples to twenty to forty gods! Sociologists have
estimated the growth rate of Christianity. In the year 100, seventy years
after the death of Jesus, there were fewer than 8000 Christians in the
world. Fifty years later the number had grown to roughly 40,000, still
a mere 0.07 percent of the population. Another hundred years passed;
in the year 250 Christians numbered over one million, but even that
was just 2 percent of the population. By 350, though, 31 million pro-
fessed Christianity, more than 50 percent of the population. The annual
growth rate to arrive at this stunning number? A mere 3.4 percent per
year![2] The faith never consumed huge crowds in a single swath, but grew
quite gradually.

This faith was unstoppable, spilling into the Rhône Valley, extend-
ing to the far isle of Britain. Missionaries and preachers risked life and
limb and spoke with conviction and inspiration. St. Patrick entered Ire-
land in 432, and Clovis baptized thousands in France in 498. When
Gregory the Wonderworker became bishop of Neocaesarea in Cap-
padocia about 240 CE, there were only seventeen Christians in the city;
when he died thirty years later, there were only seventeen pagans left in
the city. Somehow Nestorian Christians got to China by 635, during
the T'ang dynasty, planting churches that would endure more than a
dozen centuries of persecution, even weathering the Cultural Revolution under Mao Tse-tung between 1966 and 1976.

For Christianity was its own cultural revolution. Acts portrays a community we might call "communist": "All who believed were together
and had all things in common; they would sell their possessions and

goods and distribute the proceeds to all, as any had need. . . . No one claimed private ownership of any possessions, but everything they owned was held in common" (Acts 2:44–45; 4:32). So why are we not surprised by the next sentence? "And with great power the apostles gave their testimony to the resurrection of the Lord Jesus, and great grace was upon them all" (Acts 4:33). The quality of the transformed lives of these Christians persuaded neighbors and coworkers and shed social convention. Foes of Christianity unwittingly blurted out the truth in Philippi: "These men . . . are disturbing our city; they . . . are advocating customs that are not lawful for us as Romans to adopt or observe" (Acts 16:20–21). Imprisoned, Paul and Silas sang hymns at midnight with such joy that even the jailer wanted whatever it was that moved them. Opponents unwittingly blurted out the truth also in Thessalonica: "These people who have been turning the world upside down have come here also. . . . They are all acting contrary to the decrees of the emperor, saying that there is another king named Jesus" (Acts 17:6–7).

TALKATIVE IN THE CORNERS

From the beginning, the growth of Christianity was greeted by onlookers with puzzlement and even hostility. Minucius Felix described Christians as "a tribe obscure, shunning the light, dumb in public though talkative in the corners."[3] Their radical faith, their ethical determination, their refusal to bow to the powers that be put them at odds with business, religious, and political leaders, and even with friends and family. The pagan Celsus, late in the second century, belittled them, mocking their assertion that God came down to earth. By definition God cannot undergo change or endure loss; a genuinely powerful God would have no need to come down. But there is rich irony in Celsus's critique of their life of fellowship: "Their agreement is quite amazing, the more so as it may be shown to rest on no trustworthy foundation." He criticized them for worshiping in secret, for being "talkative in the corners." Just to survive they had to be "dumb in public." At the same time, their secretive nature led to misunderstanding of who they were and what they did. Suspicious critics, knowing only enough of the truth to be dangerous, accused them of cannibalism, drinking blood, ritual murder, or promiscuous intercourse. Most importantly, and not at all erroneously, they were labelled as unpatriotic, easy targets because of their peaceful and unarmed ways.

The emperor Nero, looking for scapegoats after Rome burned, tarred Christians and burned them as torches to light his garden. According to the *Quo vadis* legend, Peter was crucified upside down on the Vatican hill. Paul, James, Ignatius, Apollonia, women, men, and children by the hundreds were killed. Byron surveyed the Colosseum in Rome and said, "Heroes have trod this spot,"[4] noting how Christians were forced to fight as gladiators and thrown to wild beasts (a claim disputed nowadays). Countless martyrs preferred death to renouncing their faith. Ironically, persecution fueled the rapid growth of the church. Tertullian wrote that "the blood of the martyrs is the seed of the church."[5] And it was not merely that they died, but rather the way they died. When the bishop of Smyrna, Polycarp, was burned at the stake in the year 156, he refused to curse Christ, saying: "Eighty-six years have I served him, and he has done me no wrong; how could I blaspheme my king who saved me? You threaten the fire that burns for an hour, but then is quenched; you are ignorant of the fire of judgment to come. Why delay? Do what you wish."[6] Onlookers, including the proconsul, were awed by the joy and peace on his face, even as he perished in the flames. In modern times, Dietrich Bonhoeffer was hanged in a Nazi concentration camp on April 9, 1945. His last words were, "This is the end; but for me, the beginning of life." The camp physician wrote: "I was most deeply moved by the way this unusually lovable man prayed, so devout and so certain that God heard his prayer. . . . In the almost fifty years I worked as a doctor, I have hardly ever seen a man die so entirely submissive to the will of God."[7] Tertullian reported that when Christians were brought into the arena to be killed, the crowds would shout, "Look how these Christians love one another!"

We have the detailed correspondence of Pliny to the emperor Trajan regarding how to handle dissident Christians. Showing them statues of the emperor and the Capitoline gods (Jupiter, Juno, and Minerva), Pliny would demand a sacrificial offering and verbal denial of Christ. Some recanted and were spared, although Pliny observed that "real Christians" could not be forced to do so. Celsus understood that the cohesion of Roman society was at stake in worship of the emperor: "If you overthrow this doctrine, it is probable that the emperor will punish you. If everyone were to do the same as you, there would be nothing to prevent him from being abandoned, alone and deserted, while earthly things would come into the power of the most lawless and savage barbarians."[8]

THE TRIUMPH OF CONSTANTINE

Of course, earthly things did come into the power of Christians. At first, the faith flourished among the poor, the socially marginal, even up-and-coming merchants. But the very powerful were more resistant. Indeed, the Church's ability to include the powerful was a challenge, as Robin Lane Fox has noted:

> By its own image and moral stance, the Christian community stood opposed to the open pursuit of power. It did not resolve "inconsistency" by offering a new outlet: rather, it claimed to sidestep status and power altogether. . . . Christianity was least likely to attract the people who were most embedded in social tradition, the great families of Rome, the upper families who filled the civic priesthoods and competed in public generosity for the gods.[9]

But eventually they were attracted, and the fortunes of the church turned decisively, although not entirely for the good. The last grand persecutor was the emperor Diocletian. His own wife and daughter had converted to Christianity. One day he consulted the oracle of Apollo at Miletus. A female intermediary passed along Apollo's warning that the Christian oracles were false. So on February 23, 303, Diocletian had the Christian cathedral opposite his imperial palace destroyed and issued an edict banning Bibles, prayer books, and all assemblies of Christians. Sacred vessels were confiscated, the clergy arrested.

But the battle for power after his abdication eventually was won by Constantine. With inferior forces Constantine invaded Italy. His rival, Maxentius, in a rash show of overconfidence, came out from the security of the walls of Rome and crossed the Tiber, only to be routed by Constantine at the battle of Milvian Bridge. The year was 312. So stunning was his victory that heavenly favor had to be credited. The Roman senate built an arch (which still stands near the Colosseum) commemorating his triumph, chalking it up to "the Unconquered Sun." But evidently Constantine had a dream just prior to battle and placed the Christian symbol for Christ, the Chi-Rho, on his shields and standards. In gratitude, he granted respite to the church from persecution, bequeathed massive basilicas to the Christians for worship, granted endowments of land and exemption from taxation, and even took the lead in assembling the great orthodox council of theologians at Nicaea. Constantine was no saint; he was not even baptized until he lay on his

deathbed, twenty-five years after the battle of Milvian Bridge! His soldiers and most government officials remained pagan, despite his official
recognition of the church. Yet over the next few decades, Christianity
became common, established as the norm.

The startling rise of the church after 312 was a pyrrhic victory if there
ever was one. A Christian empire! Surely this is the Church's fantasy. But
then again, if everybody is a Christian, then is anybody really a Christian? Before Constantine, it took real conviction to be a Christian; after
Constantine it took conviction to be a pagan! In Western civilization,
we are just now stumbling back into a time when the church is a minority, and many of us feel this is our greatest hope—for a faith taken for
granted is no faith at all. For once in power, the Church learned hard
lessons about the incompatibility of faith and power.

Celsus had complained that the Church drained energy from the
workings of society. Ironically, after Constantine's triumph the empire
co-opted the Church and drained its energies away for less noble aims.
In the Middle Ages, St. Dominic made a pilgrimage to Rome. Pope
Innocent III took him on a personal tour of the gilded, opulent Lateran
Basilica of St. John. Alluding to the reply of Peter and John to the lame
man in Acts 3:6, the pope boasted, "No longer need we say 'Silver and
gold have I none.'" But the humble Dominic answered, "Yes, and at the
same time the church can no longer say 'Rise up and walk.'"[10]

STUPIDITY AND CRUELTY

But not only was the Church denuded of its countercultural mission.
Power inflicted perversions upon the Church, well described by Wendy
Farley: "The tools we are given to taste the beauty of the divine—scripture, the church, religion, theology, even the Messiah—cease to be windows to God and become mirrors that reflect back our own stupidity and
cruelty."[11] The roll of dishonor includes the Crusades. On November 27,
1095, in a field just outside Clermont, Pope Urban II proclaimed a great
crusade, a military venture to reclaim the Holy Land. The wild popularity for this notion had built up over time, in no small measure due to the
inflammatory preaching of Peter the Hermit. On a pilgrimage to
Jerusalem, he was mistreated by some Turks; traveling around France he
clamored for revenge, feeding on prejudice, ambition, greed, and fear.
One abbot reported that Peter "was surrounded by great throngs,
received enormous gifts, and was lauded with such fame for holiness that

I do not remember anyone to have been held in like honor. . . . Whatever he did or said was regarded a little short of Divine, to such an extent that hairs were snatched from his mule as relics."[12]

The dangers involved in warfare were ameliorated by foolish offers of plenary indulgence for past sins, the glory of martyrdom, the potential for fiefdoms and more. At the end of the pope's speech, the frenzied crowd shouted with certainty, *Deus vult!* (God wills it!). Led by Godfrey of Bouillon, Robert of Normandy, and Stephen of Blois, tens of thousands marched off on this holy errand. Their true colors were exposed when, to give just one example, one contingent stopped in Worms, where Luther would defy the empire and instigate the Reformation centuries later. Count Emich of Leiningen rounded up the Jews of Worms and let them choose: conversion or execution?[13] Some Christians in the city tried to shelter them, but with little success, as 800 Jews were massacred. Today the old Jewish cemetery stretches beneath the city, Hebrew headstones still standing in the field as mute reminders (and perhaps even warnings) of the potentially vicious cruelty of men quite certain they are doing God's will.

Pressing all the way to Jerusalem, the Crusaders knew their Scriptures and attempted a reenactment of the battle of Jericho. They fasted, prayed, repented, and processed barefoot around the holy city, no doubt expecting a miracle. When the walls did not come a-tumblin' down, they took God's will into their own hands. Prayer availing nothing, they resorted to the battering ram and the siege tower, broke through the fortifications, and slaughtered the inhabitants. In the hot summer of 1099 they thanked God for victory with pious prayers at the Church of the Holy Sepulchre, where, for reasons unknown, the true God did not come down and strike them all dead.

Dark chapters in Church history were written by the popes. Eamon Duffy's chronicle of the papacy is appropriately titled *Saints and Sinners*, the sinners getting the upper hand at the end of the Middle Ages. Consider Leo X, who voiced his hedonism by telling his brother, "God has given us the papacy, so let us enjoy it." Alexander VI held bullfights in the piazza of St. Peter's. Celibacy became a joke. Alexander VI made his bastard son, Cesare Borgia, a cardinal. He tried to silence his harshest critic, the Dominican friar Girolamo Savonarola, by making him a cardinal; when Savonarola refused the red hat and demanded a "hat of blood," his wish was granted. He was tortured, hanged, and burned in Rome.

When popes did take stands for goodness, their supposed subjects bolted. Craving a male heir, Henry VIII divorced Catherine of Aragon in 1527 and disregarded papal opposition by simply assuming the church's power himself, breaking with Rome and establishing the Church of England. Catherine's own daughter, Mary Tudor, nicknamed "Bloody," got some measure of revenge, burning Thomas Cranmer, Hugh Latimer, and Jasper Ridley (and hundreds more) at Oxford in 1536.

In more modern times, we have haunting photographs of German pastors, like Hitler's protégé Reichsbishop Müller, in their holy regalia toting swastika banners and saluting the führer, and documentaries of Latin American bishops laundering money in support of brutal regimes. The Church, and all churches, need regular services of repentance. Seemingly, every time the Church cozies up to the powers that be, Christ is hauled once more before Herod, before Pilate, and crucified once more. Romano Guardini put it shrewdly: "The church is the cross on which Christ is crucified. And yet Christ is never far from his cross."[14]

THE PERSISTENCE OF REFORMATION

That is the wonder, the paradox of Church history. For as insidiously wicked as the Church can be, God persists in raising up voice, challengers, reformers. Hitler was not left unchallenged. Heroes we will hear from later, such as Karl Barth, Martin Niemöller, and Dietrich Bonhoeffer, thundered against Nazi pretensions. During the Crusades, Francis of Assisi waged an alternate kind of warfare. Jesus had spoken to him from a romanesque crucifix in a broken-down church in Assisi called San Damiano, saying, "Go and rebuild my church, for as you can see, it is falling into ruin." His reforming spirit led him to join Leopold of Austria, John of Brienne, and thousands of heavily armored knights in the Fifth Crusade at Damietta in Egypt in the summer of 1219. Francis, barefoot and with no shield or sword, walked bravely across no man's land toward the enemy lines. The Muslims at first drew their sabres to kill him. But he was so pitiful, so defenseless, that they spared him, leading him to the sultan, Malik el-Kamil. Were it not for the sultan's fear of his own soldiers, Francis might have pulled off the most unlikely conversion in history.

The problematical era of Constantine witnessed the advent of the greatest theologians for centuries to come: Ambrose, Augustine, Jerome, Basil, Gregory of Nyssa. And, as if in anticipation of how the church might sell out under the empire, the desert fathers emerged from cities and went out into the wilderness, to live simply and in discomfort. St. Anthony, greatest of those fathers (who lived to be 105 years old, dying in 356), wrote, "A time is coming when men will go mad, and when they see someone who is not mad, they will attack him saying, 'You are mad, you are not like us.'"[15]

Of course, the very word "reformation" will be forever associated with a single reformer, a fastidious monk in Germany who was revulsed by one pope's fundraiser. Legal custom for centuries had allowed criminals to pay fines in lieu of other punishments. In weak moments, church prelates seized on this notion and raised fortunes from sinners hoping to avoid hell or purgatory, building cathedrals and funding theologians, but also financing crusades and a lavish lifestyle. Leo X was sorely in need of funds, as he had wars to wage—not to mention his desire to pamper Michelangelo, Raphael, and Titian. So he declared a special "jubilee" fundraiser to rebuild St. Peter's in Rome. One peddler of indulgences, Johann Tetzel, took virtually a circus on the road, with jugglers and music, pledging, "As the coin rings in the bowl, the soul flies out of purgatory toward heaven." Martin Luther, a brilliant but personally conflicted professor of Bible at Wittenberg, called it a fraud and nailed his famous Ninety-five Theses onto the church door for discussion. A firestorm ensued, with Leo complaining to the Almighty that "a wild boar has invaded your vineyard." No more coins rang in Tetzel's bowl, and Luther wound up on trial at Worms, a moment Carlyle called "the greatest moment in the modern history of man." The Reformer brusquely announced, "Here I stand. I can do no other!"—adding, "God help me!" Forced into hiding, he grew a beard to disguise himself as Junker Georg.

But the Reformation was far from in retreat, spreading to Switzerland, first under the leadership of Huldrych Zwingli and then centering in Geneva under John Calvin. Henry VIII wrought a peculiar brand of reform in England, which had much to do with his marital woes and lust for power, yet thrived on the liturgical wisdom of Thomas Cranmer and theological sense of Richard Hooker. Catholics should not be seen as the victims, the mere foil of reform. During the sixteenth century itself, the Church was forever reshaped by Teresa of Avila, Ignatius Loyola, John of the Cross. In modern times, Pope John XXIII stunned the world by summoning the Second Vatican Council. The opening statement released on October 20, 1962, revealed its intent: "Under the guidance of the Holy Spirit we wish to inquire how we ought to renew ourselves, so that we may be found increasingly faithful to the gospel of Christ." This *aggiornamento,* renewal, updating, is always the Church's burden, its vocation. On the eve of the Cuban missile crisis, the Council's consequent pleas for peace and justice could not have been more timely. In Latin America, the subversive voices of Oscar Romero and Gustavo Gutiérrez made not only their own governments tremble but elicited considerable paranoia from the CIA during the Reagan administration. Henri Nouwen characterized the dramatic impact of Gutiérrez:

> There is a little man in Peru, a man without any power, who lives in a barrio with poor people and who wrote a book. In this book he simply reclaimed the basic Christian truth that God became human to bring good news to the poor, new light to the blind, and liberty to the captives. Ten years later this book and the movement it started are considered dangerous by the greatest power on earth. When I look at this little man, Gustavo, and think about the tall Ronald Reagan, I see David standing before Goliath, again with no more weapon than a little stone.[16]

But reform carries within itself the seeds of division. If we consider the emergence of Lutheranism and Calvinism in Europe alongside the transition of Catholicism into the Church of England, we may refrain from crowning the sixteenth century as the noblest in Church history. For the very need for reform and then the very division that results from reform expose in painful ways a universal Church at odds with itself, passionate about doing and believing the good, unable to stick together in the process, with reform movements themselves rapidly in need of their own reform. Within its first century, the Church of England was persecuting not the heathen but their own brethren, as Britain was ravaged by civil war. The surviving Church was so innocuous that a priest like John Wesley, trained at Oxford, took his preaching out into the streets, to the coal mines, effecting a reformation of a tepid Church and leading to yet another split, the advent of Methodism.

AMERICAN VERSIONS OF CHRISTIANITY

Trailing Columbus across the ocean were *conquistadores* like Cortés and Pizarro, whose paths in turn were followed by Franciscans, Dominicans, and Jesuits planting missions. Their zeal to convert the natives was compromised by cruelty and greed. On the Sunday before Christmas in

1511, a Dominican, Antonio de Montesinos, preached a sermon calling for the white man's repentance:

> By what right do you keep these Indians in such cruel and horrible servitude? For with the excessive work you demand of them, they fall ill and die, or rather you kill them with your desire to acquire gold. . . . Are these not men? Have they not rational souls? Be certain that in such a state as this, you can no more be saved than the Moors or Turks.[17]

Better known perhaps is Bartholomé de Las Casas, who came to the New World in 1502. For a dozen years he lived the leisurely life of an *encomendero* with Indian slaves. But while attempting to preach on Sirach 34:21–27 ("If one sacrifices ill-gotten goods, the offering is blemished. . . . To deprive an employee of wages is to shed blood"), he was himself converted, the Bible having done its work. No one would tolerate his awakened preaching against slavery and oppression. Returning to Spain, he spent the rest of his life campaigning for the welfare of Indians. His preaching was not of the triumphant Christ ruling in heaven, but rather "the scourged Christ of the Indies," whom he knew was there "suffering affliction, scouring and crucifixion."[18]

To pay close attention to the history of the Church in America is revealing, exciting, sobering. Some of the first settlers were exemplary in their faith. The Pilgrims who arrived at Plymouth in 1620 believed America to be their promised land, and themselves the chosen people; their biblical mission was to establish a new Jerusalem, to be a city set on a hill, to bring salvation to all people. Their disappointment was grave. Not only were the land and its inhabitants inhospitable, but wave after wave of settlers seemed more drawn to tobacco, liquor, and money making than to holiness. Varying denominations got along no better here than in Europe. By the early 1700s, a paltry percentage of Americans attended church. Revivals erupted now and then, featuring fiery preachers like Jonathan Edwards and George Whitefield in New England, and intrepid circuit riders like Francis Asbury in the south. We know that some of the founders of the United States were very pious indeed, while others were very cynical about religion, many with a mere intellectual belief in a remote kind of God who created the world and established its laws but is generally uninvolved. The Church has seen its fortunes rise and fall, its influence strong for a period and then invisible for a time.

It is important to keep in mind that the American Church as we know it occupies a tiny place and but a brief moment in this 2,000-year global history of the Church—and we are odds in striking ways. Ours is an emotional faith, focused on warm, fuzzy feelings. Ours is a selfish faith, expecting God to grant us success, comfort, health. Ours is a wishy-washy faith, where truth can be almost anything you want it to be. Ours is a lonely faith, as—uniquely among Christians through history—Americans think they can have a solo relationship to God without any commitment to a Church. The history of the Church teaches us that perhaps, for all the good that happens in and through our churches, we have veered off and need radical reform.

THE PERILS OF EVANGELISM

Not surprisingly, given the kind of "manifest destiny" many Americans have sensed over the decades, evangelism has been of particular importance. And the study of Church history reminds us that evangelism is always problematical. Heroes, like those of early Christianity, have continued to brave every barrier to take the message to people all over the globe. Ignatius Loyola, having become an invalid in 1521, read about the saints of old and ignited a movement that sent Jesuits to Brazil, China, Malaya, India, Japan. I have a friend whose father lost his life to the Communists in China in the late 1940s; I have another friend who has given up a comfortable life in America and serves now as a medical missionary in a backwater community of a still-Communist China.

Inevitably, many well-intended evangelists have misunderstood the distinction between theology and culture, unwittingly imposing Americana more than inviting people to the faith. Barbara Kingsolver's *Poisonwood Bible* tells of a missionary to the Congo who condemned the women for their bare chests and then insisted the men be baptized in the river; as the river was riddled with crocodiles, they wanted no part of his gospel. Failure in mission has at times proven to be a healing balm for the church. John Wesley's fervor for the gospel was such that he ventured to James Oglethorpe's colony of Savannah to convert the "Indians." So unsuccessful, so distraught was he, that he slumped in despair and quit, only to have his faith renewed by the buoyant joy of Moravians on his ship; so his failed mission proved to be the impetus for a grand revolution in the Church of England, where Wesley's message was more warmly received.

Indeed, to many, the dominant image of Christianity in our day has been the crusade, with preachers like Billy Graham speaking to hundreds of thousands all over the globe by way of television. At a worldwide evangelism conference in New York in 1900, John Mott declared the Church's task to be "the evangelization of the world in this generation," that we would "win the world for Christ." Now many work for a more modest, yet more worthy goal—not to win the world, but to *care for* the world. Missionaries nowadays are doctors, horticulturalists, teachers, Christians who, like Mother Teresa of Calcutta, see that the world is God's, and we evangelize, if at all, only when we care for God's world and the people in God's world.

THE SAINTS

The example of Mother Teresa invites us to consider perhaps the most precious finds in the study of Church history: the lives of the saints. James McClendon argues,

> In or near the community there appear from time to time singular or striking lives, the lives of persons who embody the convictions of the community, but in a new way; who share the vision of the community, but with new scope or power; who exhibit the style of the community, but with significant differences. It is plain that the example of these lives may serve to disclose and perhaps to correct or enlarge the community's moral vision, at the same time arousing impotent wills within the community to a better fulfillment of the vision already acquired.[19]

Throughout history God has raised up heroes of the faith. Or perhaps we should state it as an even more stupendous fact: the same Church that is beleaguered by its own stupidity and cruelty has produced saints, striking evidence that the Church is of God, that Christ indeed is never separate from his Church.

In fact, Christ has been imitated, mirrored, embodied in every epoch. G. K. Chesterton, noting how Francis of Assisi sought to fashion himself after Christ, how Francis "is a most sublime approximation to his Master," "a splendid and yet a merciful Mirror of Christ," shrewdly suggested that

> if St. Francis was like Christ, Christ was to that extent like St. Francis. And my present point is that it is really very enlightening to realise that

Christ was like St. Francis. . . . St. Francis is the mirror of Christ rather as the moon is the mirror of the sun. The moon is much smaller than the sun, but it is also much nearer to us; and being less vivid it is more visible. Exactly in the same sense St. Francis is nearer to us, and being a mere man like ourselves is in that sense more imaginable.[20]

The saints are not pastel figures cast in stained glass and statues, but real flesh-and-blood heroes who read the Bible, followed the one to whom the Bible bears witness, and thus breathe life and hope into all of us.

Francis of Assisi threw his wealth away into the hands of the poor. Ignatius Loyola put "What would Jesus do?" into practice. Thérèse of Lisieux loved Christ with an intimacy that embarrasses us—mostly because we have never dared to get that close. Dorothy Day turned the front of her Manhattan apartment into a soup kitchen; from the back she published a newspaper advocating justice and social change for the hungry. Martin Niemöller, after being dressed down by Adolf Hitler, climbed into the pulpit declaring, "Christ is my Führer!" and landed in a concentration camp. Back in the 1950s, down in Georgia, Clarence Jordan read the book of Acts and implemented what he read, a commune style of life, including blacks and whites, drawing the violent ire of the Ku Klux Klan. Mother Teresa's entire life was a profound exegesis of Matthew 25:31–46. As she fed the hungry, bandaged lepers, and clothed the naked, many agnostics found it helpful to consider that Jesus was like Mother Teresa.

Yet many Protestants, and perhaps modern people in general, harbor a certain cynicism about saints. The process of canonization seems long, exacting, and politically biased, with many luminaries failing to qualify.[21] The notion of praying to the saints worries Protestants, although it is not difficult to conceive that Mary, Francis, and Thérèse dwell right now in heaven with God and may well have perception of us, their brothers and sisters still on earth. Truly we truncate the life of faith to our detriment if we pay no attention to the saints. We need heroes; our minds are being reshaped all the time by celebrities who merely titillate our fancy. Francis reminds us of Jesus and what the Christian life looks like.

The production of intricate icons and illuminated miniatures that are treasured now by art historians reveals to us how Christians studied the faces of saints, each image capturing perhaps a dramatic moment from the saint's life. Such icons help us to pray. There is a tenderness to iconography, eyes expressing love and hope, arms extended to the viewer, the saints of old embracing you and me. And we not only look at icons; they are watching us! St. Jerome wrote, "Whenever I have been angry or had some bad thought upon my mind, or some evil fantasy has disturbed my sleep, I do not dare enter the shrines of the martyrs. I quake with body and soul."[22] Saints have for centuries lived as examples, protectors, companions.

In the early centuries of the Church, Christians gravitated to the tombs of saints, sensing their graves to be hallways between heaven and earth; as Peter Brown put it, there was perceived to be a "fault that ran across the face of the universe. . . . Death could mean the crossing of that fault."[23] Tombs became altars. Relics were especially revered. To touch a bone or fingernail or strand of hair of a martyr was salvific; proximity to a relic, especially when housed beneath a sanctuary's altar, achieved proximity to God. The chains that shackled Peter are the epicenter of a church in Rome (San Pietro in Vincoli); his remains were buried beneath Christendom's primal church at the Vatican. Dimly but persistently, worshipers have grasped for the presence, power, and spiritual vigor of the deceased who were not really dead at all, but surely in paradise.

We will return to this theme in our final chapter, but for now we note the vitality of Christianity's belief in the communion of the saints, that the great saints have a continuing vocation in heaven, that they surround us and give shape and hope to the Church—and not only the famous, canonized saints. Charles Williams, describing the Church, wrote that "her spectacles and her geniuses are marvellous, but her unknown saints are her power."[24]

QUESTIONS FOR DISCUSSION

1. What values do you think we gain by studying the history of the Christian church?
2. Where do you see "reforming" movements within the Christian church today?
3. What lessons do the lives of the saints teach us? Do you know persons you would call "saints"?

5

The Development of Doctrine

Faith Seeking Understanding

Is it not true that four hundred years after his own lifetime Paul not merely had an impact but did something really new for Augustine, and that eleven hundred years later he said something really new to Luther? Might it not be that Jesus of Nazareth said things in John's Gospel and the rule of St. Francis and Grünewald's "Crucifixion" and the novels of Dostoevsky that he did not say in the Synoptic Gospels?

—Karl Barth[1]

The saints lived and the martyrs died because they believed certain truths, and with a passion that surprises us, so lackadaisical are we about such matters. Interestingly enough to us modern people, Christianity emerged in a world of many religions, in an atmosphere of easy tolerance. The average person living near the Mediterranean in the first century could sample from a varied smorgasbord of religions, with no pressure applied, no judgments rendered.

So imagine, when they were greeted by the missionary zeal of Christians, the shocked faces of good citizens, who were accustomed to laissez-faire in matters spiritual. Christianity presented ideas that demanded a clear choice, not tolerance. Ramsay MacMullen has shown that the Church was unique because of "the antagonism inherent in it—antagonism of God toward all other supernatural powers, of God toward every man or woman who refused allegiance."[2] Tyrannical, this religion's claim to truth, brooking no rivals, granting no quarter.

So demanding was this new faith, so adamant were the Church's theologians about truth, that for most of the Church's history there has been such a thing as heresy, false doctrine. From the very first, Christians cared intensely about truth and thought getting it straight was a matter of life and death. Heretics were more dangerous than invading armies or the drought, for when heeded, they led persons away from God to eternal oblivion. But heresy was not so easily diagnosed and discarded. Schleiermacher said that heresy has every appearance of being

79

Christian, while contradicting the essence of the faith. And it is that essence of faith for which the Church toiled diligently. Every generation was forced to grapple with hard questions about what is true, and what only seems to be true.

It is this story of questioning and reckoning with truth we are about to tell. The beauty of the story is this: when we ask questions about God, about Christ, about faith, hope, and love, we discover that these have already been addressed many times over and by heroes of intellect and holiness. By listening to them, we inherit their wisdom, we avoid their false leads, we find our simplistic illusions shattered—and we discover what Bernard of Chartres meant when he suggested that if we can see very far, it is because we are like pygmies on the shoulders of giants. Those giants, long in their graves, still live,[3] and we dare not ignore them. James Packer spoke truly: "The Spirit has been active in the Church from the first, doing the work he was sent to do—guiding God's people into an understanding of revealed truth. The history of the Church's labour to understand the Bible forms a commentary on the Bible which we cannot despise or ignore without dishonouring the Holy Spirit."[4] Twenty centuries of faithful men and women studying the Bible: this is theology.

PERSONALITIES

The personalities involved are fascinating. Augustine, bishop of Hippo in Northern Africa (d. 430), was embroiled in the half dozen most important doctrinal controversies of the early church and settled most of them for all time. Yet he always did so as a marvelously anxious soul. You can sense his homesickness, his grief over his mother Monica's death, his voluble passion for God, to whom his *Confessions* were addressed. We listen in on their conversation and hear Augustine tell God, "I write this book for love of your love," and more famously, "You have made us for yourself, and our hearts are restless until they rest in you."[5]

The greatest genius of early Christianity was Origen. Born in 185 in Alexandria, Origen was zealous in his commitment to the Christian life and unsurpassed in his profound reflections upon the Scriptures. Legend has it that his father, Leonides, would kiss his son's chest as he slept, reverencing his body as a shrine of the holy, and thank God for the privilege of rearing such a precocious boy. Leonides lost his life during the persecution under Septimius Severus; Origen was still a teenager. As a young man he moved to Caesarea in Palestine, where he was eventually imprisoned and tortured, surviving Decius's persecution only to die of poor health within a year of his release. Origen was the model scholar, devoted to prayer and the church, passionate about holiness, consumed by study, which he believed brought him and others closer to God.

His work was twofold. He produced the massive *Hexapla,* whose six columns compared the Hebrew Bible with various Greek translations. Carelessness with the text would be, for Origen, the beginning of bad theology. "We need great application when we are reading divine things, so that we may not be precipitous in saying or understanding anything concerning them."[6]

Obsessed with detail, Origen construed among those details a profound theology that awed even skeptics; Origen's grasp of philosophy exceeded that of anyone outside the Church. His masterwork, the *Peri Archon,* clarified what the Church believed and how it made sense in the light of philosophical thought, and taught centuries of theologians how to plumb the depths, the hidden meanings of Scripture, and how its myriad stories hung together.

In the Middle Ages, theologians began to construct complex systems of thought, what Gilson called "cathedrals of the mind." No cathedral was more cavernous and awesome than that of St. Thomas Aquinas. Born in a castle, the youngest son of Count Landulf, Thomas as a boy was heavyset, taciturn, blurting out an occasional question like "What is God?" His father's ambition was that he would be a prestigious abbot, but Thomas forsook that destiny and joined the Dominicans, the begging friars. His father and brothers raged after him and locked him up in a tower; perhaps it was his sisters who let him out. Albert the Great, his mentor in theology at Paris, defended him against a sarcastic critic: "You call him a dumb ox? I tell you, this dumb ox will bellow so loud that his bellowings will fill the world." Those bellowings filled massive volumes of his *Summa Theologiae,* a stunning feat of brilliance. Aquinas applied prodigious powers of reason and logic to the Bible, not veering off from Bible, but understanding it more comprehensively, mounting one of its stones upon another to form a cathedral of contemplation, wisdom, and truth. As Thomas lay dying, friends nearby heard a voice from above: "Thomas, you have spoken well of me. What reward would you ask for yourself?" And this author of dozens of magisterial volumes of dogma replied, "Nothing but yourself, O Lord."[7]

If Aquinas built a cathedral, John Calvin filled a library with lawyer's case volumes. Again we see a saint disappointing his father: Gérard

Calvin wanted his son to be a priest, but John studied law at Orléans. An admired Latinist, Calvin mastered ancient literature, Demosthenes and Cicero, Plato and Aristotle; but not long after his conversion in 1533 he was thrust into the teaching of Bible. His textbook of theology, *The Institutes of the Christian Religion,* is a masterful display of biblical learning and a careful, zealous construal of who God is and what that means for us. But Calvin intended it to be not a great summation of theology but, rather, a guide to help readers approach the Bible and know what to look for, and how to find it.[8] His steely determination that the city of Geneva embody what the Bible was about bumped up against the recalcitrance of human nature and against theological foes like the heretic Servetus, who was summarily burnt alive. Calvin's legal mind and inexorable logic circled in to his now-unpopular doctrine of predestination. Grossly misperceived by onlookers today, predestination is the very biblical notion that God is all-powerful, that nothing escapes God, that God's will quite simply is always done. Calvin would be surprised that we find this notion so repulsive, for to him it was intended as all comfort: "When [the believer] recognizes that the devil and all the company of the wicked are held firmly in the hands of God as by a bridle, so that they can neither conceive any evil . . . save in so far as God commands them . . . in that he has enough for his consolation."[9]

In the previous chapter we spoke also of Martin Luther, St. Anthony, and Dietrich Bonhoeffer, and we may begin to think theology is the preserve of men. Women too have taught us to think and believe. Teresa of Avila lived a cloistered life until her death in 1582. Her health was always fragile. Perhaps because of her wretched health, or perhaps as a special gift to which she was open because of her dire need, she was often ravished by the presence of Christ, seeing angels and hearing God's voice in a manner so enthralling that Pope Paul VI bestowed upon her the rare title "Doctor of the Church"; Teresa (later joined by Catherine of Siena and Thérèse of Lisieux) was the first woman so honored among almost three dozen men. Legend suggests that Teresa frequently had to cling to the altar rail during prayer to keep from floating upward. But she taught us about discipline, that regularity in prayer, reading, and the sacraments yields a deep relationship with God. She also taught us how to open up the emotional life to God. Desire must be captured if we are to be close to God. What we bring to God is not great holiness and wisdom but brokenness and profound need, a virtually desperate desire to be loved, held, and swept up into the very heart of God. Our weakness is not something to be corrected, but becomes the very crucible in which intimacy with God is established. When we expose our weakness, we understand what Teresa meant when she wrote, "God delivered me in such a way that, even against my own will, He seems to have contrived that I should not be lost."[10] Besides her autobiography, *The Life of Teresa of Jesus,* she wrote *The Interior Castle,* a provocative journey into the vastness of our unexplored selves. Her mapping of the steps to the life of prayer (self-knowledge, aiming at purity, renunciation, absorption into God, union, crucifixion of self, radiation of love, joy, and peace) are alluring and yet terribly challenging, at least for most of us who expect spirituality to be easy.

The greatest theologian of the twentieth century was so surprised by the public's response to his commentary on Romans that he said it was as if he had felt his way up the stairs of a dark church tower and, trying to steady himself, had unexpectedly caught hold of a bell rope instead of the handrail, and was shocked to hear the massive bell ringing above his head. Karl Barth (1886–1968) began his career as a pastor in Safenwil, Switzerland, during World War I and finished as a distinguished professor in Basel. When Barth, while teaching in Germany, refused to take an oath of allegiance to Adolf Hitler in 1934, he was making not a political statement, but a theological declaration that there is one God only. He was dismissed from his position in Bonn and exiled from Germany. During his years of teaching in Basel, very few knew that each year on Christmas Day he left his family and went to the local prison to preach sermons that reveal his astonishing belief in the power of God's Word, his hope for all people, his commitment to Christ's Great Commission.

There is a humility about Barth, who recognized that every human doctrine about God, every attempted formulation, is flawed and correctable. He gave glory to God through his *Church Dogmatics,* which stretched into a dozen massive volumes, each brilliant and eloquent.

> As great as this achievement was, and continues to be, he wisely remarked that in heaven we shall know all that is necessary, and we shall not have to write on paper or read any more. Indeed, I shall be able to dump even the *Church Dogmatics,* over the growth of which the angels have long been amazed, on some heavenly floor as a pile of waste paper.[11]

His eleven honorary doctorates, in the same way, would have to be handed in at the cloakroom. Hanging in Barth's office was a copy of Matthias von Grünewald's painting of the crucifixion, which features

John the Baptist pointing his index finger toward Christ. Barth said, "I want to be that finger." Theologians are not great personalities but fingers that point to Christ. And they point first by digging into the pages of the Bible.

BIBLE

What is striking about early Christianity—and the entire history of the Church, for that matter—is its obsession with the written word. For a while, documents were copied and recopied on rolls of parchment—that is, until the advent of the codex.[12] The world at large was only mildly interested in this new device, whereby hundreds of pages could be stitched together into something resembling a book. But for Christians, this was a wonder to behold, a book easily held in the hands; unlike an unwieldy scroll, the codex was accessible, as the reader could quickly flip from Luke's Gospel back to Isaiah, then forward to Romans. Such wonder attached to the Bible that no labor was spared in the production of fantastic editions, marvelously intricate manuscripts, colorfully illuminated, many encrusted with jewels, some requiring a lifetime to prepare.

All this is surprising since in the ancient world the literacy rate in the world lagged at no more than 10 percent, and the rate among Christians was probably even lower, given the faith's appeal among the poorer classes, who had neither the ability nor the leisure to read. Illiterate Christians adored books they could not read, for they heard them read aloud in worship, first in private homes, then in the catacombs where Christians huddled for prayer and the Eucharist. Scrawled in paint on those catacomb walls we can still see their favorite stories depicted: Daniel in the lions' den, three men in the fiery furnace, Jonah's rescue from the fish, Jesus raising Lazarus from the tomb. Books were read in churches whose walls and windows were graced with frescoes and stained glass illustrating defining moments in God's story. Icons put faces on those stories, as churches and homes were adorned with simple images of Jesus, Peter, Paul, and Old Testament characters. The emperor Leo III, who declared in 726 that icons were in violation of the commandment to have no graven images and should be destroyed, discovered that his subjects were recalcitrant and simply would not give up their icons. King Henry VIII and his daughter Queen Elizabeth could declare England to be Protestant, but their subjects clung to the iconographic treasures of their Catholic past.[13]

The zeal of literate and even illiterate Christians for the Bible tells us everything about how to go about theology. Luther's Reformation would have died with a whimper, had it not been for Johannes Gutenberg.[14] In 1457 he published a Bible on a printing press. Church officials were mortified: what might happen if people read the Bible and misconstrued it, that is, read it contrary to our official, self-protective interpretation? William Tyndale, whose teaching already offended church authority, translated the Bible into English not long after Luther stood up at Worms. To some friendly advice, "It would be better to be without God's law than the pope's," Tyndale responded, "If God spare me, ere many years I will cause the boy that driveth the plough to know more of the Scripture than you do." Henry VIII's henchmen tracked him down all the way to Antwerp, and Tyndale was burned at the stake. The greater fire, though, was the power of the printed text, not merely in old Church Latin, but in German, then French and English, as the Bible was put into the hands of the people.

Garrison Keillor once mused that God made a mistake by letting so many copies of the Bible be printed. For nowadays Bibles are everywhere, and the easy availability among the literate has fostered apathy, as leather-bound, gold-edged coffee-table Bibles are dusted with the rest of the furniture. But in many countries in the world, Bibles are still precious, smuggled in and paid for at great price. For the Church has always known that the way to reach God was through these pages—or rather that we are reached by God, for whom these pages are fingers that beckon, instruct, and grasp us.

So theology was defined forever when the first apostles and teachers settled on this group of books as their text, their constitution, if you will. The selection of books took time, probably even into the fourth century. But this decision was not arbitrary and was not particularly difficult. The books in the canon were those that had already for decades been the ones that had formed the very Church making such a momentous decision. The fact that debate continued—that Marcion rejected the whole Old Testament, that Luther could make snide remarks about James (the "epistle of straw")—tells us something not just about the Bible (as a motley collection of varying apprehensions of God and life that do not cozy up to each other easily) but also about the Church.

For the Church preferred this awkwardness in the book they so adored to a smooth consistency. Tatian devised his clever harmony of the Gospels, the *Diatesseron,* to simplify everything, but, as we have seen, that condensed story was ruled invalid; the Church was more prepared to cope with embarrassments than to jettison the real, mortal stuff that gave birth to this faith. Like Luther at the Diet of Worms, we are forever "captive to the word of God." And despite every criticism, the Church has always declared that the Scriptures are sufficient for doctrine and life, whatever their age and prickliness.

THE TWOFOLD CHALLENGE OF INTERPRETATION

The history of Christian theology is the story of teachers coping with this body of material, which always requires interpretation. Just to restate the Bible is impossible or even misleading, for, as Jesus experienced and Shakespeare reminded us, "The devil can cite Scripture for his purposes."[15] Interpreting the Bible has always encountered a pair of challenges. The first is internal to the Bible itself. How do we discern what it's about? What threads are woven through this diverse, seemingly chaotic collection? Is there a plot? How does it all hang together? The early statements of faith, such as the Apostles' Creed, were something of an answer, the creed serving as a plot summary, a guide to the reader, a simplified announcement of the highlights, the pivotal moments, and primal affirmations inherent in the long sprawling narrative.

The second challenge was external—how to attach those moments and affirmations to real life in the world at some ever-lengthening remove in time from the events recounted, how to discern the way my life, my church's life, the events of the world are enfolded in the plot of the biblical story. We call this art "hermeneutics," and we are astonished by the boldness and dexterity with which each age has articulated that connection.

The most daunting task has been to make sense of the faith to those who do not have faith in this God, who do not assume that the Bible should be reverenced and lived. Could the Bible's message be voiced in categories that made sense to outsiders? And in trying to fulfill this task, is Christian theology thereby corrupted or enriched? Late in the second century, Tertullian asked, "What has Athens to do with Jerusalem?" A philosopher prior to his conversion, Justin Martyr (d. 165) thought of Christianity as "true philosophy," and wrote his famous "apology" to the emperor, Antoninus Pius, asserting that Socrates had partial access to the truth, that Plato's god is the God of the Bible. Beyond question, the earliest Christian theologians relied heavily upon the thought patterns of Plato and Plotinus as they sorted through the complexities of the faith.

Partly, sheer survival was at stake. Pagan intellectuals like Celsus (d. 180) belittled Christians, mocking their assertion that God came down to earth, since by definition God cannot undergo change or endure any loss; a powerful God would have no need to come down. Christians replied not merely by tossing out Bible verses, but by mounting ambitious arguments designed to answer criticisms and by even daring to persuade the sophisticated. Impressive, this Christianity. Robin Lane Fox marveled that the church won over not only the masses but also the intellectual elite: "Christianity's theology combined simple ideas which all could grasp but which were also capable of infinite refinement and complexity."[16]

When Athens has attacked Jerusalem, the faithful have been forced to think thoroughly, and have thus been the beneficiaries. Augustine spoke of the Christian's license to use methods and knowledge from philosophy and the sciences in terms of that curious moment in the exodus when the Israelite slaves took off with all the gold jewelry of the Egyptians.

> If those who are called philosophers . . . have said things which are indeed true and are well accommodated to our faith, they should not be feared; rather, what they have said should be taken from them as from unjust possessors and converted to our use. Just as the Egyptians had not only idols and grave burdens which the people of Israel detested and avoided, so also they had vases and ornaments of gold and silver and clothing which the Israelites took with them secretly when they fled, as if to put them to a better use. They did not do this on their own authority but at God's commandment, while the Egyptians unwittingly supplied them with the things which they themselves did not use well.[17]

The pinnacle of theology was reached in the early thirteenth century, and only after the rediscovery of Aristotle; his dialectic and logic empowered a depth of thought not possible a century before. Critics have suggested Aquinas followed the earthy Aristotle at the expense of the more heavenly Plato; but they may hear G. K. Chesterton's reply: "St. Thomas was, if you will, taking the lower road when he walked in the steps of Aristotle. So was God, when He worked in the workshop of Joseph."[18]

The relationship may even be said to have a coy kind of coquettishness. Repeatedly through the history of the Church, some theologian has flirted with a great thinker, only to leave him on the dance floor.

Erasmus of Rotterdam (1469–1536) pugnaciously cried out for a Reformation by appealing to Scripture and the Church Fathers. He did Luther a great favor by studying ancient languages, arguing that Matthew 4:17 did not say "do penance," as the Latin Vulgate suggested, but merely "repent"; Erasmus thereby undermined the Church's institutional penance (and corruption) in favor of personal faith. But Luther turned on him on the issue of free will and harried his legacy, branding him somewhat unjustly as a peril to the Church.

Critics of Christianity rear their heads in every age and place, innovative in their attacks, probing with their questions. Modern thinkers have been most prickly. G. E. Lessing argued that "the accidental truths of history can never become the proof of necessary truths of reason." Ludwig Feuerbach claimed that we have created the gods, who are nothing but the embodiment of our aspirations, needs, and fears. The enormity of evil in the twentieth century is such that you cannot blame historians like Barbara Tuchman for chiding the naive: "We must not forget that the gods are a concept of the human mind; they are the creatures of man, not vice-versa. They are needed and invented to give meaning and purpose to the puzzle that is life on earth. . . . They exist to bear the burden of all things that cannot be comprehended except by supernatural intervention or design."[19] We are still in the throes of answering Friedrich Nietzsche, who thundered, "Where is God gone? God is dead! and we have killed him!"[20] Plenty of people on the street would agree with him that civilization is now at a stage that we may dispense with God.

So the Church continues to think, to question, to rethink, to reply. And we learn now and then that our most forceful reply to the world at some moments is not to make sense or apologize for ourselves, but simply to state our ancient truth with conviction, with courage. The Barmen Declaration of 1934, a heated protest to Nazism, did not dare couch itself in Hitler's categories and could not have spoken more forcefully to the folly and pretensions of the Führer:

> Jesus Christ, as he is attested for us in Holy Scripture, is the one Word of God which we have to hear and which we have to trust and obey in life and in death. We reject the false teaching, that the church could and should acknowledge any other events and powers, figures and truths, as God's revelation. . . . We reject the false teaching, that the church is free to abandon the form of its proclamation and order in favour of anything it pleases, or in response to prevailing ideological or political beliefs.[21]

TWO SCANDALS

To speak of Jesus Christ, as he is attested for us in Holy Scripture, presents enormous challenges. The man Jesus, called the Christ, stands as a pair of scandals in a way. Obviously from the beginning the crucifixion of a divine being was utter craziness to the thinking world. That the Divine could suffer, that God could be revealed in the darkness and shame of a brutal execution, fits no mental categories available. Yet that scandal thrusts us into a second, related scandal, that of the Trinity. To speak of a God who is not one but three begs for ridicule. Even today, many critics regard the Trinity as a fabrication of the early centuries of the Church.

Although the doctrine of the Trinity caused a certain embarrassment to theologians like Tertullian, Athanasius, and Augustine, they had no choice, given the biblical witness, but to tell the truth that the God of the Bible is somehow a community of three, yet a unity of one. And why? There is the formula "Father, Son and Holy Spirit" used in Jesus' Great Commission (Matt. 28:19). Furthermore, in the story of Jesus we see a narrative of relationships among Father, Son, and Holy Spirit. When baptized in the Jordan, Jesus was announced from heaven as "my beloved Son," and the Spirit descended like a dove. The Spirit drove Jesus into the wilderness. Jesus prayed to Abba, his Father. Jesus spoke of his union with the Father and said that the Spirit would comfort the disciples after his departure. At Pentecost the Spirit birthed a new community that follows the Son in obedience to the Father.

Theology had to make sense of this and groped for appropriate language, such as "three persons in one substance." Over time, heresies were sniffed out. Modalists, such as Sabellius, taught there was a single God, first wearing the mask of the Father, then intruding into the human realm in the person of the Son, then continuing in the Church as Spirit. But however appealing this may be to us logically, it fails miserably to explain what actually went on during the life and death of Jesus.

The mystery of the Trinity has always been grasped in praise and prayer more profoundly than by the theologians; this surely has been God's intent. An artist like Andrei Rublev may have oversimplified Trinitarian dogma in his famous icon; but his image of the three—Father, Son, Spirit—sitting at table, with the fourth side open toward the viewer, is full of truth. For Augustine was right: God is a community, loving together so profusely that we are the overflow of their passion, that we find ourselves drawn into their fellowship. Or so have holy women and men perceived God, them, and us. Augustine prayed humbly: "God the Trinity, whatsoever I have said in these Books that comes of thy prompting, may thy people acknowledge it: for what I have said that comes only of myself, I ask of thee and of thy people pardon."[22]

DEBATES ON CHRISTOLOGY

The most crucial reckoning in theology has dealt with the question, who is Jesus Christ? The very name suggests a double identity: Jesus, a man with a typical Hebrew name, mortal, vulnerable, walking, eating, talking—but then also Christ, not a last name, but a hint at his significance, even at his divinity. This man Jesus is the Messiah of Jewish anticipation, the one who unveils the truth about God.[23] Again, the biblical narrative compelled faithful theologians to gravitate toward a formula: Jesus Christ is fully human, fully divine; not half human, half divine; not a divine mind visiting in a human body. Two bands of heretics had to be defeated to maintain this unique truth. The Docetists suggested that Jesus only "seemed" or "appeared" to be human; they reasoned that Jesus most certainly was God, and God surely cannot be mixed up in human toil and suffering. The followers of Arius (d. 336) similarly wished to guard the transcendence and uniqueness of God; for them, Jesus surely was merely part of the created order, divine only in a derivative sort of way—a demigod, if you will.

Ironically, the warrior Constantine (whose theology was feeble) wanted peace in the empire, so in 325 he summoned church leaders from all over his world to Nicaea, where they forever defined the nature of Christ in a creed, the Nicene, still used in churches today. Jesus Christ is "true God of true God, begotten not made, of one substance with the father." Obviously this creed is using terminology not to be found in the Bible. But the makers of the creed had to answer questions not anticipated openly within the Bible, and they had to do so using language that made sense to the thinkers of the fourth century, not the first. So Athanasius, the genius of Nicaea, developed new words that, while not explicitly *in* the Bible, make good sense *of* the Bible.[24] Unsatisfied, Arius and two friends refused to sign and were summarily excommunicated.

It is important to emphasize what the Council of Nicaea was *not*. Movies like *The DaVinci Code* and many bestselling books that trash

Christianity imagine that Nicaea was a power play, Constantine shoring up his authority, foisting on the Church made-up beliefs (such as Jesus' divinity or the Trinity). Without romanticizing the council, we can say that nothing new was introduced at Nicaea. Brilliant theologians argued tenaciously about the best conceivable interpretation of the Bible. Somewhat democratically, they actually voted.[25] Crowds gathered to cheer or hiss, and the beauty of it is that people cared enough about the truth of God to labor to get it right.

Questions persisted into the next century, until Cyril of Alexandria, perhaps not as brilliant as his predecessors Tertullian, Athanasius, and Augustine, articulated a superb construal of the Bible, validated at the Council of Chalcedon in 451: we cannot distinguish or separate Christ's two natures, for the divinity and humanity are one in him, "perfect in godhead and perfect in manhood." Cyril was aware of philosophical questions and speculations. But he proved to be a hero of early theology—as he simply and plainly (and therefore even embarrassingly from a purely intellectual perspective) reiterated what he read in the Gospels about Jesus Christ.[26] For Cyril knew what was at stake: our salvation. Jesus Christ must be human, and he must be divine, or else we mortals are lost.

WRESTLING WITH HUMAN NATURE

What we think about Christ is inextricably linked to what we think about humanity, about ourselves. Or perhaps we should say that inadequate notions of Christ hook up with inadequate notions of humanity. Not surprisingly, as the early Church wrestled with understanding who Jesus Christ is, they simultaneously diagnosed what is wrong with the people to whom he came. The watershed dispute was held late in the fourth century between an immigrant from Britain, Pelagius, admired for his moral luster, and a bishop in northern Africa, Augustine, whose checkered life gave him a sixth sense when it came to reading the Bible and human nature.

Pelagius enthralled crowds in Rome with a message that would strike most modern people as somehow correct, were it not for Augustine. To Pelagius, we are able to do good, to choose what is right. Perfection is possible, and therefore obligatory. God would not ask something we are incapable of doing. Pelagius did not forget the grace of God; but to him, grace is precisely the gift of being able to do what God commands. He scoffed at the very idea of "original sin." We sin, indeed, but we can do better. To Pelagius, evil is a tough but beatable foe.

Pelagius's tough foe was Augustine, a more subtle thinker, a more realistic perceiver. The hot contest between these two giants, who never met face to face, was observed with great interest by Christians around the Mediterranean. Riots broke out in the streets! Augustine knew the Bible better, probed more deeply into human nature and into the heart of Christ. Augustine won the day, not so much because of his great rhetorical skills or cleverness in argument, but because he spoke the truth—a truth not immediately evident, a truth that is still hard to hear, a truth so humbling and downright embarrassing and yet, for precisely that reason, so honest and liberating and hopeful.

Augustine taught us about who we are: sinners who are not even free to stop sinning. Reminiscing over his life, Augustine knew himself to be a sinner even in infancy, lacking only the power to wreak worse havoc. As an adolescent he and some friends swiped some pears, and he had the insight to recognize in such a trivial incident the way we are seduced by whatever is prohibited, so flammable is our sinful desire. And the risk in indulgence? "For in truth lust is made out of perverse will, and when it is served, it becomes habit, and when habit is not resisted, it becomes necessity. By such links, joined one to another, a harsh bondage held me fast."[27] The apostle Paul had shrieked in exasperation that he was unable to do the good he wished to do: "I see in my members another law . . . making me captive" (Rom. 7:23).

The Church has always argued there is such a thing as "original sin." We need not be distracted by thinking of original sin genetically. But surely we all sin, we all are sucked into some vortex of selfishness, away from God, a sinkhole not of our own devising but yet into which we heartily plunge. Augustine knew that the dark specter of evil is not to be trifled with, that there are forces on the loose that can seize individuals and even whole cultures by the throat and squeeze the very life out of them.

More seriously, Pelagius minimized the cruciality of Christ. Pelagius seemed to lay the burden of salvation squarely upon the individual. And nothing is more sad and hopeless than being required to shoulder the responsibility for salvation when you look in the mirror and see someone who, like Paul, is lacking the interior equipment to do or be what God asks. For Augustine, Christ existed, not so much as an example to us (although no higher or better example could ever exist), but primarily to save us, precisely when we fail to follow that perfect example. And that "when" was years ago; it was just a few minutes ago; it is now; it will be tomorrow morning as well. In one sense, there is no cure for sin. And yet there *is* a cure, which does not rest in my determination but is mingled in the blood flowing from the wounds of Jesus on the cross.

ATONEMENT AND JUSTIFICATION

If proof were needed of the intractability of human sin, flip back to the previous chapter and re-read what transpired in the history of the church. The Protestant Reformation, although political and social turmoil contributed to its origins and final shaping, was at its heart a theological revolution. For centuries the Church had wrestled, not only with, Who is Jesus Christ? and What is wrong with us?—but also with, What did Jesus accomplish? Textbooks typically point to three theories of the atonement. Picking up on passages like Romans 3 that speak of the cross of Christ as a sacrifice, Athanasius wrote that Jesus "changed our sufferings for his happiness. For, being life, he died that he might make us alive."[28] In short, because of our sin we owe a debt to God so immense that we desperately need a substitute, some payment on our behalf. The most eloquent expression of this notion was *Cur Deus Homo* ("Why God Became Man"), written by St. Anselm of Canterbury (d. 1109). A hapless dialogue partner with the (seemingly to us unfortunate) name of Boso stumbles through questions and learns that God made us to be righteous, but through sin we are now impotent to obey God. Satisfaction must be made for our sin, and only a God-man would be capable of offering the satisfaction or payment to God we could never muster. The change wrought is in God, not in us. Aquinas taught this, as did Karl Barth, who could speak of Christ as "the Judge judged in our place." Much modern revivalistic preaching clings to this understanding of the work of Christ.

Anselm's contemporary, Abelard, interpreted the cross as creating change, not in God, but in us. For him, the cross is the ultimate demonstration of God's love. "The purpose and cause of the incarnation was that Christ might illuminate the world by his wisdom, and excite it to love of himself." That love moves us, lures us, transforms us. Our sins are forgiven, as Anselm taught, but we are also subjectively roused to love God ourselves.

A more ancient, but less familiar interpretation of Christ's work was developed by Origen and Gregory the Great, who argued that the devil had acquired rights over fallen humanity. But the devil overreached his limited authority when he grasped for the holy and sinless Son of God. As Gregory put it, the devil tried to devour the bait of Christ's humanity, but the hook, the divinity of Christ, did him in, and Christ emerged victorious. On this view, the result of the cross is not just the forgiveness of sin or our being moved by God's love. We are released from bondage to powers greater than our own. Readers of C. S. Lewis's *Chronicles of Narnia* will find this plot to be familiar. The white witch rules Narnia; Aslan surrenders himself and is killed, but fractures the stone table and returns victorious. As the great lion tells the children, "Though the Witch knew the Deep Magic, there is a magic deeper still which she did not know."[29]

We need not debate which of the three theories is the right theory. Each voices a melody resonant in the New Testament, and each carries some dissonance due to cultural influences (such as the way Anselm's view of God seems jaded by medieval feudalism), and due to the fact that an abstracted "theory" inevitably falsifies in some measure what it tries to explain. Robert Jenson is right:

> The Gospels tell a powerful and biblically integrated story of the Crucifixion; this story is just so the story of God's act to bring us back to himself at his own cost, and of our being brought back. There is no other story behind or beyond it that is the real story of what God does to reconcile us, no story of mythic battles or of a deal between God and his Son or of our being moved to live reconciled lives. The Gospel's passion narrative is the authentic and entire account of God's reconciling actions and our reconciliation, as events in his life and ours. Therefore what is first and principally required as the Crucifixion's right interpretation is for us to tell this story to one another and to God as a story about him and about ourselves.[30]

Perhaps no theologian grasped so profoundly the inner plot of this story as Luther. An Augustinian monk teaching Bible in Wittenberg, Luther's zeal for righteousness was his undoing—so overly anxious was he about being good enough for God. His pastor, John Staupitz, upbraided Luther during confession: "Look here, if you expect Christ to forgive you, come in with something to forgive—parricide, blasphemy, adultery—instead of all these peccadilloes!" The unreachability of a life wholly and purely devoted to God left Luther exasperated, as he wrote just before he died:

I hated that word "righteousness of God," which, according to the use and custom of all the teachers, I had been taught to understand philosophically regarding the formal or active righteousness, as they called it, with which God is righteous and punishes the unrighteous sinner. Though I lived as a monk without reproach, I felt that I was a sinner before God with an extremely disturbed conscience. I could not believe that he was placated by my satisfaction. I did not love, yes, I hated the righteous God who punishes sinners. I was angry with God. . . . At last, by the mercy of God, I began to understand that the righteousness of God is that by which the righteous lives by a gift of God, namely by faith. . . . Here I felt that I was altogether born again and had entered paradise itself through open gates.[31]

Luther went on to say that "from that moment, I saw the whole face of Scripture in a new light." Indeed. The commandments—try as we might to obey them—only make things worse. We cannot be humble; the law humbles us. Luther denied that we are free beings. We may feel free, but we are not. I am very much trapped by sin, as if I have tumbled into a tangle of barbed wire from which I absolutely cannot extricate myself. I am not free to decide for or against God; rather, it is the unmerited grace of God that sets me free. Luther put it shrewdly, "Faith is the humility which turns its back on its own reason and its own strength."[32]

This revolutionary discovery is "justification." The righteousness of God is not something we try to do and is not the judgment of God upon our failure. Rather, righteousness is a gift God freely bestows on us. What needs to be altered is not this or that behavior, but rather the whole of human nature. Justification is waking up to realize that we have been set into a right relationship with God, through no doing of our own. Our receiving of this free gift we call "faith."

But the gift is all gift, simultaneously veiled and unveiled in the cross of Christ. As his pastor, Staupitz had directed Luther to the suffering and wounds of Christ. God is most fully made known, not in some obvious victory, but in the apparently contradictory moment of the crucifixion. It is when God hides himself, when God is absent, when all is darkness, in the middle of suffering, that God is genuinely present, embracing our mortality and suffering. In the Ninety-five Theses, Luther stated, "God works by contraries so that a man feels himself to be lost in the very moment when he is on the point of being saved. Man must first cry out that there is no health in him. In this disturbance salvation begins. When a man believes himself to be utterly lost, light breaks."[33]

THE SOCIAL GOSPEL

Light broke early in the twentieth century, a century in which humanity believed itself to be lost. As the horrors of World War I dawned on the world, Walter Rauschenbusch, just a year before his death, delivered lectures at Yale that became the stellar book *A Theology for the Social Gospel.* Rauschenbusch's work swayed the young mind of Martin Luther King Jr., the catalyst of the civil rights movement. The twentieth century's singular contribution to theology was its insistence that theology was not just for the individual, not just for the church, but for the world, to be lived out in the world. As we have seen, Karl Barth stated clearly in the Barmen Declaration that every sphere of life belongs to Christ. As a pastor to poor workers in Safenwil, he studied the Bible but also delved into factory practices, safety laws, and trade unionism, and found himself embroiled in fierce struggles on behalf of laborers.[34] Other movements, especially in Latin America and South Africa, perceived theology's rightful intrusion into the political and social spheres, something as old as the great prophets Amos, Isaiah, and Jeremiah. To explore the faithful words and courageous lives of Desmond Tutu, Oscar Romero, and Gustavo Gutiérrez is to shatter "the great fallacy," the bogus notion that "religion and politics don't mix." The great observer of liberation theology Robert McAfee Brown told the truth: "In sum, the appeal of the Great Fallacy is that it frees us from having to face challenges to the present state of affairs. It is a way of opting for the status quo."[35] The refusal to get involved in whatever is "political" is a lame excuse to keep things they way they are, which is usually to the advantage of the one refusing to get involved.

And so we will be forever uncomfortable because of the guerrilla warriors of twentieth-century theology, forever questioning whether our vested interests are jading our thinking, forever having to explain our mental beliefs to the poor and despised children of God in remote places (and right before our eyes!), forever probing every corner of life in this world, forever bringing the gospel to bear upon reality, and thus to change that reality—a subject about which we will say more in chapter 7. In his Yale lectures, Rauschenbusch claimed that this social gospel, which is "neither alien nor novel" to the Scriptures and nature of Christianity, "is a permanent addition to our spiritual outlook, and that its arrival constitutes a stage in the development of the Christian religion."[36]

QUESTIONS FOR DISCUSSION

1. Why was it important for early Christians to hammer out precise statements of Christian doctrines?
2. Why is it crucial for Christian faith that Jesus Christ be recognized as "fully human" and "fully divine"?
3. Why is the insight that righteousness is "a gift God freely bestows on us" such a radical and revolutionary idea?

6

Theology

What We Believe

I can only teach in such a way as to engender in him the questions, as if he were saying to himself, "If it were true, it's a big enough truth that would pull me together." In a sense, that's what a sermon is for: to hang the holy possible in front of the mind of the listeners and lead them to that wonderful moment when they say, "If it were true, it would do." To pass from that to belief is the work of the Holy Spirit.

—Joseph Sittler[1]

Having surveyed the Bible, and what Christians have been doing with it through history, we now ask, what do Christians believe? The Nicene Creed begins with the most obvious sentence: "We believe in one God." A little poking around inside that sentence will help point us in the right direction.

It is a "we" that believes. Believing is something we do with others, people we talk to and see right now, people in other parts of the world, people who have lived in other centuries. The last chapter demonstrated that Christianity is something old, something ever fresh, something we receive. We do not believe alone. Good thing, too. How sad it is if I think that ultimate truth is something that is inside me and me alone, that God is somehow captured in my private ruminations and biases. Our culture declares that you can and should have your own little private denomination of belief.[2] But how likely is it that even the brightest person's opinions, that even the most passionate person's pious feelings, are in fact the truth about anything rightly called God? Nobody can believe for me or you. But I don't want to believe by myself; I want to believe with others, with you, in community.

What do we mean by "believe"? What is faith? Certainly a faith worth bothering about isn't easy or cheap. Faith is serious, not just a little nicety added on. Faith is not pretending that horrible things must somehow be good. Faith is not a mere surge of feeling, although in American religion we've been duped into thinking that if we don't get that swooning rush, akin to falling in love, then we have no faith at all. Maybe the life of faith is like a marriage or a deep friendship: at the beginning, or at turning points, there may be an intensity of feeling, but most of the time the relationship is pretty mundane—more like a commitment. By faith you look at things differently. Faith is our freedom. I don't have to be like Atlas, the weight of the world on my shoulders. Faith is not getting a grip on our chaotic lives. No, faith is letting God get a grip on us, to lift us and sweep us into an eternal adventure. Faith is trust.

Faith wants to know. Some people talk about faith as a blind leap, when you grit your teeth and swallow some otherwise unbelievable story. To correct this notion, we turn to the banner document of medieval Christian thought penned by Anselm of Canterbury in 1078. The subtitle of his *Proslogion* is *Fides quaerens intellectum,* "faith seeking understanding." In its first chapter, Anslem declares, *Credo ut intelligam,* "I believe in order to understand." This pair of Latin phrases is the inversion of modern thought, which either insists on understanding before believing, or else divorces the two as incompatible. For Anselm, faith bears within itself a desire to know, not the kind of knowledge that is merely in the head or is geared to mastery and control of an object, but the kind of knowledge that a lover has for the beloved, ever wanting to perceive more.

Maybe in our day and age, faith is a lot like courage. Faith is what Maggie Ross called "a willingness for whatever,"[3] the courage to be and do whatever God has for us. Luther compared unfaith to the experience of someone who must cross the sea but is frightened and doesn't trust the ship. Faith is getting on board, launching out into God's way, God's future. Faith is not something we do once, and then we've done it, admission ticket to heaven firmly in hand. Faith is like breathing, growing, walking. Faith permeates every decision, every thought, how we spend our money and time, whom we hang around with. Faith is everything, or it is nothing. Faith that is just pasted on the outside is really no faith at all.

And we do not merely believe, but we believe in *God.* Karl Barth saved twentieth-century Protestant theology, which was sliding imperceptibly into an emotionalism that said the religious life is about me and my religious feelings. Barth heard the Bible's thunder and alerted us to the fact that the religious life is about God. A mocking public may laugh if we start with God, for the public is not at all sure there is a God or, if there is a God, what that God may be like. In Arthur Miller's *After the Fall,* Quentin, a lawyer in his forties, alone on stage, sadly states: "I

think now that my disaster really began when I looked up one day—
and the bench was empty. No judge in sight. And all that remained was
the endless argument with oneself—this pointless litigation of existence
before an empty bench. Which, of course, is another way of saying—
despair."[4] Try as I might, I cannot begin just now with some compelling
proof that there is a God, that the bench is not empty. If God is, if God
can be known, this God is known only in the telling of the story and is
proven only in the living out of that story.

Of course, as soon as we try to explain the story, we immediately
distort the nature of things and even of life, which can never be dis-
tilled into categories or terminology.[5] To talk about the things of God,
though, requires that we risk all and use words. Some of those
words—ancient words like creation, sin, justification, sanctification,
faith—carry freight that may even insulate us from the story, from
God.

We need to hear afresh what faith might be, who God is, what Jesus
was about, and all that means for me and for you. We do not begin by
presuming we know who or what God is, and then exploring how the
story fits or doesn't fit what we know God to be. Instead, we read, we
listen, we live, we practice, we hope, and perhaps only then do we discover that we have passed by the sirens and not crashed upon those dangerous rocks.

But then we enjoy a curious luxury. We begin at the beginning of the
story, and yet we know how the story ends. As in an intriguing detective
story,[6] events happen, unexplained moments loom, we wonder who did
what and how it will all turn out. Then the insightful detective steps into
a room where all the parties involved, suspects included, are present, and
he unfolds a concise little narrative explaining who did what, why, and
how. To our amazement, as we look back over the story, we understand it
all and see connections and clues that formerly were meaningless but now
are the very threads tying it all together. So it is as we look back across the
Bible at our story, at God's story, at what we believe. We know the whole
story, and the ending determines the beginning in surprising ways.

CREATURES CAME FORTH

The Bible begins in the beginning, when God created heaven and earth.
The giants onto whose shoulders we have climbed—Augustine,
Aquinas, Luther, Calvin, Barth—all agree that the God in question is

the Trinity, the Father, Son, and Holy Spirit. Those faces were not at all discerned by the writer of Genesis, but yet they were there, the cause of everything. God is love, God is a community of three, and the intensity of love in that community is such that an unfathomably massive universe has been cast into being. Scientists have dated the beginnings of the universe to some fifteen billion years ago. But the telescope cannot see far enough; the microscope cannot look closely enough. Some scientists believe; others wonder.

Thomas Aquinas, the "dumb ox," saw the truth of creation: "In God's hand were all the ends of the world: when his hand was opened by the key of love, the creatures came forth."[7] Creation, all of the universe, is grace, love. The world is not God. God is not "in" the world. The world is not divine, but it isn't worthless or meaningless, either. The world is the theater of God's glory, the open hand of God's love.

God creates by speaking: "Let there be . . ." God works verbally, by commanding, by inviting. This God who made everything did not just wind up the world like a clock and leave it to tick on its own. "He sustains all things by his powerful word" (Heb. 1:3). God's creative activity continues as God conserves life and the universe.

Creation has a purpose, a goal. We feel as though we have time and space to live and enjoy the world. Theologically, we discover that we have time and space to be invited into God's life, to be grasped by God's open hand. We realize the hidden purpose of that fifteen-billion-year explosion of love is Jesus Christ himself, the ultimate embodiment of God's love, the crown of mundane reality, the one who makes sense of it all. This will seem absurd to those who have not risked everything and gotten inside the story, who haven't been tipped off on how the story ends. St. Anselm acknowledged our position: "The unbelievers, who laugh at our simplicity, charge that we do God injury and insult when we assert that he descended into the womb of a woman . . . and—not to speak of many other things that seem inappropriate for God—that he bore weariness, hunger, thirst, blows, and a cross."[8] How we make sense of Christ, and even claim his participation in creation, will have to wait.

ALL PRAISE IS YOURS

Students of Luther's *Small Catechism* recite, "God created me, along with all creatures." For we too have a purpose. The fact of creation elicits and requires a twofold response from us as the beneficiaries of and participants in that creation: praise and stewardship. Praise is our amazement at creation, our recognition of the power and tenderness of the creator, our sense of belonging, of loyalty or fealty. Praise enjoys and celebrates God's love, and as such is "an attempt to cope with the abundance of God's love."[9]

Praise is what we were made for. And yet in our culture, praise is an alien kind of mood, an unfamiliar activity. We are so functional: What works? What is being produced? What is its value to me? Praise doesn't "work," it is not productive, it isn't even about me. Praise means being lost in adoration of the beloved, being awestruck by beauty. Praise is downright wasteful in terms of possible ways to spend your time. To think of God like a lover, one on whom you might dote for hours, requires considerable imagination, a radical retreading of the soul. To learn praise we need a guide, someone like Annie Dillard, who goes out and notices minute wonders in nature; someone like Charles Wesley, who wrote hymns every day extolling God's greatness; someone like St. Francis, who wrote his famous canticle:

Most high, all-powerful, all-good Lord,
All praise is yours, all glory, all honor and all blessing.
To you, alone, Most High, do they belong.
No mortal lips are worthy to pronounce your name.
All praise be yours, my Lord, through all that you have made.

He proceeded to praise God for "my brother sun, who brings the day. . . . Of you, Most High, he bears the likeness"; then he turned to "sister moon and stars, brother wind, sister water, brother fire, and sister earth." Poignantly, Francis composed these lyrics not long before his death, while racked with pain, suffering constant hemorrhaging, his eyesight almost gone. Francis and other saints have taught us a paradox in praise, how the very effort to praise God is an antidote to despair.

For the wonders of the world are a generous gift of God to us. And yet these wonders are not intended solely for our pleasure. They are windows to their maker. St. Augustine suggested that the world's beauties are God's engagement ring: "Starting from all those things which we love here, let us long all the more for him."[10] Francis perceived in the birds and flowers intimations of the holiness of God. Not that every person who looks at a sunset or a rose in bloom actually discerns the face of God. But the wonders of creation are evidences of a treasure we share with all people, even with all religions.

The rest of the Bible's story makes no sense without grasping how it unfolds in this theater of God's glory, just as a theater is merely a dark cavern without the players staging the drama. Try as it must, praise never rises fully to its task:

> How my weak words fall short of my conception,
> which is itself so far from what I saw
> that "weak" is much too weak a word to use! (Dante)[11]

Yet even weak, lame words—precisely because of their weakness and lameness—tell the truth. Alice Walker imagined two unlettered young women expressing theological wisdom more profoundly than even Augustine, Aquinas, Luther, or Barth. Shug proposes a notion, which elicits questions from Celie:

> Listen, God love everything you love—and a mess of stuff you don't. But more than anything else, God love admiration.
> You saying God vain? I ast.
> Naw, she say. Not vain, just wanting to share a good thing.
> . . . People think pleasing God is all God care about. But any fool living in the world can see it always trying to please us back. . . . It always making little surprises and springing them on us when us least expect.
> You mean it want to be loved, just like the bible say.
> Yes, Celie, she say. Everything want to be loved.[12]

Everything wants to be loved, and is loved. We are loved. The Bible expresses this by the daring claim that we are made in the "image" of God. "Let us make humankind in our image" (Gen. 1:26). There is a likeness, a connection, a relationship between God and mortals like you and me. We are not chattel, we are not robots, we are not beasts. Our most precious treasure is that we have this kinship with the God who hurled the universe into being:

> When I look at thy heavens, the work of thy fingers,
>   the moon and the stars which thou hast established;
> what is man that thou art mindful of him,
>   and the son of man that thou dost care for him?
> Yet thou hast made him little less than God,
>   and dost crown him with glory and honor.
> Thou hast given him dominion over the works of thy hands.
>   (Ps. 8:3–6 RSV)

We are glorious beings, and therefore much is expected of us. "From everyone to whom much has been given, much will be required" (Luke 12:48)—which leads to the second appropriate response to creation.

Adam and Eve were put in the garden "to till it and keep it" (Gen. 2:15). Our vocation is to be good stewards of God's world. We have talents and abilities, things and money; we find ourselves with responsibilities in a world where things grow, where resources must be distributed. As Christians we are charged with the privilege and duty to use all that exists for the glory of God. To know that God is the Creator, to recall that the world belongs not to us but to God, summons us to shelter the environment. Every sparkling stream, every feathered species, every creature in the deeps of the ocean and in rocky mountain haunts, every created form is a voice in creation's chorus of praise to the Creator. When we destroy a species or pollute the earth, we silence part of the harmony of praise to God.

As stewards we are to work tirelessly for justice, human rights, the alleviation of poverty. Our marching orders emanate from our Lord's Prayer: "Thy will be done on earth as it is in heaven." More than mere philanthropy is required. We are not the proud possessors of funds and abodes, who then paternalistically shower our leftovers upon the pitiable needy. We are all brothers and sisters. There is enough in God's world for all of us, and those who have must share as God makes them able, must go where God's children are hurting. At creation, when human beings are given "dominion" over the earth, they are being asked to *take care of* God's world, not to *take over* God's world.

THE HUMAN PREDICAMENT

Taking over God's world, usurping God's place. Now we delve into the regions of sin. Modernity recoils at the very notion. Thoughts and behaviors long bracketed under the category of "sin" now are explained in psychological categories.[13] Dysfunctional families, hormonal imbalances, or sociological pressures bring on our troubles. Little wonder the new high priests of our society are not the priests, but lawyers and therapists. We cast a wary eye upon anyone speaking of sin, for beyond any doubt, the Church has been manipulative in its usage of the word "sin," attaching it to trivialities, burdening people with shame when they are victims, co-opting God in their tawdry enterprises.

In fact, a good case can be made that the confession "We have sinned against your holy laws" is nonsensical in our era, for very few are even aware of those holy laws, and no particular weight is attributed to those laws. To such people, we may need to shift our diagnosis of the human predicament in order to gain a hearing; a truer mental image of our problem may be conceived. For years, the Church has upbraided us for being like Prometheus, defiantly scaling the heights, proud titans lusting after power. But people do not feel much like Prometheus. Most people in our culture, if they sit down and bare their souls, admit that they are above all else exhausted. We are a weary, hollow, fatalist people, seemingly condemned like Sisyphus to roll a massive stone uphill, never to arrive, never to rest.[14]

The Bible knows this about us. Genesis 3 not only portrays sinful rebellion against God, but further understands the sweat, toil, frustration of existence. Paradise just barely but persistently eludes us, and like Cain we are banished "east of Eden," wanderers, weary, homeless, homesick. Philosophers have written very biblically on the subject. We may wish Socrates were wrong when he said we are like leaky jars, never fulfilled. We wish Hobbes could have been gentler, but life really is "solitary, poor, nasty, brutish, and short."[15]

For such wandering, homeless people, we may hear the beckoning call of the saints who have gone before us. We are glad that Augustine began his *Confessions* by peering so clearly into our souls ("Our hearts are restless until they find rest in thee") and that Dante, with words near the end of his *Divine Comedy,* can guide us ("I see man's mind cannot be satisfied unless it be illumined by that truth beyond which there exists no other truth").[16] The Apostles' Creed leaps rather forgetfully from creation directly to Jesus, as if the Old Testament's cast of characters and story lines were dispensable. But in Hebrews 11, a weary, harassed band of Christians is bolstered in their faith by a litany of heroes from ancient Israel: Abraham, David, Isaiah, Daniel, women and men who knew homelessness, who yearned for fullness, who suffered much, yet believed as we must. Kings, sons and grandsons of David, came and went, most mere pretenders; yet they were tenacious legates of a promise, ancestors of the true Messiah who would not merely pretend to be a king. Prophets spoke and were hounded and martyred, their voices declaring God's involvement in the very world in which God's own Son would also be hounded and martyred. Priests routinely prayed and burnt incense and poured blood across stone altars in unwitting anticipation of a priest who would once and for all put an end to their work by fulfilling their work as both the priest and the sacrifice offered. All those saints from the Old Testament, home-less and weary as they were, shuddered over the reality of sin. Even Sisy-phus was not merely tired.

CURVED IN ON OURSELVES

Genesis tells the full truth about the human predicament. We sin. While our vocation, our delight, should be praise and stewardship, we veer off into those perversions of praise and stewardship called idolatry and self-ishness. Selfishness isn't really the right word. Sin indeed is living as if I am the center of the universe, as if everything exists for me and my pleasure. Not content to serve and worship God, we prefer to be God. Luther spoke of sin as being "curved in" on yourself.

And yet to the eyes of faith we know that sin is the most self-destructive thing imaginable. There is a deeper kind of selfishness that says, "The absolute best thing I can do for myself, and for others, is to praise and serve God." C. S. Lewis put it most profoundly in his even-song sermon at St. Mary's, Oxford, on June 8, 1941. He began "The Weight of Glory" by hazarding the guess that good men in our century regard "unselfishness" as the highest virtue, whereas the great Christians of old would have thought of "love." We have substituted a negative, assuming somehow that desires should be denied, smothered, cooled. Then he added:

> Indeed, if we consider the unblushing promises of reward and the staggering nature of the rewards promised in the Gospels, it would seem that Our Lord finds our desires not too strong, but too weak. We are half-hearted creatures, fooling about with drink and sex and ambition when infinite joy is offered us, like an ignorant child who wants to go on making mud pies in a slum because he cannot imag-ine what is meant by the offer of a holiday at the sea. We are far too easily pleased.[17]

Jesus paradoxically lured the disciples in by saying, "Whoever wants to be first must be last of all and servant of all." "Those who want to save their life will lose it" (Mark 9:35; 8:35). The goal isn't merely being last and losing, but fulfilling our God-given destiny, which is life, glory, joy.

Life, glory, and joy cannot be found just anywhere. We are constantly titillated by peddlers pledging these elusive goods, but only God can deliver. All sin turns out to be a collision with the first commandment:

"You shall have no other gods before me" (Exod. 20:3). We are not so dumb as to prostrate our bodies before a handsomely carved block of wood. But we most assuredly are idolaters. Luther said that your god is whatever you look to for the good life, whatever you turn to in time of need: "That to which your heart clings and entrusts itself is really your God."[18] God craves our love, and we are above all else lovers. Sin therefore is a disordered love, a passion pointed at various lovers who are unreliable. Martin Luther King Jr. painted the disaster involved:

> There is so much frustration in the world because we have relied on gods rather than God. We have genuflected before the god of science only to find that it has given us the atomic bomb. . . . We have worshipped the god of pleasure only to discover that thrills play out and sensations are short-lived. We have bowed before the god of money only to learn that there are such things as love and friendship that money cannot buy. . . . These transitory gods are not able to save or bring happiness to the human heart. Only God is able.[19]

We fawn after other gods that promise us the moon but are nothing but a nightmare. We get lied to and perversely enjoy it, gullible fools that we are.[20] We look into the mirror and, like Narcissus, hope we see the source of all hope in our own face; and we wind up broken and alone. And if we are honest with ourselves and as a culture, can we not see the extent to which our sin and our giddy pursuit of bogus gods are nothing more than fear?

Whole cultures stumble into sin. For centuries the Church warned us about the "seven deadly sins" (greed, sloth, lust, gluttony, anger, envy, and pride)—but our culture celebrates all seven, and calls them "the good life." Gandhi spoke of the "seven social sins": politics without principle, wealth without work, commerce without morality, pleasure without conscience, education without character, science without humanity, and worship without sacrifice. Systems, institutions, governments, and cultures can and do assume the aura of sin, making absolute claims, sucking in our loyalty, spreading invisible toxins. Little wonder then that our proclivity to sin feels like being normal, like being stuck, like fear, or suspicion, or distrust—and all those moods are further entanglements in our wayward souls.

For we do get entangled and cannot extricate ourselves. To speak of turning away implies God has been clear about what is to be done, and turning away implies we have the freedom to do so. Freedom is something of which we are downright proud; in America, heroes have fought for freedom, and politicians are elected based on their zeal to shelter our freedom. We have misused our freedom to the point that we are no longer free. Like prisoners, we can choose to sit in this part of the cell or that part, but we are still behind bars. Like Augustine relishing his stolen pears, we love our wrongdoing, and it becomes delightfully necessary. Lust served does become habit and then necessity.[21]

Or perhaps the real habit is not so much getting chained to one craving but our flitting about among endless cravings. Today we speak of "affective contrast": we experience something "up," something fun or tasty, but then there is an aftereffect, a bounce "down." To get rid of the aftereffect, people seek another positive experience. Soon luxuries become necessities, but they fail us before long, as Barry Schwartz notes:

> There is an inevitable disappointment that comes with consumption because repeated consumption of the same commodities provides people with doses of pleasure that do not live up to their expectations. . . . As a result, people are driven to pursue novelty, to seek out new commodities whose pleasure potential has not been driven down by repeated consumption. But these new commodities will also eventually fail to satisfy. The lesson in this is that the pursuit of pleasure is a perpetual wild goose chase.[22]

Ironically, the most futile wild-goose chase is the avoidance of sin. Sin is sin, but in the Bible the most heinous sin rages among the holiest of people: self-righteousness. The Bible's harshest judgment is reserved not for the grimy wicked, but for the squeaky-clean righteous ones. And why? In the Bible, the way to God is all mercy, and never can be traversed by human achievement, for "the antithesis of sin is not goodness, it is love."[23] From the beginning God waged complex campaigns of love, strategies to restore us homeless sinners. In a sense, the Old Testament is the grand saga of God's patient healing and nurturing of God's people. Is the story comedy or tragedy? Surely elements of both cohere, as the noblest souls stumble embarrassingly, and the coarse and spiritually suspect prove to be the very ones God uses most powerfully. To read Genesis, or to contemplate the drama of the prophet Hosea, is to sense that God is a pained lover, a grieving parent, yearning for our love, unwearying in bringing us home. Genesis 12 declares the strategy God will employ: to save the whole world, God zeroes in on a single man, Abraham, and makes a covenant by which God will use him and his descendants to save everybody else. That promise is toyed with, flung away foolishly by Abraham himself and everyone in his prolific family. But that promise is never thwarted, for it is God's plan.

From the beginning, God put mechanisms into place so people could be reconciled and forgiven. Holy acts, sacrifices, all were designed to offer a merciful means for the humble to be restored to God and to each other. God always provided a way to return. The Day of Atonement was the ultimate ritual during Old Testament days, when the high priest would offer sacrifice, after which a dead bull would be burned outside the camp, and a goat would be driven out into the wilderness. Symbolically, sins were transferred to the "scapegoat" and removed from daily life in the city. Not surprisingly, the early Christians saw Christ as the high priest making sacrifice for them, even being that sacrifice himself, put to death outside the city walls.

THE DENIAL OF MORTALITY

In anticipation once more of the story's end, we may ask about death. God's dealing with us involves death: that of a sacrificial lamb, that of God's Son, and our own. The human predicament, sin, homelessness, greed, weariness, all focus in on the brutal fact of our mortality, loath as we may be to talk about it. Ernest Becker has noted how death poisons our lives: "The idea of death, the fear of it, haunts the human animal like nothing else; it is a mainspring of human activity—activity designed largely to avoid the fatality of death, to overcome it by denying in some way that it is the final destiny for man."[24]

If we read the Bible's story and "get it," then the most revolutionary conversion takes place: we need not fear or deny death. In his last, painful days, St. Francis added one final strophe to his canticle of praise:

> All praise be yours, My Lord, through Sister Death
> From whose embrace no mortal can escape.
> Happy those she finds doing your Holy will.
> The second death can do no harm to them.

We are made mortal by God. Human life is packaged with limitations, and to be limited is no evil. The problem is how we cope with our limitations. We are not God. We are not able to do and be all we wish. We are mortal. Evil is rooted in our revolt against what are natural limits, as we refuse to accept our finitude. Limitation is not bad; but our defiance of our limits, our game struggle to be independent, self-sufficient, indestructible—this is our undoing.

QUESTIONS OF OMNIPOTENCE

So if God is love, if God's desire for us is life, if we have this potential for revolt, we must ask why: Why all this risk and loose possibilities with God? Why was that dangerous tree planted in the garden of Eden? Why did God arrange our genetic makeup so poorly that, morally speaking, we have "shabby equipment, badly deteriorated" (T. S. Eliot)? Why did God fashion a world in which mortality reigns, in which weariness bedevils us, in which God is not praised and served? These nagging questions are the subject of many books, including one of my own, *The Will of God: Answering the Hard Questions*. The key thought of that book is captured in two unsettling yet inviting sentences:

> God is not interested in control.
> God is interested in love.

The problem always is that we intellectually define who God is, what God must be, with impeccable definitions and attributes. Our brains tell us that God is omnipotent, infinite, omniscient. We admire power and success and assume God must be better at these than we are. Armed with this presupposition, we scratch our heads and try to figure out how to fit the atrocities of the world and of our own lives into the all-embracing control of such a God. When everything goes smoothly, it is pleasing indeed to think that God has masterminded my cozy world. When disaster strikes, many find comfort in the notion that it isn't meaningless or haphazard, that despite horrid appearances, God still is in control.

To such a theology there are two objections. One is that many people refuse, and with good reason, to be comforted by such thoughts. Dostoevsky's all-too-true fictional character Ivan Karamazov protests all blithe platitudes that justify God and evil: "It's not worth one single tear of the martyred little girl who beat her breast with her tiny fist, shedding her innocent tears and praying to 'sweet Jesus' to rescue her in the stinking outhouse. It's not worth it, because that tear will have remained unatoned for. . . . I prefer to remain with my unavenged suffering and my unappeased anger—*even if I happen to be wrong*."[25]

From Job to Auschwitz, people have screamed in horror, not only over the immensity of evil, but also in recoil from a simplistic theology that blithely asserts, "It is God's will."

But when we hear such voices, we might chalk it up to a lack of faith, were it not for the second objection—which is that the Bible simply, strangely, yet wonderfully tells of a God who is not first of all omniscient, infinite, omnipotent, all-controlling. Jürgen Moltmann explains it beautifully: "Finally, a God who is only omnipotent is in himself an incomplete being, for he cannot experience helplessness and powerlessness. Omnipotence can indeed be longed for and worshiped by helpless men, but omnipotence is never loved; it is only feared."[26] Such a powerful God "cannot weep, for he has no tears." The Bible's God yearns, hurts, risks, feels rage, exposes God's own heart to the vagaries of wayward people. To love, you must make yourself vulnerable to another person. When I say "I love you—Do you love me?" I am giving myself over to you, and you may return my love and bring me immense joy, or you may reject or deflect my attentions and grieve my heart. When I love you, I hand my fragile self over to you, fully aware that you may cradle me to your bosom or drop me to the floor, shattering my self. From Genesis through Revelation, this is the Bible's God, willing to be broken for love of our love, determined at great cost within God's own self to love us and bring us into fellowship with Father, Son, and Holy Spirit.[27]

GOD'S DARING PLAN

And so in a way, Quentin's question as he looked up and saw that the bench was empty is misdirected. In Jan Karon's novel *At Home in Mitford*, one evening the rector walks through the sanctuary and unexpectedly hears a lone man's chilling question: "Are you up there?" Father Tim slides into the pew next to him and says, "Perhaps the question you need to ask is, 'Are you down here?'"

God did come down here. The embodiment of God's eternal decision to reach out, to reach down to us, to let divine love overflow onto us and all creation, took place in a small tract of land at the juncture of three continents. In one of her eloquent sermons, Barbara Brown Taylor imagined the angels and God discussing how best to rescue a wayward world. At length God suggested he create himself as a baby. At first the archangels were silent, but then they tried to talk God out of such a foolish plan. They would worry, for he would be putting himself at the mercy of wayward creatures. No security in such a plan. But God decided to take the risk. He was willing to risk everything to get as close as possible to his creatures, in hopes they might love him again.

> It was a daring plan, but once the angels saw that God was dead set on it, they broke into applause—not the uproarious kind but the steady kind that goes on and on when you have witnessed something you know you will never see again. While they were still clapping, God turned around and left the chamber, shedding his robes as he went. The angels watched as his midnight blue mantle fell to the floor, so that all the stars on it collapsed in a heap. Then a strange thing happened. Where the robes had fallen, the floor melted and opened up to reveal a scrubby brown pasture speckled with sheep and a bunch of shepherds sitting around drinking wine. It was hard to say who was more startled, the shepherds or the angels. Looking down at the human beings who were trying to hide behind each other, one angel said in as gentle a voice as he could muster, "Do not be afraid, for I am bringing you good news of great joy for all the people: to you is born this day in the city of David a savior, who is the Messiah, the Lord." And away up the hill, from the direction of town, came the sound of a newborn baby's cry.[28]

This was no emergency measure, but the very purpose of God's creation in the first place, the crown of the universe, lighting the way to our destiny. "The Word became flesh and lived among us, . . . full of grace and truth" (John 1:14). Or as Luther put it, God became small for us in Christ, showing us his heart, so our hearts might be won. A peasant girl of Nazareth, glorified and ossified into statues and stained glass, Mary, was given a startling vocation, unique and yet similar to mine and yours, to let God become flesh in her life, to disrupt everything she had arranged, even to suffer ridicule and pain, for Christ to become flesh. St. Francis again helped us when in 1223 he came to Grecchio, organized a great processional, and staged perhaps the first manger scene; he wanted people to see the humility, the humanity, the inconveniences of the holy family, with ox and ass standing by. A man named Giovanni even saw a child in the manger, which Francis roused as from sleep; Francis's first biographer, Thomas of Celano, wrote that Jesus had been sleeping in forgetfulness until then. In those days, Bethlehem was a trophy for the Crusader knights. But Grecchio showed we have no need to go on crusade, but that Bethlehem is everywhere, and can be anywhere.

HANDED OVER

In the previous chapter, we explored the way Christians have thought about the nature and identity of Christ. The creeds codified that nature and identity, and in a way that echoes the words Judas sang to Jesus in *Jesus Christ Superstar*: "You've begun to matter more than the things you say." The creed leaps forgetfully once more from Jesus' birth to his death, skipping right over his teachings and deeds. But Jesus' words and actions matter only because of his birth, and more so because of his death, and then what transpired on the third day.

Even during his life, Jesus' teaching and doing grind to a surprising halt. In the first half of each Gospel, Jesus is in command, boldly striding into new territories, conquering demons, healing diseases; he is a doer, in control of everything, even the wind and the sea. But then the mood changes abruptly. Jesus becomes reflective, darkly hinting at his fate. He ominously walks straight into danger in Jerusalem. He is "handed over" by Judas to the authorities, and he does not fight back; he says nothing. He is no longer active, but passive. In a sense, this is hopeful for us, for our lives often traverse that same ground, as we grow old or sick and are increasingly forced to be dependent on others. We fear our identity is lost if we are not active, productive. But Jesus shows us that who we are, who he was, is found not in our activity but in what we suffer, in what we receive.[29]

But there is more. Jesus was not merely passive. He gave himself up. He deliberately chose to let them act upon him. God even gave him up. God didn't kill Jesus, but he did choose to let the powers that be have their way with him. And why? "For God so loved the world that he gave his only Son" (John 3:16). In this moment we see God; in this darkest of hours God is brightly glorified. On the cross, God seems absent. But there God is most surely present.[30] God's love made vulnerable, risking everything, suffering as love inevitably suffers—and yet since it is this one who suffers, history is turned upside down. When Jesus endured the brutality of crucifixion, a horrific execution reserved for the despicable, God entered fully into our mortality, our abandonment, our pain. Theologians may overanalyze what this is about, but the devout through the ages—painters, hymn writers, a dying mother clutching a crucifix, an old man breathing his last, a tortured prisoner, an abandoned child, a martyr at the pyre—have known that in those hours of agony Jesus was taking onto his own heart all of the misery, the sin, the sorrow, the loneliness, the hopelessness of all people in all ages. All are held tightly by his outstretched arms close to the bosom of God. The window to God's heart has been flung open, the curtain ripped asunder, our forgiveness not merely offered but embodied, our hope assured.

To talk about it is to trivialize it, but talk we must. Anselm wrote that our "debt was so great that, while man alone owed it, only God could pay it, so that the same person must be both man and God."[31] Abelard worried that this kind of God seemed more concerned for his honor than for our salvation; for him there is sacrifice, but its purpose is not to make amends but to tell the truth, stir love in us: "his son has taken upon himself our nature and persevered therein in teaching us by word and example even unto death—he has the more fully bound us to himself by love; with the result that our hearts should be kindled by such a gift of divine grace, and true charity should not now shrink from enduring anything for him."[32] God's honor is our salvation; God's delight is this suffering love, which we understand only in prayer, perhaps as St. Francis prayed when his devotion to Christ's wounds wrought actual bleeding from his own hands, feet, and side:

> My Lord Jesus Christ,
> Two graces I ask of you before I die:
> the first is that in my life I may feel, in my soul and body,
> as far as possible,
> that sorrow which you, tender Jesus,
> underwent in the hour of your most bitter passion;
> the second is that I may feel in my heart, as far as possible,
> the abundance of love with which you, son of God, were inflamed,
> so as willingly to undergo such a great passion for us sinners.[33]

Often we rush too quickly away from the cross of Christ and fail to contemplate the grief in God's heart, that unfathomable love, the embrace of our sorrow. But rush we must, as the disciples did that first Easter, to find death and hopelessness rolled back, the grave having given up this Jesus, so that nothing will ever separate us from the God who always yearns for us to trust, to rest in his arms. In Christ, God did not merely climb down into a dark hole with us. Rather, God lifts us up out of the pit, into the light, into life.

The resurrection is not the million-dollar prize for living a nice life. Rather, God loves us, we love God, and not even death can sever that relationship. Questions of historicity dog us, as they dogged the first

Christians. The resurrection is not a provable kind of thing, although Moltmann may be right: "The message of the resurrection brought by the disciples on their return to Jerusalem could hardly have lasted a single hour in the city if it had been possible to show that Jesus' body was lying in the grave."[34] What catapulted the disciples back into the city, most assuredly, was not an empty tomb, or anything hollow, but the presence of the risen Lord, the fullness of joy and hope. The implications of this resurrection for the Christian life, the hope for our future, and even the cosmic consequences of this ultimate act of God, will be laid out in the last three chapters of this book.

But for now we take note that the resurrection is Christianity's center of gravity, the inescapable fact that is truer than mere fact, the turning point of the universe. When we speak of the resurrection, we do not mean the mere resuscitation of a corpse, the endless continuation of this earthly life. The risen Jesus is not recognized, but then is recognizable. He can be touched, but then he pulls back. He cooks a meal and eats, but then he materializes and vanishes. Paul, who saw the risen Christ at some remove in space and time from the grave and garden outside Jerusalem, spoke of "spiritual bodies" in the resurrection. Bodies, yes, but spiritual—not mere spirits, but bodies, transformed. We cannot measure the pulse or weight or genetic makeup of such a body.

But whatever resurrected life is like, we trust it will be entirely good, as the ultimate expression of God's love for us. This really is the plot line: not that God rewards us for good deeds or even for having faith, but rather that a relationship begins at our birth, God loving, nurturing, guiding us, patient, bearing much. And this love is of the kind that even death cannot quench, for God would have that relationship go on forever, not forever in its current ambiguity and messiness, but face to face, transformed, fulfilled.

THE HOLY SPIRIT

The second chapter of Acts narrates the sudden, surprising gift of the Spirit to the disciples. Mere words cannot express what happens to them. They pour into the streets, talking in such a way that people with widely varied native languages all manage to understand them. Because of this remarkable story, the Spirit has often been associated with paranormal phenomena, with experiences of ecstasy. For people like me, with a decent command of English but just a smattering of foreign languages from school days, tongues and such "spiritual" things seem alien.

Some Christians proudly claim, "We've got the Spirit in our Church," implying that maybe others don't. But the Spirit isn't something I have or don't have. The Spirit isn't something God gives me; rather, the Spirit *is* God, very present with us. And with all of us. If there is such a thing as the Spirit of God, it is for everyone, not just for the ultrapious or holy elite. The Spirit is there, whether or not we feel it, whether or not we are even aware of it.

In the Bible, the Spirit does not exist so that we can have a tumultuous, heartwarming, fuzzy experience. Jesus came, not so that we could *feel* different, but so that we could *be* different. The Spirit hurls people out into the street to live a different kind of life in the world. The Spirit is an ethical force that alters our behavior and attitudes. After all, if God gives extraordinary gifts to people, why would God want them to hide inside church walls? For "spiritual" does not equal "invisible." There is no invisible, spiritual world into which we may flee and have our life with God. "Spiritual" means that which is led, inspired, directed, and changed by God—and that should be tangible, measurable, something you can taste and see.

In the Bible, the Spirit gives life—and so if you are spiritual, you work tirelessly for life, to combat hunger and illness, to resist the tyranny of violence in our cities. We recognize the Spirit when we see glimpses of what Jesus was about. There must be continuity between the things Jesus did and where we look for the Spirit. The Spirit weaves us together as a community, drawing forth our diverse gifts for the good of the whole, invading our lives so thoroughly that we treat each other with compassion and mutuality.

Basil of Caesarea, a great teacher from the fourth century, said that the Spirit's function is the "perfecting" of creation,[35] of life, of our lives. We need perfecting. If we dare to be different, we may discover the Spirit, described so beautifully by Hildegard of Bingen:

> The Holy Spirit is life that gives life
> Moving all things.
> It is the root of every creature,
> And purifier of all things,
> Wiping away sins,
> Anointing wounds.
> It is radiant life, worthy of praise,
> Awakening and enlivening all things.[36]

This brings us back to the primal question: is there a God? The proof is in the reality of living it, or there is no proof at all, which leads us to think together about the Christian life.

QUESTIONS FOR DISCUSSION

1. In what ways has creation suffered from humans interpreting God's command to have "dominion" over the earth to mean to "take over" God's world? What can be done to change this?
2. Where do you see examples of humans being "curved in on ourselves" in the world? In your own life?
3. Where do you recognize examples of the Holy Spirit at work to bring life in the world? In your own experiences?

PART III

The Christian Life

7

Christian Life and Ethics

The Practice of Faith

The truth of faith is made good in the living of it or not at all.
—James Wm. McClendon[1]

Søren Kierkegaard told us about geese who waddled into their goose church every Sunday and heard an inspiring sermon by the goose preacher, who proclaimed, "We need not be confined to the ground. God has given us wings, so we can fly, and soar to the sky!" The geese clucked their hearty "Amens," sang their goose hymn, and then waddled back to the barnyard again.[2]

In this chapter we will look at the Christian life, at Christian ethics, at the kind of lifestyle that makes sense, given what we believe, the manner of being that finally *is* what we believe. When it comes to the Christian life, we waddle off in several directions. First, we think that being Christian is a matter of avoidance. Christians "don't . . ."–and you can fill in the blank. Lawyers and business leaders speak of "ethics," and they mean you don't break the law or swindle anybody. But Christianity is not a mountain of prohibitions. Christ came to set us free, to embrace an active life of doing and being, an abundant life of holiness and service.

Second, and worse, ethics is perverted into a weapon of judgment. Our talk about morality is little more than venting our anger upon those who are different from ourselves. The harshest judgments in the Bible, Jesus' most strident denunciations, were reserved for those who self-righteously pointed the ethical finger at others. There is a judgment, an accountability for us all, but that work is reserved for God, and "it is part of God's mercy that we do not have to undertake that heavy part of his work, even when the judgment concerns ourselves."[3]

Third, our morality gets entangled with our emotions. Does it feel right? Does it feel good? What does my heart or my conscience tell me? Feelings and conscience are deceptive, so muddied are they with self-centeredness or the peculiar ways we were brought up.[4] Our faith gropes for some mood or sentiment, and we forget that Jesus did not come so we could merely *think* or *feel* different. He came so we could *be* different. An emotional high may actually be counterproductive. Maggie Ross once wrote that there are always those people who want a religious experience instead of God.[5] The whole point of faith isn't me and my feelings. Faith is all about God. Dietrich Bonhoeffer, whose faith earned him a cell in the Flossenbürg concentration camp during World War II, wrote that the Christian life is "not in the first place thinking about one's own needs, problems, sins, and fears, but allowing oneself to be caught up into the way of Jesus Christ."[6]

Most commonly, we think of ethics only when we have a big decision to make. Should I move to Toledo? Should I get married? Should I have an abortion? Often we aren't equipped to make a particular decision because we haven't taken seriously the adventure of an entire life focused upon God. Christian ethics is a matter of formation. Our souls are being shaped, reeducated, all the time, but unfortunately the dominant tutors are television and other media.

PERFORMING THE SCRIPTURES

The Bible is not just to be read, but practiced and performed. I play the piano. I didn't just "decide" to play Chopin one day. Rather, for years I had teachers, took lessons, studied, and practiced, with a metronome ticking. Then one day I knew how to play and could even delight in the music. Nicholas Lash has spoken of "performing the Scriptures," noting that "the fundamental form of the Christian interpretation of Scripture is the life, activity and organization of the believing community."[7] Biblical texts are to be "performed," in patterns of human actions that evidence some continuity with the words, life, and death of Jesus. When faith is not embodied, it is like people sitting around a table and making chitchat about F-sharps, triplets, whole notes, and treble clefs on a page of music. The intent of the music is not that it be talked about, but rather that the musicians pick up their violins and trumpets and perform. The Christian life is a skill earned over time, requiring practice, improvement, failure, ever greater facility.

Certainly, even a knack for "improvisation" is essential.[8] The Scriptures are like a script, and the actors on stage at times must live into their parts if the drama breaks down, or in response to some unforeseen moment in the performance. The Bible doesn't give clear directions for everything, but we develop our characters and act accordingly. For this embodiment of the Scriptures, we really need a teacher or two, women and men who have lived their faith, from whom we can learn, whose moves we may imitate. The saints are our teachers.

Consider St. Francis. Earlier biographers called him "almost a second Christ given to the world for the salvation of the people," all because of his naive, startling conformity to Christ:

> He was always with Jesus:
> Jesus in his heart,
> Jesus in his mouth,
> Jesus in his ears,
> Jesus in his eyes,
> Jesus in his hands,
> he bore Jesus always in his whole body.[9]

The wonderful stories of Francis befriending robbers at Monte Casale and then the wolf of Gubbio, and of Francis strolling unarmed into the camp of the sultan during the Crusades and making peace with the Muslims, show how he took quite literally Jesus' mandates: "Love your enemies," and "If your enemy is hungry, feed him."[10] Francis shows us the way, and demonstrates the possibility, of an affluent, comfortable man changing everything and actually performing the faith.

The saints pose a seemingly irresolvable conflict for us, though. They are doers, actors, achievers in the Christian life. Yet they all would remind us that we are not saved by a mountain of good deeds. As Martin Luther said, "The cause of despair is not the multitude or magnitude of our sins; despair comes from thinking we must rely on our good works, that everything hinges on me and my abilities."[11] Pelagius, as we saw in chapter 5, had reason to despair, for all our doing will never be sufficient, will never be more than a laughable stumbling behind Christ. But when Luther said that faith is the surrender of action, he did not mean that how we live is irrelevant. On the contrary: we surrender the foolhardy bias that everything depends on us, and instead surrender ourselves to the Spirit of God. The spiritual life is not an invisible life, but rather a life wooed, choreographed, drawn forward by the Spirit of God. Faith is "a willingness for whatever."[12] The Christian who has trained diligently at the feet of the saints, who has loved and followed Christ with zeal, understands that the ethical life is not some grand human achievement but is itself a pure gift from God, the remarkable discovery that we no longer live under compulsion to do as the world dictates, but that we have been set free to be the people we were made and destined to be.

DEAD MAN WALKING

Our destiny has the most peculiar shape. We may pinpoint the fulcrum of Mark's Gospel as that moment when Jesus tells the disciples that he is setting out for Jerusalem, where he will be unjustly convicted and executed. And what does this dark turn mean for them, and therefore for us as we pursue the Christian life? "If any one would come after me, let him deny himself and take up his cross and follow me. For whoever would save his life will lose it, and whoever loses his life for my sake and the gospel's will save it" (Mark 8:34–35, au. trans.). Struggling to tell his friends what following looks like, Jesus compares what's at stake to the situation of a prisoner condemned to death: Take up your cross. In the Roman world, a "dead man walking" would be forced to carry the *patibulum,* the crossbeam to which he would be nailed, to the site of execution; with ironic horror the condemned was compelled to bear the instrument of his own death. We would prefer that Jesus have painted a warm, sunny picture of the life of discipleship. How exactly is the Christian life like that of a prisoner condemned to death?

Perhaps two modern prisoners can unveil some things for us. Aleksandr Solzhenitsyn, who won the Nobel Prize for his haunting exposés of the Soviet gulag, in which he was incarcerated in 1945 for remarks offensive to Josef Stalin, wrote about becoming a condemned prisoner:

> From the moment you go to prison you must put your cozy past firmly behind you. At the very threshold, you must say to yourself "My life is over, a little early to be sure, but there's nothing to be done about it. I shall never return to freedom. . . I no longer have any property whatsoever. . . Only my spirit and my conscience remain precious and important to me." Confronted by such a prisoner, the *interrogation* will tremble. Only the man who has renounced everything can win that victory.[13]

Renunciation, putting your cozy past behind you: such is the life of faith. A Russian Jew, Natan Sharansky, was abducted by the KGB in 1977. For advocating free speech and openness to emigration, he suffered solitary confinement, severe hunger, brutal handling. Always clutching a pocket Psalter, he described the gulag as "the place where I had emerged victorious, defended my freedom, retained my spiritual independence against the kingdom of lies."[14] For Sharansky, freedom and independence curiously were attainable inside the gulag in a way that eludes those of us on the outside. Shrewdly, he observed:

> In freedom, I am lost in a myriad of choices. When I walk on the street, dozens of cheeses, fruits, and juices stare at me from store windows. [A]n endless series of decisions . . . must be made: What to drink in the morning, coffee or tea? What newspaper to read? What to do in the evening? Where to go for the Sabbath? Which friends to visit? In the punishment cell, life was much simpler. Every day brought only one choice: good or evil, white or black, saying yes or no to the KGB. Moreover, I had all the time I needed to think about these choices, to concentrate on the most fundamental problems of existence, to test myself in fear, in hope, in belief, in love. And now, lost in thousands of mundane choices, I suddenly realize that there's no time to reflect on the bigger questions. How to enjoy the vivid colors of freedom without losing the existential depth I felt in prison? How to absorb the many sounds of freedom without allowing them to jam the stirring call of the shofar that I heard so clearly in the punishment cell? And, most important, how . . . to retain that unique feeling of the interconnection of human souls which I discovered in the Gulag?

The fundamental choice, good or evil, testing myself in fear, hope, belief, love: this kind of testing requires some discipline, some training—like playing the piano, but much harder.

SELFISH GENES

The pedagogy required for the Christian life bumps immediately and persistently up against a grim difficulty. For we do not naturally gravitate toward the good. In earlier chapters we probed the sad paradox that a good God installed in our moral selves "shabby equipment, badly deteriorated." Richard Dawkins, the provocative and brilliant biologist, has written that "we are survival machines—robot vehicles blindly pro-grammed to preserve the selfish molecules known as genes. . . . A pre-dominant quality to be expected in a successful gene is ruthless selfishness."[15] Now we know that genes are not agents; as bits of code they "intend" nothing at all. Yet the inherent pattern suggested is accu-rate: as life marches through the millennia, the fittest actually do sur-vive. Strength, street smarts, agility, and a ruthless seizure of limited resources: these work and seem to be virtually innate, not just in the ani-mal kingdom out there, but in our very human souls. Selfishness is just natural.

Even as people of faith, our natural inclination is to use Christianity to pursue what society paints as the "good life," as if Christianity were a prescription for a happy, successful life. But conformity to this pre-tended "good life" is the ruin of faith and has nothing whatsoever to do with the existence of the "dead man walking." The deeper killing is the way we use up ourselves, as Merton put it, chasing experiences, power, affection,

> to clothe this false self and construct its nothingness into something objectively real. And I wind experiences around myself and cover myself with pleasures and glory like bandages in order to make myself perceptible to myself and to the world, as if I were an invisi-ble body that could only become visible when something visible cov-ered the surface. But there is no substance under the things with which I am clothed. I am hollow. . . . And when they are gone there will be nothing left of me but my own nakedness and emptiness and hollowness, to tell me that I am my own mistake.[16]

Our cozy past is to be just that: a thing of the past, not the objective of our future, a mistake leaving us hollow.

Yet there is a mystery here, a paradox at the heart of life. Christian-ity comes at us like some demolition crew, but the saints in the hard hats tell us they love us and want only the best for us. Early in his ministry Karl Barth wrote, "God is not with us as an alien stranger but as our nearest most intimate acquaintance, his will not a strange rule which lies athwart our free feelings, but as the pulse of our own organism, our own deepest, truest, freedom."[17] Our desires, as played out in daily life, are too weak and require redirection and considerable strengthening. We thirst for God and God's way, but poke around in all the wrong water-ing holes. Commands discipline us, reshape us, help us to delight in what is genuinely good, in what fully satisfies. The dual command to love God and neighbor is "a pick which wrenches open the lock of self-love" (Kierkegaard)[18] and draws us into a new world, a new life, our cozy past squarely behind us, a startling adventure lying ahead.

Even the atheist biologist Dawkins admits to a grudging hope:

> There are special circumstances in which a gene can achieve its own selfish goals best by fostering a limited form of altruism. . . . Be warned that if you wish, as I do, to build a society in which individuals cooperate generously and unselfishly towards a common good, you can expect little help from biological nature. . . . Let us try to *teach* generosity and altruism, because we are born selfish. Let us understand what our own selfish genes are up to, because we may then at least have the chance to upset their designs, something that no other species has ever aspired to. . . . We have the power to defy the selfish genes of our birth and, if necessary, the selfish memes of our indoctrination. . . . We have the power to turn against our creators. We, alone on earth, can rebel against the tyranny of the selfish replicators.[19]

Paul, Augustine, Luther and Barth would pat him on the shoulder and say, "No, we don't have the power, but if we turn to instead of against our Creator, there is hope." The good news is that change is not only required but actually possible, not by our own determination so much as by the power of God seizing our priorities, our time, our pocketbooks, and our relationships. For like a symphonic score, the Bible is something to be performed not solo, but rather together, in the company of others. We have the Church, which should be a school of ethics, an orchestra playing beautiful music. More will be said about the Church in the next chapter, but for now we take note that in the Christian life we encourage each other and hold each other accountable. We take responsibility not just to be ethical in private or among ourselves. We reach out, recognizing that the Church is responsible to care for the world, to be an agent for transformation, the very hands and feet of Christ.

SPIRITUAL DISCIPLINES

So there are habits to be broken, genes to be defied, skills to be learned. The Christian life therefore requires a certain training regimen to overcome our inertia, that sorry flabbiness of soul and life that weighs us down. Such a regimen recognizes that Christianity isn't just one big decision but comprises a thousand little decisions every day. Every thought, each word, the smallest act, whatever I see and hear—every time I do anything at all, I am changed into somebody I wasn't just a moment before. Life is the accumulation of countless thoughts, acts, events, and I am who I am as a result of them all. Therefore diligent attention must be paid to my schedule, what I'm soaking up, what I do all day. I want to learn to be a Christian, to perform the score.

John Wesley prescribed four disciplines that he called "means of grace": prayer, fasting, "Christian conference," and Bible reading. The Christian life involves consistency in all four. Reading the Bible: to become like God we study God's Word, welcoming its painful disagreements with our superficial lives, taking its blows like the marble struck by Michelangelo, who conceived his mission as liberating a beautiful body imprisoned in rough stone. We do not by rote memorize this rule and that rule, to cover every conceivable situation in life. Rather, like learning a foreign language, we finally get inside the grammar of it all. We begin to think God's thoughts, our imaginations transformed.

If we think of Jesus as the "score," if we take his teaching and behavior seriously, we have radical changes to make in everything we do, the ways we think, what we value. In desperation we explain Jesus away, noting how the times were different back then, how our world is more complex, how Jesus after all was divine (and I'm not!). But Jesus *is* the pattern of the ethical life.

Jesus' most ruthless competition in our culture is money, the great high god that pretends to be the fulness of life. Perhaps the most influential theologian of money is still Andrew Carnegie,[20] who believed that capitalism is good, that discrepancies in wealth are well-justified, and that faith enters in only after the money has been made, and then only to cajole us toward charity, which should be given exclusively to the "deserving poor" (not those who deserve to be poor, but the poor who deserve a chance). But Christ would ask about how we make our money and why more is better. Christ would unmask the slimy side of our moneymaking, and would remind us that all we have belongs to God. Christ would inquire into the way we make necessities out of luxuries, while children whom we conveniently keep out of sight and mind nod off to sleep shivering and hungry. Christ would remind us that all people, whether we regard them as deserving or not, do belong to God; therefore the way we disburse our money has to make sense in light of Jesus' suffering and death. Our faith cannot just be something pious pasted on the outside of an otherwise unaltered life.

We will have more to say about "Christian conference" in the next chapter. For now we can state that the Christian life cannot be lived alone and that we desperately flounder unless we have the support and accountability of others, almost like an Alcoholics Anonymous group in which we push each other, having established an atmosphere in which we can discuss and honor the things of God.

FASTING AND PRAYER

Nothing is more alien to our culture than fasting. But consider Moses, Elijah, David, Paul, Jesus himself, Augustine, Francis, Luther, Calvin, Teresa: all knew that renunciation is the only route to fulfillment. Fasting is not giving up something harmful, like smoking or double martinis. Fasting is giving up something good in itself, something I have and love, but which I do without for a time for the sake of God. When we satisfy every desire as often as possible, our deeper desire for God comes to be masked over, desensitized. I need to fast as a reminder that I have a deeper quest than the satisfaction of my animal desires. I blunt those desires in order to whet my appetite for God. When hunger gnaws, I discover how hollow I am inside, how superficial I can be. Richard Foster, in his helpful book on spiritual disciplines, says, "Our human cravings and desires are like rivers that tend to overflow their banks; fasting helps keep them in their proper channels."[21]

We also learn a solidarity with the needy, who by no choice of their own are denied simple pleasures and satisfactions. There is the danger of self-pity and self-righteousness in fasting. Francis of Assisi once planned to fast for forty days, but on the thirty-ninth day he broke the fast, eating half a loaf of bread—in order to avoid vainglory, as he might be tempted to think he was as holy as Jesus. Doing without the basics, and even shedding a luxury or two, should lead to simplicity, as the Christian life knows the freedom of which the Shakers sing:

'Tis the gift to be simple,
'Tis the gift to be free.

Every day we have thousands of choices. If over and over we choose the simpler way, if in various ways we choose renunciation, then we are less and less enmeshed in the world and have more freedom, an available space, for God.

And of course, the Christian prays. The saints teach us much about prayer. Barth called prayer "the beginning of an uprising against the disorder of the world." Origen taught that we should not think of prayer as a way to gain some benefit, but rather as a means to become more like God. We pray, not so much to get a chaotic world under control, but rather to yield our chaotic world and lives to God. Prayer is not easy; it too is a skill to be learned. Bonhoeffer, as clouds of evil gathered over Europe in 1939, wrote:

> The phrase "learning to pray" sounds strange to us. If the heart does not overflow and begin to pray by itself, we say, it will never "learn" to pray. But it is a dangerous error, surely very widespread among Christians, to think that the heart can pray by itself. For then we confuse wishes, hopes, sighs, laments, rejoicings—all of which the heart can do by itself—with prayer. Prayer does not mean simply to pour out one's heart. It means rather to find the way to God and to speak with him, whether the heart is full or empty.[22]

Bonhoeffer wisely illustrates this learning by an analogy. Children do not just know how to talk. Rather, "The child learns to speak because his father speaks to him. He learns the speech of his father." So it is as we learn to pray. And the child must be shaped and molded in ways that may not suit the child's immediate desires.

> If we are to pray aright, perhaps it is quite necessary that we pray contrary to our own heart. Not what we want to pray is important, but what God wants us to pray. If we were dependent entirely on ourselves, we would probably pray only the fourth petition of the Lord's Prayer. But God wants it otherwise. The richness of the Word of God ought to determine our prayer, not the poverty of our heart.

Prayer is not merely conversation, but pulsates in the direction of meditation. We simply reflect, rest, and focus, perhaps on an icon, maybe listening to music, but generally in silence. Sabbath is the lost practice, the failed habit of Christians in our day—the demarcation of sacred time just to rest, to be still, to declare by my inactivity that not everything depends on my feverish activity. I can be still and know then (and only then) that God is God (Ps. 46:8).[23] Silence and solitude feel like unwelcome threats to us who so frantically fill our moments with noise and our spaces with company. Yet it is in the quiet, when we are alone, not just with our thoughts but with God, that we burrow out a space for God and listen and are called. Perhaps we can conjure up again the image of the condemned prisoner, for whom solitary confinement is designed to break the convict's will. In solitude we may comprehend what our wills are up to when prayer is so difficult. As Merton suggested, "Much of our coldness and dryness in prayer may well be a kind of unconscious defense against grace."[24] We may blame prayer, as it seems boring or ineffectual; but really we are clinging to our flabby lives, when the secret to joy resides in letting go, in togetherness with God, for whom we were made in the first place.

So far we have been talking about what Wesley called "inward holiness," cultivating the spirit, growing our souls deeper into God, seeking purity of heart. For we have a desire somewhere in the recesses of our soul to be clean and whole, a God-given urge toward integrity. God sees us, knows us, and we want our minds, our souls to be conformed to God's image, transformed into Christ's likeness. Much of what the world counts as "feeling" really requires discipline. Consider gratitude or forgiveness. We think of gratitude as a feeling that either you have spontaneously, or you just don't—and generally we don't. We nurture grievances and file complaints. Advertisers incessantly lull us into a sense of dissatisfaction so that we will buy their products. Henri Nouwen understood how gratitude takes practice:

> The discipline of gratitude is the explicit effort to acknowledge that all I am and have is given to me as a gift to be celebrated with joy. Gratitude as a discipline involves a conscious choice. I can choose to be grateful even when my emotions and feelings are still steeped in hurt. It is amazing how many occasions present themselves in which I can choose gratitude instead of a complaint. I can choose to be grateful, even if my heart is bitter. I can choose to speak about goodness and beauty, even when my inner eye looks for something to call ugly. I can choose to listen to the voices that forgive and to look at the faces that smile, even while I still hear words of resentment and grimaces of hate. . . . The choice for gratitude rarely comes without some real effort. But each time I make it, the next choice is a little easier, a little freer, a little less self-conscious. Acts of gratitude make one grateful.[25]

The same pattern is true of forgiveness. Forgiveness is not merely an emotion you happen to feel toward someone. Rather, forgiveness is a discipline, a set of practices that require work, effort, and community, including judgment, confession, penance, reconciliation, a changed life.[26]

CARING FOR THE POOR

But holiness is not only inward. There is also an "outward holiness," actions of compassion for the poor, exhibiting tangibly the love of Christ for people in need. Dorothy Day, the great hero of outward holiness in the twentieth century, once said: "Does God have a set way of prayer, a way that He expects each of us to follow? I doubt it. I believe some people—lots of people—pray through the witness of their lives, through the work they do, the friendships they have, the love they offer people and receive from people. Since when are *words* the only acceptable form of prayer?"[27] Her own life reveals how radical acts of service to the poor, even with the poor, are not just good things to do for God. These acts simultaneously stretch our faith, hold our selfishness in check, and bring joy, the profound kind of joy known to those who have met Christ, not just in the comfort of worship, but in the discomfort of the world. Mother Teresa taught us that service is not somehow the outcome of prayer or something done when not praying. Serving the poor and opening the heart to Christ are one and the same. "The Missionaries of Charity do firmly believe that they are touching the body of Christ in his distressing disguise whenever they are helping and touching the poor. We cannot do this with a long face." She taught the sisters "to pray while working, doing it *for* Jesus and doing it *to* Jesus. This brings a tremendous closeness with him."[28] Or as Gutiérrez put it, "It is through encounters with the poor and the exploited that we shall encounter the Lord."[29]

And wise Christians have understood that genuine, outward holiness is not when the haves dole out to the have-nots. Rather, we live together and build relationships, knowing that we are all poor or, rather, that in God's eyes we are all rich and that the learning and growth in Christ goes both ways. People on different sides of the world's socioeconomic divide look at the score of God's great symphony and know that it is to be played, now, together.

CALLING, NOT CAREER

The altering of life is comprehensive and pushes us to ask questions, not merely about what is right and wrong, but about our calling. We are all—not just the clergy, but all of us—called by God, just as Jesus called fishermen by the shore of Galilee. Francis, as we have seen, was called by God to "rebuild my church." On a train to Darjeeling in 1946, a young teacher heard God tell her to reach out to the poorest of the poor in Calcutta; Mother Teresa in turn helped thousands of women discover their calling. My grandfather had the satisfaction of having followed God's call to be a rural mail carrier and fulfilled mundane tasks with a flair of mission and love.

God calls us not just to general niceness or general doing good. God has something specific to which you and I are called. God wants me here, and not there. God calls us in major life decisions (such as a vocation or marriage) and in smaller, daily moments (such as phoning a shut-in or writing my wife a love note).

We live in a culture that focuses instead on "career." In a career (or even, just a "job"), the goal is more money, a higher rung on the ladder, a bigger office, more plaudits. But calling implies a place within the broader community, doing something for the common good, contributing to the adventure of the kingdom of God. In the movie *It's a Wonderful Life,* Mr. Potter thinks he can buy off George Bailey with a fat salary, the nicest house in town, some new dresses for Mrs. Bailey, and the occasional business trip to New York. But George storms out of Potter's office, back to his little building and loan, with little to show for his enormous efforts—except for a wonderful life and a different kind of Bedford Falls.

We discern our calling perhaps not in a flash or with utter clarity, for which we may envy Francis or Mother Teresa. We pray, we reflect, we let our minds, desires, dreams be remolded by the Bible's stories. We seek out mentors, wise women and men of vision who can dissect our motivations, gifts, agendas. We presume nothing in advance. John Wesley established that at the New Year Methodists should offer up this "Covenant prayer":

> Put me to what thou wilt, rank me with whom thou wilt.
> Put me to doing, put me to suffering.
> Let me be employed by thee or laid aside for thee. . . .
> I freely and heartily yield all things to thy pleasure and disposal.

Obviously calling is related to but different from morality. God may call me to live in the city where I find myself, but living in this city is not morally right or wrong per se. Morality is more general, binding upon everyone. And so we turn now to the great moral issues, and how Christianity not only responds to these issues, but even dares to create them, and most amazingly to do something about them.

WHERE THE BATTLE RAGES

Martin Luther once wrote in a letter:

> If I profess with the loudest voice and clearest exposition every por-
> tion of the truth of God except precisely that little point at which the
> world and the devil are at that moment attacking, I am not confess-
> ing Christ, however boldly I may be professing him. Where the bat-
> tle rages, there the loyalty of the soldier is proved, and to be steady
> on all the battlefield besides is mere flight and disgrace if he flinches
> at that point.[30]

Christians have confessed Christ and proved their loyalty in every age.
Martyrs knew that little point and did not flinch. Thomas More refused
to approve of the Act of Succession (which declared Henry VIII's marriage to Catherine of Aragon invalid, enabling him to marry Anne
Boleyn). His silence thundered throughout Europe and eventually cost
him his head. Martin Luther King Jr. denounced racial injustice in the
name of the gospel, acknowledging on his last night on the battlefield that
"I've seen the promised land; I may not get there with you . . ." Dorothy
Day not only fed the hungry but published *The Catholic Worker,* a
provocative journal that questioned a capitalist economic system that
spawned poverty. Her views, not surprisingly, earned her several jail stints.

While in every era the Church has exercised its teaching office on
morality, recent years have witnessed fierce and protracted warfare
within the Church over society's confounding issues, such as abortion,
homosexuality, the death penalty, or gun ownership. Many Christians
wish to be insulated from such increasingly "politicized" debates, but
the Church has two commitments that allow no flinching: we believe
that Christ is Lord over all the earth, and we serve a God with a passion
for holiness. We cannot flinch where the battle rages.

Humbly, we admit we are not very good at deliberating on such
major issues. Every breath we take is drawn in an intellectual milieu that
is not successful at settling moral disagreements. When we hear some
thought about the death penalty, abortion, or homosexuality, we leap to
either "I agree" or "I disagree," which slams the window of listening
firmly shut and dismisses the person trying to talk to us. We forget how
jaded our own views are, how enmeshed in our biases, private prefer-
ences, social habits, what is beneficial to me.

And at crucial moments we suffer some bizarre theological amnesia.
Shortly after the first Gulf War broke out, I saw a televised interview

with three prominent clergy. Two of them were, at that moment, hawks, marshaling their faith in support of an American victory over Saddam Hussein. Then James Forbes countered by simply quoting some of the sayings of Jesus about loving your enemies, about the one who lives by the sword dying by the sword, about overcoming evil with love. One of Forbes's combatants shot back, saying, "That's not relevant now—we're at war!" To which Forbes shrewdly responded, "If the Bible's not relevant now, it's never relevant."

But the problem is even deeper. Many harbor a skepticism that "truth" on such matters exists at all. Like Nietzsche, we wonder if truths are "illusions we have forgotten are illusions, worn-out metaphors now impotent to stir the senses, coins which have lost their faces and are considered now as metal rather than currency."[31] Unwittingly fearful that Nietzsche might be right, we spout knee-jerk reactions that are superficial and unlikely to persuade any but the already convinced. One Christian fires off a verse from Leviticus and another from Romans, vehemently claiming homosexuality is perverse. Another Christian points to a broader notion of creation, and says "They are made that way," and blithely claims acceptance. Both forget that, with respect to each other, their very ways of thinking are "incommensurable": their conclusions do not differ so much as their premises differ; when we begin with rival premises, there is no rational way to proceed, and so we wind up sounding shrill as we shout at one another. Christians also fail to notice the inner inconsistency of their positions. If a verse or two can clinch the day on homosexuality, then a son who talks back to his father should be summarily executed, women must never cut their hair or wear jewelry, and anyone hoping to follow Jesus should immediately sell their house and stock holdings and give the proceeds to the Salvation Army; divorce would never happen, slavery would happen, and society as we know it would be no more.

Although black-and-white simplicity has its allures, the denseness of life as we know it requires a more complex, integrated, reflective approach to Christianity. If we are to think about a moral issue, we need to read the Bible, and not simplistically. We need to listen to great teachers from our tradition with both openness and a critical eye. We need to weigh apparently non-Christian thinking and ask what truth is being told. We need to listen to and sympathize with the real people involved. The Bible is messy, and our most brilliant theologians, for all their shared outlook, cannot finally claim to have cornered truth.

And humbly we need to admit that some issues simply are not

resolvable—at least not yet. At one time, amazingly enough, Christians could not figure out how to settle the debate on slavery. Noble Christians read their Bibles and made a rational case for slavery. But finally the antislavery forces won the day, clinched the argument, and now only a maniac would openly claim that chattel slavery should be reinstituted as God's will for humanity. At the dawn of the twenty-first century, the Church is at some kind of impasse on the issue of homosexuality, with neither side capable of swaying the other in a definitive manner. Some large measure of humility is required to stay at the table, to listen, to learn, to continue to think and rethink, to pray and pray again, so that some resolution might be had on this and other thorny issues.

HIGHER GROUND

Perhaps the Church has a role of peculiar but definite shape with regard to grand moral issues. We need to avoid picking and choosing from the rhetoric and entrenched positions that are bandied about on talk shows and among protesters. The Church must tell its own story and struggle mightily to avoid being used for somebody else's political agenda. For Christianity is not a prop for conservatism or liberalism; we look not so much for common ground as for higher ground.[32]

Christianity must struggle uphill just to keep our language and conceptualities straight. On abortion, for instance, both sides talk about rights, the right to life, or the right to choose. But the whole notion of "rights," even outside the Christian sphere, is problematical. Political discourse in America is impoverished by the incessant and shrill talk about rights; such utterly individualistic and selfishly uncompromising stances say nothing about community, sharing, or responsibility, and clashes can never be won so long as both sides assert absolute rights. But certainly in the Bible and Christian theology, Alasdair MacIntyre's verdict is on target: "There are no such rights, and belief in them is one with belief in witches and in unicorns."[33] For Christianity, life is not something to which we have a right. Life is a gift. We are to be good stewards of that life and of the life-bearing potential we find within our own bodies.

Much talk on moral issues involves self-fulfillment, and again that is society's agenda, not Christ's. In moral talk, we must unveil idolatry, gently but firmly. If the Christian life is comparable to the dead man walking, then assertions about "controlling my body," or "providing for my family," or "pursuing my happiness" are really perversions of the life to which Christ calls us, modern idolatries to be exposed.

For truly, when it comes to moral issues, Christianity is usually *for* something. Certainly we slip into being against this and against that. But we have a vision of life that we must lift up as worthy, which requires us to be against whatever is contrary to that vision. In the introduction to this book we spoke of the lyre of Orpheus, how he played a sweeter song that the rowers followed so that they were not lured onto the rocks by the seductive sirens. We do not hate the world's song so much as we believe we have the most beautiful song. When the Church opposes divorce, and even when the Catholic Church maneuvers those who have been married toward annulment, the point is not that people should be miserable, but rather to hold up a holy vision of marriage, the virtues of commitment. Christians have traditionally opposed gambling and lotteries, partly because we see the dangers in addiction and crime, but more because we believe that work and discipline are good, that getting "lucky" is not the greatest good that could befall someone, that having a huge bag of money is not the fullness of life, but that Christ, and community, and holiness are that fullness.

In the Church we have an ethic that would discourage premarital sex (and extramarital sex), not because the unmarried must miss out on the fun, but because there is a fragility in our intimacy. We dare not squander our precious selves in anything less than a lifelong relationship of grace. So we cannot merely assert that extramarital sex should be avoided; we have to fashion a more alluring song. Young people need to hear about the delights of the Christian life that might make them more zealous to embrace a higher ethic and identity than to indulge in mere sexual play.[34]

WE WILL TAKE THE CHILD

Most importantly, the Church's job is not simply to trumpet what is right and wrong, but first to poke around a bit, asking about the root causes of the problem and daring to take responsibility. Dom Helder Camara fingered what can happen when the Church pulls the veil off an issue: "When I feed the hungry, they call me a saint; but when I ask why they are hungry, they call me a communist." But we ask, and our talk about morality always assumes that we as the Church are prepared to do something. Mother Teresa stunned the world when she accepted the Nobel Peace Prize in 1979. Not only did she give away the prize money and refuse the customary banquet; she spoke out on abortion, calling it "the greatest destroyer of peace today . . . because it is a direct war, direct murder by the mother herself." The sharp edge on her words carried a different kind of authority, though, for she could point to thousands of children taken in by her sisters around the world: "Please don't destroy the child; we will take the child."[35] Before the church can talk about an issue like abortion, it needs to be eager to say with Mother Teresa, "Give the child to me."

This kind of morality requires considerable immersion in reality, shunning the kind of idealism that trumpets moral truths and never grapples with the murky reality. We may make only small improvements. We may make none at all. But the rule of faith is love, and loving in the real world may require what seems like compromise. In his Gifford Lectures, Alfred North Whitehead thought of Jesus' humble origins and tender life: "Love neither rules, nor is it unmoved; also it is a little oblivious as to morals."[36] Or perhaps it is that our morality is of some higher order, cognizant of the human predicament, pulsating with the grace and mercy of God, all the while laboring compassionately for life, moving however tentatively toward the fulfillment of God's kingdom, never giving up. Accepting the Nobel Peace Prize in Oslo in 1964, Martin Luther King Jr. said: "I refuse to accept the idea that the 'isness' of man's present nature makes him morally incapable of reaching up for the eternal 'oughtness' that forever confronts him."[37]

Perhaps this is an appropriate place to revisit modernity's hard question: Is there a God? Throughout history, the most persuasive evidence has always been changed lives. Perhaps Chesterton understood best why the faith can be held in such suspicion nowadays. He suggested that the problem is not that Christianity has been tried and found wanting. It has hardly ever been tried.

QUESTIONS FOR DISCUSSION

1. Why is it important to realize that the Christian life is lived out in the context of community with others? What are some implications of this insight?
2. In what spiritual disciplines would you like to participate? In what disciplines do you participate?
3. What is your sense of "calling" by God in living your life? With your work? With your service to others?

8

The Church

The Body of Christ

The biggest paradox about the Church is that she is at the same time essentially traditional and essentially revolutionary. But that is not as much of a paradox as it seems, because Christian tradition, unlike all others, is a living and perpetual revolution.

—Thomas Merton[1]

In Lorraine Hansberry's *A Raisin in the Sun,* Beneatha declares what she has learned and come to believe while off at school:

I'm just tired of hearing about God all the time. What has He got to do with anything? Does he pay the tuition? God is just one idea I don't accept. I get tired of him getting credit for all the things the human race achieves through its own stubborn effort. There simply is no blasted God—there is only man and it is he who makes miracles.

Her Mama studied her daughter, rose slowly, crossed the room, slapped Beneatha across the face and said, "Now—you say after me, in my mother's house there is still a God."[2]

A white wooden church on a hillside in the rural Midwest. A stone spire, which once towered over the buildings of a city on the East Coast, now dwarfed by bank skyscrapers. A Gothic cathedral, which took more than a century to build, perched as majestic as ever at the center of a city in France. A small but proudly elegant adobe mission built by Franciscans in Mexico. A squarish cinder-block structure, for decades a factory, now restored and functioning as a sanctuary in China. In myriad ways, in every era, Christians have joined hands and built, not just sanctuaries, but communities. And each one is a slap of sorts, a stubborn testimony that there is still a God.

Christianity is a vast gathering of churches. Christianity is the Church; the Church is Christianity. To speak of "Church" evokes a variety of images in our minds. We may think of the Church as a global or spiritual phenomenon or as a building down the street. Avery Dulles observed six "models" that writers use to describe the Church: an institution, mystical communion, sacrament, herald, servant, and a community of disciples.[3] H. Richard Niebuhr reflected on how Christianity relates to civilization, and discerned five visions adopted by various writers: Christ opposing culture, Christ agreeing with culture, Christ as the aspiration of culture, Christ in creative tension with culture, and Christ as transforming culture.[4]

IMAGES OF AN INSTITUTION

The Church certainly is an institution, and an impressive one. As a corporation, however unwieldy, the Church has planted "franchises" literally everywhere, involving countless millions, all instigated by a band of a dozen men in Palestine. At its most heroic times, this institution—or the occasional hero emerging from this institution—has been at odds with the culture; at its most embarrassing moments, this institution has been thoroughly enmeshed in the culture. In chapter 4 we surveyed the proud and embarrassing history of the Church, including that dramatic moment when St. Dominic, sizing up the pope's riches, sadly noted that such a Church loses its ability to bring healing. Dominic's contemporary, Francis of Assisi, refused gifts of property from his own bishop, arguing, "If we had goods, we would also have to have arms to defend them. It is from wealth that questions and lawsuits come, and thus the love of God and the love of neighbour are hindered in many ways. Therefore we do not want to have any possessions in this world."[5]

Christians have habitually gotten fixated on the care and feeding of the institution, lamely forgetting why the institution exists in the first place, and to whom it belongs. Frederick Buechner may be right:

> Maybe the best thing that could happen to the church would be for some great tidal wave of history to wash it all away—the church buildings tumbling, the church money all lost, the church bulletins blowing through the air like dead leaves, the differences between preachers and congregations all lost too. Then all we would have left would be each other and Christ, which was all there was in the first place.[6]

Indeed, as St. Ambrose said, the Church is like the moon, having no light of its own, existing only to reflect the light of Christ, the glory of God.

Yet our wariness of the institution is not entirely noble. In modern times, even Christians have been swept up in the mood of our culture, which is suspicious of all institutions (government, education, and certainly the Church). More and more Christians believe they can be Christians apart from the Church, and perhaps even be better Christians without having to grapple with buildings, committees, denominations, and disagreeable people. But it is the people, and the curious work we try to do together, that define the Christian life. The Bible, and the two thousand years of Christian history, know nothing of a solitary Christianity. This faith is something we do together, something that presses us up against people with whom we normally might have no contact at all, only to discover that with regard to what really matters, we are brothers and sisters in God's quirky family.

Even the building matters. Many preachers criticize "mere churchgoers" who spend their lives going to and working on some building, as if such an exercise were sheer futility, a tragic case of being so close to and yet so far from the real thing. But W. H. Vanstone is wise to say, "Attachment to a Church building is by no means to be dismissed as sentimentality: it may well contain a profound, though possibly inarticulate, understanding of what that building is."[7] Church buildings, varied, beautiful, ostentatious, tacky, ramshackle, and the Church as an institution: this is our burden, and yet this is our opportunity.

A HOME, A BODY

Perhaps the best thing that could happen to the Church would be for some great tidal wave of imagination to reconfigure our perceptions and expectations. Back in the fifth century, a new church building was constructed, octagonal in shape, in the city of Capernaum. When a team of archaeologists dug down into the foundations of that church, they found a neighborhood, a little network of houses dating to the time of Jesus. Most of the interconnecting houses were identical: stone walls, dirt floors, fishing hooks and broken pottery lying about. But one house was unique: the walls were plastered, with painted religious graffiti, featuring a monogram of Jesus, being called Lord, the name "Peter," along with an "Amen," and a "Lord have mercy."[8] The foundation of that octagonal church was a home, where a family ate and slept, and a place of hospitality for visitors, where the sick were brought for prayer.

Or consider another find: near the theater in ancient Corinth, archaeologists found a gray, Acrocorinthian limestone pavement with an inscription, its bronze inlay pilfered long ago by looters, that reads, *Erastus pro aedilit[at]e s[ua] p[ecunia] stravit* ("Erastus in return for his aedileship laid the pavement at his own expense"). We believe this is the Erastus mentioned by Paul in Romans 16:23; if so, a high public official with sufficient wealth to pave a major street was a member of the fledgling church in Corinth. At the same time, in Corinth (as in all cities on the early Christian map) membership was still dominated by the poor. In the ancient world—as is too often the case in our world—rich and poor usually knew each other (if at all) only as employer and servant, never as friends or equals. So, some social revolution was afoot when Erastus worshiped with poorer citizens of the city.

When they came to worship, since there was no church, they met in the largest available home. Jerome Murphy-O'Connor offers an educated guess that the Corinthian church met at the house of Gaius (Rom. 16:23), a typical villa with an atrium of perhaps 55 square meters (590 square feet), and a triclinium (or dining room) of perhaps 36 square meters (390 square feet).[9] With spouses and servants the church had perhaps fifty members, not all of whom could begin to fit into the triclinium. The well-heeled host would quite naturally invite his closest friends into the triclinium, where they were accustomed to recline at dinner, while the rest would have to sit in the atrium. The affluent would not merely be the host's friends, but would also have the leisure to arrive early, while the poorer manual laborers would be detained at work until later. Roman custom dictated that different kinds of food be served to different categories of guests: oysters, turtledoves, and fine wine would be served in the triclinium, while nothing but scraps would be shovelled over into the atrium.

No one in ancient Corinth would have been stunned by such an arrangement. But Paul castigated them, especially the host and early arrivals who inappropriately imported their social mores into the church. Obviously they had not yet learned that, to quote Jürgen Moltmann, "the opposite of poverty is not property, but the opposite of both is community."[10] For community to happen, all must be welcome and treated equally. If anything, Christianity is to have a preference for the poor, a kind of humility that offers the best seat, and the finest portions, to those who are usually denied or deprived.

MEMBERS AND FRIENDS

The Church may be imagined not only as a home, with room for all at the table. Paul painted another picture of the Church for the Corinthians, a portrait in this case. The Church is the body of Christ.[11] Paul invites a diverse band of people to see themselves as various body parts, all coordinated and part of a larger body. Being part of a "body" freed people to be together, to discover their peculiar gifts, to delight in being part of something bigger than me and my concerns.

Christians become "members" of a church, parts of the body. Being a "member" is not the surrender of our individuality, but rather is the only true exercise of our freedom. For Paul, you are really yourself only in community. We are called, not to an individual relationship with Christ, but rather into mutual relationships with others, a collective body that worships and serves Christ together. Body members are not identical, but are certainly complementary. As C. S. Lewis put it, church members are not identically dressed and identically trained soldiers standing shoulder to shoulder.[12] We are more like a family, bound together profoundly, not like interchangeable parts; you cannot subtract or add a family member without the whole family being totally altered. There is a unity to this body, as people who are different find their place, as a dizzying variety of gifts is put to use.

For Church is a fellowship. When the book of Acts speaks of "fellowship" in the early Church, the Greek term so translated is *koinonia*, which really means "sharing everything." The first Christians were virtually what we might call communists, in that they held no private property, holding all things in common (Acts 2:42–47, 4:32–36). Such a vision of the common life may lead us to rethink what friendship is all about. The Quakers call themselves the Society of Friends. Church is about friendship, but an alternative kind of friendship. Usually either friendship happens or it doesn't, and it is based on having fun or common interests. Yet in all our many friendships we yearn for something deeper. In her famous diary, Anne Frank wrote, "No one will believe that a girl of thirteen feels herself quite alone in the world. I have strings of friends, I have relations, a good home—no, I don't seem to lack anything. But it's the same with all my friends, just fun and joking, nothing more. The root of the problem is this: I have no real friend."[13] Back in the 1930s, C. S. Lewis met with J. R. R. Tolkien, Charles Williams, Owen Barfield, and others (calling themselves the "Inklings") to talk about politics, religion, and life, and read what they were working on—

now famous works like *The Lord of the Rings* and *The Screwtape Letters.* The criterion for being in the Inklings was simply this: do you care about truth? Members did not need to agree on the answers but had to be passionate about the questions.

Aristotle wrote about "real friends" at the very end of his *Nicomachean Ethics.* Friendship is not just enjoyable but formative, reshaping who we are, our values, and our decisions. When we are passionate about morality, we are striving for a certain kind of society. But Aristotle knew that morality *required* a certain kind of society.[14] John Wesley understood what we required and what Church might look like. In 1743 he penned a description of a little society of church members, to which he urged every Methodist to belong: "A society is no other than a company of men having the form and seeking the power of godliness, united in order to pray together, to receive the word of exhortation, and to watch over one another in love, that they may help each other to work out their salvation."[15] Participation in such a group was no easy thing. When you arrived, after prayer and singing, you would be sternly questioned about your spiritual life. What sins have you committed since our last meeting? What temptations have you encountered? Were you delivered? What have you thought or done or said that is sinful? Friendship is hard work, but the hard-won friends are real friends. As Kierkegaard put it, "To help another human being to love God is to love another man; to be helped by another human being to love God is to be loved."[16]

THE MARKS OF THE CHURCH

So what distinguishes this particular group of friends, this body of Christ? What must be in place for the Church to be itself? Luther once asked, "How can a poor confused person tell where such Christian holy people are to be found in this world?"[17] He answered by detailing seven "marks" of the Church: "the possession of the holy word of God," "the holy sacrament of baptism," "the sacrament of the altar" (the Lord's Supper), "the office of the keys" (order and discipline), "the consecration or calling of ministers," "prayer, public praise and thanksgiving" (including the catechism, the teaching of beliefs), and finally "the holy possession of the sacred cross" (the bearing of trials, misfortune, and suffering for the sake of Christ). These seven "holy possessions" are the work of God's Spirit in us, through us, in spite of us. We do them clumsily, and our clumsiness may cloak God's Spirit. But as we inevitably cloak the Spirit, we may thereby unveil God's mysterious activity and give it some tangibility.

The New Testament calls Jesus' followers "disciples," a word that means students, learners. The Church is a body of friends unusually devoted to the possession of God's word, the teaching of beliefs, a life-long learning about the things of God. In the early Church, before you could be baptized or receive the Lord's Supper, you underwent a full year of instruction, of catechesis. So specific were the beliefs of the Church, so demanding its life, that Christianity was "too great a shock"[18] for young believers to absorb all at once. What society celebrated, the Church shunned as sinful. Normal habits of living had to be broken, with a new routine of behavior and thinking instilled. A long pedagogy in lifestyle was needed.

As students, we never arrive; we never master the material. Over the centuries, the wisest saints have demonstrated that the Bible is a rich mine that is never exhausted, that we are at best dullards who constantly need to be tutored and deepened in what God would teach. For the subject is not cast in stone. The content of our faith is old and has some antiquity about it; yet it is something living, moving, ever fresh.[19] Pasolini's film about Jesus (*The Gospel according to St. Matthew,* 1964) captures something of this vitality. Jesus is always on the move, walking briskly, teaching on the way, the disciples breathlessly trying to keep up with him. Christian learning happens not merely in the stillness of a classroom, but also out in the world. The Bible can indeed be studied around a table upstairs in the church building with people like yourself; but the Bible is perhaps more profoundly explored out in the world, at a homeless shelter, reading with people who are different, trying out what the Bible is talking about in risky practice.

T. S. Eliot exposes the nature of this schooling: "Why should men love the Church? Why should they love her laws? She tells them of life and death, and of all that they would forget. She is tender where they would be hard, and hard where they like to be soft. She tells them of evil and sin, and other unpleasant facts."[20]

Where else will you go to be reminded that you are not just a bundle of desires, that you are more than a worker for some company's profit margin, that you have a spiritual side? Where else will you hear any word even subtly challenging our culture's ideology of money, sex, pleasure? Where else will you hear a thing about death, or about the mind of God? Without the Church, you may harbor religious thoughts and feelings. But how will you prevent those thoughts and feelings from getting watered down into nothing more than your own private wishes and prejudices? Indeed, this education is countercultural, not at all geared toward the simple betterment of the life I brought with me when I came to Church. Satisfying people's conscious "needs" is not the Church's function.

Therefore, the Church always has a countercultural feel about it, as if we are aliens, strangers, mere sojourners on this earth, quite intentionally out of sync with the values and happenings of the world in which we find ourselves, cognizant that "our citizenship is in heaven, and it is from there that we expect a Savior" (Phil. 3:20). Of course, our delight is knowing that we are not alien; rather, the world has let itself become alienated from God, and we exist as a bridge back from that alienation for all people who do not yet grasp their true citizenship.

In the last chapter we spoke of ethics and the Christian life. One of Luther's "marks" of the body of Christ is "the office of the keys." In Matthew 16, Jesus hands over to Peter the keys of the kingdom, to bind and to set free, thereby charging the Church with the weighty responsibility of order and discipline, to assume authority over the lives of Christians, as if members of the body of Christ are likely to need a firm hand with their lives. Through history, Christians have submitted to the authority of priests and bishops, trusting in their seemingly God-given right to dictate behavior and thought. To us, however, nothing could seem more alien than to invest such authority in mere mortals.

And yet should the Church relinquish its office of the keys as some relic of the past? Should our understandable wariness of abuse force us to give up on any kind of authority in the Church? Is there a way to offer sorely needed direction to floundering Christians seeking guidance? Oliver O'Donovan makes a helpful distinction between the Church's offering "commands" and "counsel." We have these commands in the Bible, but when we meet with people, we counsel them, using commands gently, solidly, yet giving space for an owned response.

> Counsel, indeed, is the church's most characteristic form of address to the individual, because it respects his status as one whom God also addresses directly, and whose particular decisions are partly hidden from public gaze. It is not, however, that the church pretends to know nothing about the rights and wrongs of individual decision. When the church counsels, it points to the authority of God's revelation in Christ and to the moral teaching of Jesus, the prophets and

the apostles; for it knows that right attitudes and decisions, however hidden and inscrutable in their detail, are those which come from a thoughtful obedience to that revelation.[21]

The Church cannot give anyone a thrashing; blunt mandates fall on deaf ears. And yet the Church cannot be merely supportive and soothing. We listen to and reflect on God's Word, we discern, we dare to speak humbly, we persuade, we hope.

WORSHIP AND PREACHING

Souls are shaped not only by what we teach but by what goes on in the regular cycles of worship in the Church. Hymns are sung, prayers recited, sermons preached. Kierkegaard helped us understand worship: while a service looks like performers (the minister, the choir) on stage before an audience (the congregation), the fact is that we all are the performers (minister, choir, congregation), and God is the audience. In worship we declare what is worthy of our praise, another counter-cultural act in a world where everything from soap to cars is praised. In worship we offer ourselves and what we have to God. In worship we are even transformed into people we would never be, had we not come. Amos Wilder put it pretty boldly: "Going to church is like approaching an open volcano, where the world is molten and hearts are sifted. The altar is like a rail that spatters sparks, the sanctuary like the chamber next to an atomic oven; there are invisible rays, and you leave your watch outside."[22]

Transformation hinges on the proclaimed Word of God, and the Church enjoys an historic gallery of great preachers. John Chrysostom (nicknamed the "golden mouth") preached spectacularly, first in the great octagonal church in Antioch, then in the Hagia Sophia in Constantinople. His brilliant expositions were greeted with thunderous applause, no matter how he urged them to be silent. Riots erupted. He chided the empress for her costly jewelry and was ostracized from the city, dying in disgrace. George Whitefield (1714–70), the "grand itinerant," preached in fields, near factories, three times daily, to raucous crowds. Some 20,000 pressed onto Boston Common to hear him. Even cynical old Benjamin Franklin admitted that he first came to hear Whitefield, resolving in his mind to give nothing to the collection. But once he had heard the sermon, he emptied his pockets.

Martin Niemöller preached vehemently against the emergency of Nazism. Summoned to the Führer's office, Niemöller spoke boldly to Hitler's face, when all others had cowered in fright: "The responsibility for our German nation has been laid upon our souls and conscience by no earthly authority but by God himself, and no earthly authority can take away this responsibility from our hearts, not even you."[23] Although Hitler threw a tantrum, Niemöller was unrelenting, choosing texts such as "We must obey God rather than men" (Acts 5:29 RSV). His final sermons were collected in a volume with the daring title *God Is My Führer*. Subjected to harassment, searches, and finally arrest by the Gestapo, Niemöller was convicted in a mock trial and spent eight years in various prisons, from Sachsenhausen to Dachau, enduring torture and solitary confinement. Martin Luther knew the power of the word proclaimed, and told his friend Phillip that credit for the Reformation all goes to God, whose word was working while Luther was sleeping and drinking Wittenberg beer.

BAPTISM AND THE LORD'S SUPPER

Worship is never simply preaching. Calvin wrote, "Wherever we see the Word of God purely preached and heard, and the sacraments administered according to Christ's institution, there, it is not to be doubted, a church of God exists."[24] The pillars of worship are the sacraments, which Augustine conceived as "visible words." These tangible signs, clearly enacted in the New Testament, are means of grace, which convey a mystery—not the kind of mystery you cannot fathom, but a mystery that lures us through a window punctured through our flattened lives into the depths of God's life. While Catholics have traditionally enumerated seven sacraments (including confirmation, penance, extreme unction, ordination, and marriage), Protestants have generally counted only two, Baptism and the Lord's Supper.

Baptism is a sign of union with Christ (Rom. 6:3), becoming part of the body of Christ (1 Cor. 12:13), the gift of the Spirit (Acts 2:1), forgiveness (Acts 2:38), and being born again (Titus 3:5). In the early Church, after weeks of intensive instruction and fasting, candidates would be scrutinized in preparation for an all-night vigil on Easter Eve. After the cock would crow, candidates would undress, and the bishop would anoint them with oils, believed to exorcise demons. After descending into a large pool, candidates would affirm their faith and be baptized. Emerging from the water, candidates would be anointed with the sign of the cross on the forehead, clothed in a pure white robe, and given the Lord's Supper, graced tantalizingly with a drink of milk and honey—all powerful symbols of the new life in Christ, the richness of God's promises, a radical passing from one life to another. To be baptized put the believer in certain danger, as persecution sometimes flared up and targeted the white-robed people. Yet so solid was God's promise that believers admitted to the authorities, "I am baptized," and became martyrs. Luther understood the profound comfort this grand act of grace could continue to have in the believer's life: "There is no greater comfort on earth than baptism." When he was in despair, he would remind himself, "I am baptized, and through my baptism God, who cannot lie, has bound himself in a covenant with me."[25]

How tragic, then, is the demise of Baptism, its trivialization into one more routine passage in the respectable life! Søren Kierkegaard, with blistering sarcasm, narrated a typical Baptism in nineteenth-century Denmark:

> It is a young man, we can imagine him with more than ordinary ability, knowledge, interested in public events, a politician, even taking an active part as such. As for religion, his religion is . . . that he has none at all. To think of God never occurs to him, any more than it does to go to church . . . he almost fears that to read God's Word at home would make him ridiculous. This same young man who feels no need of religion . . . marries, then he has a child. And then what happens? Well, our young man is, as they say, in hot water about this child; in the capacity of presumptive father he is compelled to have a religion. And it turns out that he has the Evangelical Lutheran religion. So they notify the priest, a young lady holds the infant's bonnet coquettishly, several young men who also have no religion render the father the service of having, as godfathers, the Evangelical Christian religion, while a silken priest with a graceful gesture sprinkles water three times on the dear little baby and dries his hands gracefully with the towel—and this they dare to present to God under the name of Christian baptism.[26]

Baptism is a comfort, a radical commitment, and the Lord's Supper nourishes and sustains that new life.

Jesus gave very few direct commands. But on the night before he was crucified, he shared a meal with his disciples, and mandated, "Do this in remembrance of me" (1 Cor. 11:25). To understand the Lord's Supper, we begin by feeling out what a meal with Jesus was like. Jesus had this striking habit of making an issue out of meals, offending against custom with one faux pas after another. He ate with tax collectors and sinners and was accused of gluttony; he rudely urged his hosts not to invite their friends or the "right" people, but rather the poor, maimed, and blind; Jesus permitted an unseemly woman to wash his feet with her hair at table; he in turn washed the feet of his unseemly disciples. Although the Church has theologized even subtle nuances of this "holy sacrament," we need always to recall the way Jesus conducted himself (or failed to conduct himself!) at table and permit *his* meal to be an event of surprise and perhaps even offense, certainly of social subversion.

Theologically, the Lord's Supper has several basic nuances: it is an act of thanksgiving (Acts 2:46), a fellowship meal (1 Cor. 10:16–17), a memorial (Luke 22:19), even a sacrifice (Heb. 9:14). Ignatius called it "the medicine of immortality," for this meal anticipates the biblical vision of the glorious banquet that heaven will be. The Church's passion to understand this mystery has wrought sad division among Christ's people. In the ninth century, two monks in the monastery of Corbie, named Radbertus and Ratramnus, debated fiercely, the former discerning a very literal presence of Christ in the Eucharist, the latter sensing a more spiritual or symbolic presence. Radbertus won, and by the thirteenth century the doctrine of transsubstantiation, the belief that God powerfully alters the elements into the true body and blood of Christ, was widely accepted. At the Colloquy of Marburg in 1529, Luther and Huldrych Zwingli, united in their aversion to the Catholic position of transubstantiation, argued over what Christ meant when he said, "This is my body." Luther asserted a "real presence" of Christ, Zwingli a more spiritual kind of fellowship of believers with Christ. Denominations continue to parry opinions, even excluding those who disagree—again, not out of stupidity but of a passion for truth in these matters. Yet is Moltmann not right when he says that the Lord's Supper is not the place to practice church discipline? For truly,

> the Lord's Supper takes place on the basis of an invitation which is as open as the outstretched arms of Christ on the cross. Because he died for the reconciliation of "the world," the world is invited to reconciliation in the supper. It is not the openness of this invitation, it

is the restrictive measures of the churches which have to be justified before the face of the crucified Jesus.[27]

It is to this work of reconciliation that we now turn.

THE MISSION ENTRUSTED TO THE CHURCH

To speak of the body of Christ is not merely to talk about our unity with other Christians. We also have this activity, a task, a mission, to be the body of Christ. A marvelous admonition has traditionally been attributed to Teresa of Avila:

> Christ has no body now on earth but yours,
>   no hands but yours,
>   no feet but yours.
> Yours are the eyes through which the compassion
>   of Christ is to look out on a hurting world.
> Yours are the feet with which he is to go about
>   doing good.
> Yours are the hands with which he is to bless now.[28]

The challenge to the church is to be the hands, feet, eyes of Christ in the world, somehow, no matter how feebly, embodying what Christ is about in the world. We feed the hungry, touch the untouchables, reach out to the lonely, heal, pray, serve; for the Church has historically understood its mission to be the imitation of Christ. The Church does not *have* a mission so much as we *are* a mission. For Paul was not merely deploying a clever metaphor when he called the Church "the body of Christ." The Church quite simply *is* Christ in the world.

St. Francis and his friars may be exemplary for us. As Chesterton shrewdly put it, Francis "seemed to have liked everybody, but especially those whom everybody disliked him for liking."[29] At its worst, the Church excludes people who are different, who think wrongly, who are from someplace else, and Church becomes a place where narcissism is celebrated. A few years ago, a friend of mine spent a week at Lourdes, the shrine in France where the Virgin Mary appeared to Bernadette Soubirous, just fourteen years old, in 1858. Thousands of gallons of water flow there each day, and thousands claim to have been cured in its streams. When my friend returned, I asked her, "Did you see any

miracles?" She said, "Oh yes, every day." "Every day? Tell me!" She
explained, "Every day at Lourdes, no matter who you are, or where you
are from, or what's wrong with you, you are welcomed, and loved." This
is the Church.

The Church is not a fortress in which Christians hide out from the
world or pass judgment on the world. The Church is in the midst of the
world, with doors opening out onto the streets where people live and
dream and hurt. Our mission is to heal, to be the light of hope, bearing
and sharing the realities of life in the world. The Church is not against
the world, but is the place where the world becomes aware of its true
need, where the "sickness of the world comes to a head"[30]—that the
Church's effort to heal (which at the same time is the Church's need for
healing) is the hope of the world. In January of 1978 Archbishop Oscar
Romero preached a sermon that perfectly named the Church's challenge
to heal:

> This is the mission entrusted to the church,
>   a hard mission:
> to uproot sins from history,
> to uproot sins from the political order,
> to uproot sins from the economy,
> to uproot sins wherever they are.
>   What a hard task!
> It has to meet conflicts amid so much selfishness,
> so much pride,
> so much vanity,
> so many who have enthroned the reign of sin among us.
> The church must suffer for speaking the truth,
>   for pointing out sin,
>   for uprooting sin.
> No one wants to have a sore spot touched,
> and therefore a society with so many sores twitches
> when someone has the courage to touch it
> and say: "You have to treat that.
>   You have to get rid of that.
>   Believe in Christ.
> Be converted."[31]

Healing inevitably involves the Church in social issues, in the political
realm, where many would prefer the Church steer clear. Beyond question, the Church has erred by getting in bed with this or that political

party, by blessing a politician by name, or by baptizing some liberal or conservative cause. The Church's task is to help society find common ground by moving to "higher ground."[32] This responsibility cannot be shirked, for as soon as we acknowledge that Christ is Lord over all, we are plunged into the thick of controversy, and we are naive to expect to avoid hostile reactions. When Luther enumerated the "marks" of the Church, he included suffering trials for the sake of Christ. In a society out of sync with God, in a culture that celebrates what we have called the seven deadly sins, in a world drunk with pleasure and superficiality, the Church will fall under suspicion, be misunderstood, meet opposition, even suffer. But the privilege is that someone, somewhere, is always standing up for the kingdom of God, daring to be the body of Christ in the same world that killed Christ the first time around.

DISSATISFACTION WITH THE CHURCH

We inevitably fail at this crucial task, as demonstrated so pointedly in chapter 4. Corruption poisons the Church in every era. Ongoing, irresolvable division into denominations, splintering now into the ironical "nondenominational" bodies, breeds confusion and cynicism. Theologically speaking, we can never wriggle free of the terrible truth that division in the Church is blasphemy, to be chalked up to sin, not to God's will.[33] Apathy and laziness lull the Church and the world to sleep. Mildest of all, and perhaps most insidious, is the pervasive "niceness" of the Church; many are pleased when the Church majors in triviality and minors in irrelevance. In every place and era the Church cries out for reform. We can never be satisfied, as Romano Guardini knew: "The Church is the cross on which Christ was crucified. And yet Christ is never separate from his cross. And so we must live with a sort of permanent dissatisfaction with the Church."[34]

Yet even without reform, the Church bears a certain hope even in its failure. Karl Barth, disillusioned when major theologians sold out, cheering on the kaiser's launching of World War I, embarked on an intensive study of Romans that, when published, rocked the Church throughout Europe and America. Yes, the Church shrank back in a pivotal hour, but we need not despair. In a flight of stunning rhetoric, Barth preached on how the hope of the Church paradoxically is manifest precisely where its guilt is proven:

And in fact all human piety does point beyond itself, for it knows that it can be no more than an imprint, a signpost and an intermediate station, a reminder and a negation. The Church—if it be aware of itself and is serious—sets fire to a charge which blows up every sacred edifice which men have ever erected or can ever erect in its vicinity. . . . And so, the Church is . . . the canal through which flows the living water of salvation. "Only where graves are, is there resurrection" (Nietzsche); rather, wherever graves are, there is resurrection. Where the Church ends—not, of course, by a human act of will, but by a divine decree—there is its beginning. Where its unrighteousness is altogether exposed, there its righteousness dawns. The divine demolition of any Church means that every Church arises as a signpost, threshold, and door of hope. It is then that the Church appears, as its were, as an arrow shot from the other bank; it appears as the messenger of Christ and as the tabernacle of God with men. . . . Broken, the church can bear its message with head erect, for the Gospel of salvation belongs to the Church which is lost. Shattered, the Church can, and indeed must, speak of God, by whose help men leap over the wall.[35]

Indeed, the liturgy used in baptism begins with the humble, glorious truth: the Church universal is of God and will be preserved to the end of time. Consider the particular church where you and I go, in our town, on Sunday morning. Barth's grandiose vision fit snugly into a little sanctuary in Switzerland, as it fits into ours:

> I believe that the congregation to which I belong . . . is the one, holy, universal Church. If I do not believe this here, I do not believe it at all. No lack of beauty, no "wrinkles and spots" in this congregation may lead me astray. . . . In faith I attest that the concrete congregation to which I belong and for the life of which I am responsible, is appointed to the task of making in this place, in this form, the one, holy, universal Church visible.[36]

For this congregation is part of a great constellation of flickering lights, with a history as long as time itself, a membership enfolding the globe, and a destiny that is and will ultimately resound as a great chorus of women and men from yesterday, today, and tomorrow, the communion of the saints.

Perhaps it is the "tomorrow" that defines us and our posture as Church. Augustine's words can lead us into our final chapter: "Whenever I have described the Church as being without spot or wrinkle, I have not intended to imply that it was like this already, but that it should prepare itself to be like this, at the time when it too will appear in glory."[37]

QUESTIONS FOR DISCUSSION

1. What do you like about the images of the church as a "home"; as "the body of Christ"?
2. In what ways do the sacraments of Baptism and the Lord's Supper nourish your faith as a member of the church?
3. In what ways do churches of which you are aware live out their "missions"?

9

Eschatology

Hope and the End of Time

Too often we think of hope in too individualistic a manner as merely our
personal salvation. But hope essentially bears on the great actions of God
concerning the whole of creation. It bears on the destiny of all humanity. It is the salvation of the world that we await. In reality hope bears on
the salvation of all men—and it is only in the measure that I am
immersed in them that it bears on me.

—Jean Daniélou[1]

Christianity has always had a peculiar perspective on time, one that
leans toward the future, investing its emotional capital in an epoch that
looms out there at some unspecified date. Theologians call this region
of thought "eschatology," which technically means "talk about the last
things." But eschatology is not merely predictions or positions on the
end of time, speculation about how it will all end. Eschatology is a posture, a mentality, always pressing forward, always waiting, expecting
something, or someone.[2]

As far back as Old Testament times, the heroes of Israel staked everything on God's promise of what God would eventually do. Abraham
was led out from Ur of the Chaldeans to a new land with a new destiny,
one he would not witness in his lifetime. Moses gazed over into the
promised land from Pisgah, glimpsing a future he would not enjoy.
David learned about the historic role his descendants would play. Isaiah's disciples penned his words on a scroll for future generations to read.
Jeremiah foretold the day when God's people would be given a new
heart. Ezekiel "saw de wheel, way up in de middle of de air," and dry
bones in a valley revivified, a vision that God's shattered people have a
vital future. Jesus himself spoke of the coming of the Son of Man on the
clouds. Paul's theology and his utterly mundane advice both presumed
the coming consummation of God's redemption of the world, when
Christ returns with his angels and gathers the elect to him.

158INTRODUCING CHRISTIANITY

THINGS HOPED FOR

Indeed, "faith is the assurance of things hoped for, the conviction of things not seen" (Heb. 11:1), and what we cannot see is the future; but it is precisely that unseen future that has been the great treasury, the vital wellspring for Christians. Polycarp, the venerable bishop of Smyrna, was burned at the stake in the year 156. Taunted by officials who urged him to cry, "Away with the atheists!" (meaning the Christians), he wryly looked heavenward and shouted, "Away with the atheists!" (meaning the Romans). The proconsul persisted: "Curse Christ, and I will let you go." Polycarp replied: "Eighty-six years have I served him, and he has done me no wrong; how could I blaspheme my king who saved me? You threaten the fire that burns for an hour, but then is quenched; you are ignorant of the fire of judgment to come. Why delay? Do what you wish."[3] Onlookers, including the proconsul, were awed by the joy and peace on his face, even as he perished in the flames.

American slaves sang spirituals of stunning joy and hope, proving that a harsh plantation could be transformed into a beachhead of heaven. When they sang, "Soon ah will be done a-wid de troubles ob de worl'" or "But some ob dese days my time will come," they latched on to a future hope when all injustice would be set right. Yet at the same time they were buoyed now and sensed the presence of God now, never moreso than when their voices were lifted in praise. When they sang, "There is a holy city," that heavenly Jerusalem seemed somehow truer, more real, than the embattled towns of America.

Beginning in the childhood of her too brief life, Thérèse of Lisieux was eager for heaven. Suffering the loss of her mother and sisters, and racked by the pains of tuberculosis, she prayed that God might take her without delay into his eternal embrace so that "I may be able to tell you of my love eternally face to face." Poetry poured from her heart:

> To die of love is what I hope for,
> on fire with his love I want to be,
> to see him, be one with him forever,
> that is my heaven—that's my destiny.[4]

Moments before her death on September 30, 1897, sensing that she was falling into the arms of God, Thérèse opened her eyes widely and looked straight up, making those near her believe it was her first clear glimpse into heaven. For her, death was not the end, but the door to her real vocation: "My mission is about to begin, my mission to make God loved as I love him, to give my little way to souls. If God grants my desires . . . I will spend my heaven doing good upon earth."

PREPARED FOR THE WORST

This conviction about the future does not mean everything will go smoothly. On the contrary: those whose citizenship is in heaven (Phil. 3:20) should expect the "troubles ob de worl." For hope is to be carefully distinguished from optimism. Optimism is the blithe notion that tomorrow will be better, that if we hang in there and try harder, all will turn out sunny, that the plot of human life is one of progress. But hope? Christopher Lasch wisely defined the heart of hope:

> Hope doesn't demand progress; it demands justice, a conviction that wrongs will be made right, that the underlying order of things is not flouted with impunity. Hope appears absurd to those who lack it. We can see why hope serves us better than optimism. Not that it prevents us from expecting the worst; the worst is what the hopeful are prepared for. A blind faith that things will somehow work out for the best furnishes a poor substitute for the disposition to see things through even when they don't.[5]

Martin Luther King Jr. was prepared for the worst when, late in life, he could say, "I am no longer optimistic, but I am still hopeful." Oscar Romero, having condemned the government of El Salvador for its ruthless oppression of its people, knowing his assassination was imminent, told a reporter over the telephone: "My life has been threatened many times. I have to confess that as a Christian I do not believe in death without resurrection. If they kill me, I will rise again in the Salvadoran people." More personally he continued: "God assisted the martyrs and, if necessary, I will feel him very close when I offer him my last breath. More important than the moment of death is giving him all of life and living for him." And again: "If God accepts the sacrifice of my life, my hope is that my blood will be like a seed of liberty and a sign that our hopes will soon become reality."[6]

Clearly the Christian hope, hanging everything on God's future, induces no paralysis in the real world, but hurls the Church into fervent action. Confidence in God's future frees the Christian to do what is right, no matter the consequences: "Hope is the ability to work for something because it is good, not just because it stands a chance of succeeding" (Vaclav Havel). And hope fosters in us a dogged participation in a this-worldly adventure that is very much long term: "Nothing worth doing can be achieved in a single lifetime; therefore we are saved by hope" (Reinhold Niebuhr). Hope does not rob us of the present, but rather is the joy of the present: "Expectation makes life good, for in expectation man can accept his whole present and find joy not only in its joy but also in its sorrow, happiness not only in its happiness but also in its pain" (Jürgen Moltmann).[7] Or as Catherine of Siena put it, "All the way to heaven is heaven."

THE SECRET OF JOYFULNESS

This is the secret of that fruit of the Spirit of which Paul spoke, namely "joy," a disposition largely unknown in our day, not to be confused with mere happiness. Polycarp was joyful amid the flames. Francis of Assisi, in bodily agony, sang canticles of pulsating joy. On his deathbed in 1791, John Wesley surprised everyone, breaking a long silence with a song (from a hymn by Isaac Watts):

> I'll praise my Maker while I've breath,
> and when my soul is lost in death,
> praise shall employ my nobler powers.
> My days of praise shall ne'er be past.

Thérèse was remembered by surviving nuns four decades after her death for her smile, which "arose from the noblest kind of modesty," which "was simply the honest fulfillment of her vocation," described in another of her poems:

> For Him I love I wish my smile to shine;
> Though He to try me hides His Face from me,
> For Him I wait, though night and pain be mine;
> This is my Heaven, this my felicity.[8]

Because of the resurrection of Christ, you just cannot walk around with a long face. The Christian hope begins and is never for a second separate from what happened outside the walls of Jerusalem that first

Easter. Foolishness to the intelligentsia of Paul's day, dismissed by philosophers as sheer wishful thinking, the resurrection was in Bible times (and still is in modern times) the ultimate surprise, the fracturing of the status quo, the pattern of cause and effect subverted, the seemingly inevitable "survival of the fittest" reversed. Interestingly, many scholars argue that the religions of Jesus' day were not focused on the afterlife, but rather pledged benefits in this world. A cloud of agnosticism hovered on the other side of death. The resurrection of Christ gave definition and certainty to the fate of people in the hour of death.

So can we say that Feuerbach was wrong when he cynically suggested that belief in the resurrection is mere fantasy, a projection of our sincere wish to live, a concoction cooked up to answer our fear of extinction? The definitive answer to such questions can be known only by people who rest in cemeteries. But our wish to live, our prevalent anxiety about death can be given a more positive evaluation. Consider the startling normalcy of death in the animal kingdom; aphids, houseflies, sparrows, all with short life expectancies, are evidently untroubled by mortality. The only unusual aspect of our view of death is not our dying, but our feelings about it. Alone among creatures we harbor this anxiety and foreboding about death. So is Feuerbach right, that we have hatched this fantasy about salvation? Or was Annie Dillard more on target?

> Our excessive emotions are so patently painful and harmful to us as a species that I can hardly believe that they evolved. Other creatures manage to have effective matings and even stable societies without great emotions, and they have a bonus in that they need not ever mourn. It would seem that emotions are the curse, not death—emotions that appear to have devolved upon a few freaks as a special curse from Malevolence.[9]

A curse from Malevolence perhaps. But more likely a gift from God, who yearns for us to detect in those feelings a calling, an invitation. We need not fear the future, but confidently embrace it. Or even better, we may let the future embrace us.

Not that the resurrection is merely about me and the benefits God hopefully will give me. The resurrection is ultimately about God, the triumph of God, the all-consuming manifestation of God's love and purpose. Christiaan Beker clarifies what is at stake in Christianity's hopeful posture: "Paul's church is not an aggregate of justified sinners or a sacramental institute or a means for private self-sanctification but the avant-garde of the new creation in a hostile world, creating beach-heads in this world of God's dawning new world and yearning for the day of God's visible lordship over his creation."[10] For we still yearn. We may say that God's promise was "validated," rather than "fulfilled,"[11] when Christ was raised. For all of creation is still given over to sin, evil, and death. The final consummation of God's purpose for creation is pledged but not yet manifest.

REVELATION'S MONSTERS

The most poignant yearning for that lordship in the pages of the New Testament can be heard in the book of Revelation. With over 500 quotations from the Old Testament, the book stands at the end of the Bible as the climax of the entire biblical journey and portrays the climax of history. The strange creatures and events in Revelation have piqued the curiosity of artists, many of whom have tried to capture them on canvas. In a sense, what John describes cannot be put onto a canvas—for he is describing something beyond comprehension, something immeasurable, too fantastic for words or measurement. Most famous have been the woodcuts by Albrecht Dürer, and the work of William Blake (himself quite a visionary). John's language is fantastic, kaleidoscopic, poetic—as he gamely describes God's awesome presence, which is obviously too wonderful for mere words.

Herein lies the flaw of those zealous interpreters throughout history who have tagged the symbolism of Revelation to events in their own day. G. K. Chesterton said that, although John saw many strange monsters in his vision, he saw no creature so wild as one of his commentators. In our generation, the beasts and symbols of Revelation have been applied to political turmoil in Russia and the Middle East, making fortunes for several authors. J. F. Walvoord's 1974 book *Armageddon, Oil, and the Middle East Crisis* is a million seller (even in its updated and reissued 1990 edition!). Hal Lindsey's *Late Great Planet Earth* was a multimillion seller through the 1970s and early 80s. At the turn of the twenty-first century, Tim LaHaye and and Jerry Jenkins sold tens of millions in their Left Behind series.

Before I offer any critique, I must declare the great impact some of these apocalyptic writings can have on people, including myself. Back in 1975, some of my religious friends were certain Christ would return during the month of August (with great humility, they claimed not to know the exact day). One day in early September, I proclaimed to my roommates, "Well, I guess Jesus didn't come back." "How would *you* know?" was the reply. "We're still here." "Yeah, but we're the ones who got left." So we decided on a test. We chose the person we thought most likely to go—if people in fact were going up into the heavens with Christ. A woman named Glo seemed the logical choice: very sweet, devout, holy. And we hadn't seen her in a couple of weeks. We drove out to her house. Her car was in the driveway. We heard the radio on inside the house as we rang the doorbell. No answer. We knocked. No answer. Silently we turned to get back in the car. Just as I lay my hand on the car door handle, Glo's voice pierced the silence: "Hey, guys!" She'd been in the back yard. I hate to admit it, but between the unanswered doorbell and her calling out to us, I was secretly wondering: "Could it be? Naahh. . . . And yet. . . . Why didn't anybody come to check to see if *I* was still around? What am I doing with my life?" The funny thing is, two of the three of us are now Methodist preachers!

Of course there is nothing new under the sun. Virtually every generation has had its apocalyptic believers. In Phrygia in the year 156, Montanus claimed to be the incarnation of the Holy Spirit, and Christians flocked to Phrygia to wait for the second coming. In the year 1000 apocalyptic dreamers watched the skies for the apocalypse. Followers of Joachim of Fiore (1145–1202) even resorted to self-flagellation, blaming themselves for Christ's failure to return on schedule. In the aftermath of John Hus's execution in 1415, one band of Bohemians went about naked, claiming to enjoy the innocence lost by Adam and Eve in the garden. In the 1500s, Martin Luther thought the world was in its final days. William Miller, a Vermont pastor with thousands of followers, calculated that the world would end in 1843.

Why are Christians so eager about this subject? There is some sheer headiness of being in the know, being privy to God's calendar. Norman Cohn argues that such movements in the Middle Ages found fertile soil among the poor, especially the poor whose world was falling apart around them.[12] The dangers are plenty. David Koresh and the Branch Davidians were intrigued by what they thought the book of Revelation was telling them to do. Ronald Reagan invited Hal Lindsey to give a lecture on a potential war with Russia to strategists at the Pentagon. Interestingly, this theme of doomsday apocalyptic is far more popular in the United States than anywhere else in the world, leaving us to wonder if America's political aspirations have bled over into people's eschatology.

But the root impulse of leaning toward the future, looking for God's climatic action is not wrong. For while Revelation is not a crystal-ball prediction of political events in Europe or Asia in our times, it still has everything to do with us and our age, and portrays with awesome imagination the truth of God that is ultimately relevant today.

The Lindseys and LaHayes overlook the fact that Revelation is a letter, addressed to the real concerns of Christians living in Asia Minor who faced an anxious future. Under severe pressure, facing mounting persecution under the emperor Domitian, Christians desperately needed, not a crystal-ball forecast of the early twenty-first century, but a word for the moment, their moment. The first recipients of the letter understood what John was talking about, just as we recognize what a donkey and an elephant mean in an editorial cartoon. The white horse, with a mounted archer, represented the dreaded Parthians who waged war against the eastern edge of the Roman Empire. To people in whose lifetime Mount Vesuvius had erupted, the sky turning black would be familiar. The ignominious "666" is a transparent reference to Nero,[13] whose rumored survival from a brush with death (and return in brutal vengeance) stirred intense fears among Christians familiar with his habit of tarring Christians and burning them as torches for his garden. Many symbols resonated with Old Testament promises of God's presence.

But the longer reading of the book has an extravagance, an excess, spilling over the bounds of reality as they knew it, or as we know it. When the final upheaval comes, when God's consummation of history dawns, no writer, artist, or musician can begin to capture the glorious wonder of it all. The climax of God's ultimate plan will be such a marvelous victory that Christians may endure any oppression now. And the sureness of that plan's dawning leads Christians, not to a sheltered passivity or flight from the world, but to a courageous resistance, daring even to stand up to the powers that be. Revelation speaks to Christians in everyday situations, calling them to invest all their hopes in a God who rights all wrongs, who is in fact coming, who will in the end draw us and all of creation to himself, in a day when time will be no more. As Cardinal Newman put it: "Christ, then, is ever at our doors; as near eighteen hundred years ago as now, and not nearer now than then; and not nearer when He comes than now. When He says that He will come soon, 'soon' is not a word of time, but of natural order."[14] As we weigh the implications of Christianity's eschatological posture, difficult theological issues catch our eye. Is there a final judgment? Does hell exist? What is salvation? Who will be saved? What is the place of non-Christian religions?

THE FINAL JUDGMENT

For the Old Testament prophets, for the New Testament writers, and for thinking believers over the centuries, the coming of God is something to be feared. A grisly God's garments are soaked in blood in Isaiah 63:6 "I trampled down peoples . . . in my wrath, and I poured out their lifeblood on the earth." Noting that the Lord will come "like a thief in the night," Paul trembles over the "sudden destruction" from which "there will be no escape" (1 Thess. 5:2–3). Jesus himself was not at all shy in speaking of the torments of hell, the gnashing of teeth.

The wrath of God is a subject we prefer not to talk about, or to discuss only with reference to our enemies. There is this ferocity in God, an attention toward us that burns with zeal, raging at our waywardness. Consider the intensity of Jonathan Edwards's famous sermon, "Sinners in the Hands of an Angry God," preached on July 8, 1741: "It would be dreadful to suffer this fierceness and wrath of Almighty God for one moment; but you must suffer it for all eternity. There will be no end to this exquisite horrible misery. . . . You will know that you must wear out long ages, millions and millions of ages, in wrestling and conflicting with this almighty merciless vengeance." Edwards is brandishing the very biblical threat that we may wind up in hell. Is there such a "place" as hell, and what sense can we make of hell theologically?

A recent Gallup poll shows that while 60 percent of Americans believe there is a hell, only a paltry 4 percent of them feel they are likely to go there. Children once were taught that hell was a subterranean region of flame and torment. Artists and writers have creatively imagined what hell is like, none as profoundly as Dante. At the entrance to the nine circles of the inferno are the words "Abandon hope, all who enter here!" Descending ever deeper, Dante encounters swamps, furies, Medusa, heretics, centaurs, tyrants, a virtual burlesque of horrors. There is fire, but then a hard frozen lake at hell's epicenter. And just as Thérèse could speak of her heaven beginning now, Robertson Davies spoke for many who sense hell's presence creeping onto earth and into our time: "I saw no reason then why hell should not have, so to speak, visible branch establishments throughout the earth, and I have visited quite a few of them."[15]

Earlier, especially in chapter 6, we dealt with the problem of evil, why a loving God allows suffering in the world. The possibility of hell raises the question from another angle: Why would a loving God allow endless suffering and torment? How can we square the gracious character of God with judgment and punishment? Logic reminds us there can be no grace without judgment. For God's love comes with a demand, or else it is not love. As Bonhoeffer taught us, grace is cheapened when we expect forgiveness without repentance and baptism without church discipline: "Cheap grace is grace without discipleship, grace without the cross, grace without Jesus Christ. . . . Such grace is costly because it calls us to follow, and it is grace because it calls us to follow Jesus Christ. It is costly because it costs a man his life, and it is grace because it gives a man the only true life."[16] So there must be a judgment, an accountability, consequences to our failure to follow Christ.

But was Jonathan Edwards right in calling God's judgment "merciless"? Judgment, as fierce and fearful as it surely is, proves to be the shadow side of what in fact is good news. Our life in the world would melt into meaninglessness without some eventual accounting. I am glad that murderers and racists, purveyors of smut and drugs, are denied the last word and will finally be denounced. I do not feel nearly so glad that I too will be denied the last word, and that much that I relish will surely hurl me into denunciation. For in the end, a strict accounting of what I did with my money, my time, my mind, my stuff will be required.

Yet we can see how judgment has hidden within its harshness a healing balm. The prophet Malachi spoke of God's coming as a "refiner's fire," as "fuller's soap" (3:2). For hidden in judgment is the Gospel itself, and it may stir in us not servile fear but joyful hope.

Judgment finally isn't on me or you, but on evil, on all that is not of God. This judgment is about the dismantling of the powers that undo us, and so is cosmic in scope. While we may reduce Christianity to something personal, a benefit for me and mine, the true God engages the massive powers of the world, staring even international evil in the eye, judging not just individuals, but systems, governments, cultures. Karl Heim hit upon the hidden meaning of history:

The repeated collapse of every earthly imperialism is the most impressive demonstration of the fact that no divinization of any earthly power can stand, that every absolutizing of any earthly absolute always carries within itself the seeds of death. God sets up his throne on the wreckage of human earthly thrones, and the history of the world is strewn with the wreckage of demolished imperialisms and smashed altars, whose debris reveals impressively the sole Lordship of God.[17]

JUDGMENT AND JESUS CHRIST

On the front wall of the Sistine Chapel, Michelangelo painted his masterpiece *The Last Judgment,* in which a powerful Christ separates the reconciled, who weightlessly glide upward, from the terror-stricken condemned, who cower in anguish. What we realize most importantly from Michelangelo's image is that judgment is executed not with respect to some timeless law code that is adhered to or broken. Judgment is related to a person, to the person of Christ. And so we may imagine a different kind of court from those we see on earth, where legality prevails, where the clever manipulate opinion and win or lose unjustly. God's judgment is a creative justice, the kind of justice determined to set things right, to restore good order, and this judgment must be meted out by the only one competent to fashion reconciliation. Moltmann wrote: "What we call the Last Judgment is nothing other than the universal revelation of Jesus Christ, and the consummation of his redemptive work . . . judgment at the end is not an end at all; it is the beginning. Its goal is the restoration of all things for the building up of God's eternal kingdom."[18]

If the Bible teaches us anything about the universal revelation of Jesus Christ, it is that he is the strangest sort of judge, a judge who passes judgment but then bears that very judgment upon himself. While Karl Barth instigated an incredible debate on this subject within twentieth-century theology, I hope that he was right when he wrote the astonishing *Church Dogmatics,* volume II, part 2. He probes the historic doctrine of predestination, following the logic that if God is all-powerful, then people are saved because of God's will; and if people are lost, this must too be God's will.[19] But herein lies the problem—for God's omnipotence could not fail at the point of even one lost soul. Barth affirmed the logic of predestination, yet turned it on its ear. There is predestination indeed, and its focal point is Jesus Christ and his work:

> If the teachers of predestination were right when they spoke always of a duality, of election and reprobation, of predestination to salvation or perdition, to life or death, then we may say already that in the election of Jesus Christ which is the eternal will of God, God has ascribed to man the former, election, salvation and life; and to Himself He has ascribed the latter, reprobation, perdition and death. . . . God, by the decree He made in the beginning of all His works and ways, has taken upon Himself the rejection merited by the man isolated in relation to Him; that on the basis of this decree of His the

only truly rejected man is His own Son. . . . This one Righteous can
be righteous in our place, can be obedient for our sake, only because
He acknowledges our sin, and drinks to the bitter dregs the cup of
temporal and eternal destruction which must follow transgression.[20]

All of hell bears in on Christ on the cross. The torment of separation
from God is precisely what Christ screams so poignantly: "My God, my
God, why have you forsaken me?" There is judgment, but for us it
becomes the forgiveness of our sins. We have nothing to offer to God
except our brokenness, our lostness, which means that as the beneficiaries of what genuinely is nothing but mercy and grace, we can only
bring God our thanks. We can only feel gratitude, and joy.

THE NATURE OF SALVATION

Salvation, therefore, is not a great prize that we win by making shrewd
choices on earth, or some great fortune distributed to those held in favor
by God. Salvation is the overflow of God's own love, the fulfillment of
God's promise, the sharing of God's very own life. A clue to the meaning of eternal life is found in the Scriptures that did not know about
eternal life. In Psalm 73 we read of someone who has suffered much,
and unjustly. He cries out to God, even contemplating giving up on
God. But he goes to the sanctuary and, despite everything, senses the
presence of God. Not expecting life after death, this psalmist declares
why he wants to live, to survive:

> Whom have I in heaven but you?
>   And there is nothing on earth that I desire other than you.
> My flesh and my heart may fail,
>   but God is the strength of my heart and my portion forever.
> . . . .
> For me, it is good to be near God.
>
> (Ps. 73:25–26, 28a).

What we hear is someone who loves God, who has in this life received
God as his only good, his deepest desire. And what is eternal life? What
is the resurrection, if not the continuation of such a relationship beyond
the fracturing of death? God's love is such that it cannot fail; not even
death can eradicate a relationship precious enough to God to endure the
hell of dereliction, the gruesome agony of the cross.

And so we may conceive of salvation, of the future of our relationship with God, as being graciously included within the life of the Trinity, as we are drawn into the circle of love that is the Father, Son, and Holy Spirit. Throughout history, theologians have taught us that salvation will be akin to divinization, that we will be transformed into beings that will be so gloriously luminous that "you would be strongly tempted to worship" (as C. S. Lewis phrased it).[21] We will see God face to face; we will know God, and goodness, and each other fully. Or might it be that as we discover more about God, we will at the same time discover more questions, so that our experience of the glory of God will continually feel like seeking rather than possessing, and that our joy will be the seeking?

We must add that salvation is not just for the individual person but is for all of creation. When asked if there would be mosquitoes in heaven, Lewis wryly answered that yes, there will be a heaven for mosquitoes, and it will be the same place that is hell for people. The animal kingdom, flora and fauna, rocks, water, and galaxies: all is incorporated in the Bible's vision of salvation. The climactic destiny of the universe is not annihilation, but transformation (as taught consistently by Irenaeus, Augustine, Aquinas, Barth); we look forward to a new creation (Rev. 21:5, 1 Cor. 15:28). This new creation is not first of all about my personal survival, but rather about the triumph of God. Ultimately, salvation is about the glorification of God, and our pleasure will be to praise and enjoy God forever.

THE SALVATION OF ALL?

But who will be there to praise and enjoy God forever? We observe a tension within the Bible and among the great theologians. An apparent majority of voices indicate that people must choose for or against God, and those who fail to believe are expelled from the presence of God; heavenly life is restricted to those who believed, who were saved, who were chosen. For the love of God to make sense, we must return God's love.

Yet there are biblical passages (such as Eph. 1:10, Col. 1:20, Rom. 11:32, 1 Tim. 2:4) that intimate a broader plan for humanity, one in which God's loving will for all is realized. In 1 Timothy 2:1 the church is asked to make supplication for all people, which, as Hans Urs von Balthasar thinks, "could not be asked of her if she were not allowed to have at least the hope that prayers as widely directed as these are sensible and might be heard."[22] This minority tradition's most eloquent exponent was perhaps Origen, whose logic insisted on there being a redemptive purpose in God's wrath. He could not imagine that God's love could fail, believing that "God's goodness through Christ may recall all his creatures to their one end."[23] Implicit in Barth is the notion that God's judgment upon all falls upon Christ, so that God's gift of salvation falls upon all as well.

Barth and Origen are looking from *God's* side at the ultimate triumph of grace over even unbelief. There is a *human* side to this, as the sheer possibility of incompleteness in heaven somehow robs heaven of its supposed fulness of joy. Merton spoke his heart: "I will have more joy in heaven and in the contemplation of God, if you are also there to share it with me; and the more of us there will be to share it the greater will be the joy of all."[24]

Mind you, belief in the salvation of all remains a minority position within Christendom. But from its theses we recognize that as Christians there can be no room for anyone to take perverse pleasure at being someone who gets in while others most deservedly will not. The Christian who comprehends the gospel will always cradle a tenacious hope that all will in fact be saved. Von Balthasar, in his provocative book *Dare We Hope that All Men Will Be Saved?* quotes Gustave Martelet at length:

> If God is love, as the New Testament teaches us, hell must be impossible. At the least, it represents a supreme anomaly. Being a Christian means, first of all, believing in Christ and, if the question arises, hoping that it will be impossible that there is a hell for men because the love with which we are loved will ultimately be victorious. And yet this love has not extinguished our freedom, for a love bestowed will always have to be also a love received.

And so, human refusal of God,

> which is absurdity itself, cannot be regarded as the ultimate word on "ultimate things." The Gospel never presents such a refusal to us as a credible possibility that Jesus could be satisfied to accept. For hell is the real absurdity. . . . If we speak of a refusal of love, then never of God who would refuse love. There will never be beings unloved by God. . . . Hell, as refusal of divine love, always exists on one side only: on the side of him who persists in creating it for himself. Thus, if there is any reaction in God to the existence of hell—and how could

there not be such a reaction?—then it is one of pain, not of ratification; God would, so to speak, find a brand burned into his flesh: we can guess that it has the form of the Cross. Our pain in the face of hell would then be only an echo of his own pain. . . . If Christ speaks to us in the Gospel of the possibility of man's becoming lost through a refusal of love, then certainly this is not in order that it should happen, but only in order that it should not happen.[25]

HE DESCENDED INTO HELL

A clue into how this can be, how there can be hell, and judgment, and salvation, even for all, may be found in the report that Christ "went and made a proclamation to the spirits in prison, who in former times did not obey. . . . The gospel was preached even to the dead, so that, though they had been judged in the flesh as everyone else is judged, they might live in the spirit as God does" (1 Peter 3:19–20, 4:6). These words are notoriously difficult to interpret; but from the earliest times, the creeds have proclaimed that Christ descended into hell, believing that during that enigmatic Saturday between Good Friday and Easter Sunday, Christ preached to the dead, offering even to those lost and dead the opportunity to hear the good news and have life. Even hell has not escaped the bright light of Christ's lordship. The abyss is not bottomless but has an opening to heaven—at least so we hope.

To get our imaginations around this possibility, C. S. Lewis may be of help, first by his clarification of the temporal issue. This "harrowing of hell" was not just for those who died before that dark day in April of the year 30, but also those who died the following day, the next week, a decade hence, into the days of Dante, Lewis, and our children's children: "It was not once long ago that He did it. Time does not work that way when once you have left the Earth. All moments that have been or shall be were, or are, present in the moment of His descending. There is no spirit in prison to Whom He did not preach."[26] For the notion that death is the cutting-off point, the moment of an absolute veering off into either bliss or oblivion, has not always been held by the Church, as the belief in purgatory bears witness.

Lewis penned a clever echo to Dante that he called *The Great Divorce.* Hell is a gray place, dreary and dull, and its citizens may actually depart whenever they so choose. But just as they did on earth, people choose separation from God, misery over joy, hollowness over reality. One ghost insists, "I don't want help. I want to be left alone." Why do they not leave hell for heaven? "There is always something they insist on keeping, even at the price of misery. There is always something they prefer to joy." Indeed, "there are only two kinds of people in the end; those who say to God, 'Thy will be done,' and those to whom God says, in the end, 'Thy will be done.' All that are in Hell, choose it."[27] And so God waits, yearns, loves, waits some more, hoping for the salvation of all.

This perspective may be flawed or totally in error. Augustine pointed out repeatedly that the Church flatly rejected Origen's teaching and carefully refuted his views as "compassionate" but "muddleheaded."[28] Calvin is sure the condemnation of the reprobate is not only richly deserved, but displays perfectly the glory of God.[29] Aquinas, Luther, and Wesley all argued, on unquestionably biblical grounds, that an act of faith is necessary for salvation. Even Origen felt that the notion of eternal punishment, even if it turns out to be a chimera, has a positive function, urging naive Christians toward faith and holiness.[30] So we are surely on safer ground, in the life of faith, to believe that a final, irrevocable judgment awaits, when for unbelievers there will be endless weeping, wailing, and gnashing of teeth.

But the possibility of universal salvation may better safeguard the character and grandeur of God as revealed in the Bible. Some may worry that if all are saved, then belief and behavior become irrelevant, that all demands are relaxed, and chaos will ensue. On the contrary, if we comprehend in the depth of our souls this kind of God, this sort of inviolable bond to God, the inevitability of God's purpose, then the resulting demand on our lives is not less, but greater. And perhaps it is only when all is grace, when all is in God's hands, even hell and its branch establishments, that we are finally set free to be the kind of people who are fit for heaven in the first place.

CHRISTIANITY AND OTHER RELIGIONS

Naturally this raises the question of religions other than Christianity. Few in our society cling to the notion that Christianity is the only way. Many feel that all faiths are manifestations of a deeper spirituality, that the one true God is above, behind, beyond all mere human religious expressions. But can we really just blend all faiths together? Are they really the same? In reality, Nirvana does not equal heaven; Brahman,

Shiva, and Vishnu are not Father, Son, and Holy Spirit in Eastern guise; Buddhist loss of self is not quite the same as Christian self-denial. Apparent agreements are encompassed in a web of disagreement. Islam claims to supersede Christianity, which in turn claims to be *the* way.

One thing is sure: we Christians don't have a corner on truth. Teachers and practitioners of other faiths have spoken truths and have lived true lives, often with more validity and persuasiveness than Christians. Other faiths may in fact enrich our own, reminding us of aspects of our faith that get watered down in our culture. We may rightly criticize Hinduism for its social stratification; but do we Christians not indulge in class consciousness and social distinctions? We may think of Muslims as militant; but contemplate the checkered Christian history of Crusades and warmongering that has not entirely subsided. Islam, once we get the ayatollahs and terrorists out of our minds, is a model of devotion, with a regimen of five mandated prayer times each day. The name Buddha means "awake," and Zen masters compare the religious quest to an alarm clock—and we surely need to be roused from our stupor. And just as we do not have a corner on truth, we also need never fear truth. Simply learning about other religions is good; as the Buddha said, "He who would may reach the utmost height, but he must be anxious to learn."

We may agree with Thomas Merton: the existence of many religions is not an evil, but a sign of God's mercy, God's pursuit of all people, or at least of their need for God. With respect to other religions, our first task is not to "win" adherents away from other religions. Our first calling is to *be* Christian, to embody the faith. We have accounts of people seeing Mother Teresa putting her faith into action, in a culture dominated by non-Christian religions—and deciding to follow Christ. But in caring for God's world and God's people, we may discover a surprising role we play with respect to other religions. George Lindbeck has suggested that

> Christians may have a responsibility to help other movements and other religions make their own particular contributions, which may be quite distinct from the Christian one, to the preparation for the Consummation. The missionary task of Christians may at times be to encourage Marxists to become better Marxists, Jews and Muslims to become better Jews and Muslims, and Buddhists to become better Buddhists (although admittedly their notion of what a "better Marxist," etc., is will be influenced by Christian norms). Obviously this cannot be done without the most intensive and arduous conversation and cooperation.[31]

Dialogue and shared labor are needed among religions, aimed not at conversion, but at benefits for all religions and people.

But does this mean it doesn't make any difference what we believe? How can we be open to various religions, without emptying all religion of its content, its substance? Can Christianity really be *the* way, without implying eternal perdition for those who have never confessed Christ? Mother Teresa once said, "I love all religions, but I am in love with my own." We are wise to learn to love religions, the beauty, the devotion, the wisdom. But this being "in love" with our own—what is so lovable about Christianity? Our faith's basics ring true, make sense, and are far from detrimental to believers. We are God's children, precious to God, loved unendingly by God. And God establishes a pattern for how to live, guidelines to help us be in sync with the world and in positive relationships with each other. Our faith isn't lazy or complacent or invisible. There is a firm mandate, a challenge, for us to share, to care about others, to put our faith into practice, to make a difference. And our faith can even embrace and take into account suffering and death. The beauty of the story of Jesus is that God touches, grasps, sweats, and even bleeds—not removed or distant from the heartache of our lives or of our century, but right in the middle of it all. The Christian story doesn't deny death or pretend it doesn't exist, but embraces suffering and insanity and cradles our pains in God's eternal love. The Christian story is no glib optimism, but pulsates with hope.

Perhaps the crucial questions, if we compare religions, are these: Is one religion more adequate than another? Can it better explain our questions, our dreams, our sorrows? Can it produce good, a better world? In one sense, it's impossible to evaluate if your religion is more adequate than another. Perhaps you took a course on Islam or Buddhism in college; but there is no way for you to climb inside another faith and mind-set, and truly comprehend what it's about, much less debunk it. Talk about our questions and dreams, or a better world, is already shaped by the religion we happen to have, and may not be shared by everyone. What I would hope to argue, though, is that Christianity does gather up into itself who we are, our dreams, our tragedies, and perhaps even who all people are, all dreams, all tragedies. And Christianity has the ability to change lives and even to change our world. Not that it has done so in any obvious way. Far from it. We are humbled by Martin Luther King Jr.'s observation that Gandhi lived more of a Christian life than any Christian he knew.

Christianity within itself does claim that Jesus Christ is *the* way. But

Christianity is not unequivocally exclusive; much in the Bible insists that God's love and mercy extend to all people in all of creation. How do we resolve this seeming contradiction? Just because many in our world have never heard about the mercy of God in Christ does not mean God is not merciful to them because of Christ. And just because many disbelieve and distrust this mercy, because the Christian message has been presented to them in such an abysmal, unfaithful manner, does not mean that God is any less merciful to them because of Christ. My children do not see, nor do they appreciate, the most significant sacrifices I make for their well-being. But they are no less loved, no less the beneficiaries of my parenting, because of their ignorance.

When people are touched and moved to seek God, Christ is present, even if unnamed, a face fuzzily perceived, labelled imperfectly. Karl Rahner coined the term "anonymous Christians." The Second Vatican Council spoke of Moslems, "who in shadows and images seek the unknown God, for it is He who gives to all men life and breath . . . and who as Savior wills that all men be saved."[32] Such inevitably is our hope, which does not dampen our zeal for Christianity, for only in this way can this single faith truly be the hope of the universe. And if it cannot be the hope of the universe, then perhaps it is not big enough to be my hope, either.

Perhaps this is a subject that requires humility, irony, even humor. The Jewish writer Martin Buber once asked a group of Christian priests, "What is the difference between Jews and Christians? We all await the Messiah. You believe He has already come and gone, while we do not. I therefore propose that we await Him together. And when he appears, we can ask Him: 'Were you here before?' And I hope that at that moment I will be close enough to whisper in his ear, 'For the love of heaven, don't answer.'"[33]

QUESTIONS FOR DISCUSSION

1. What are the places of hope and joy in the Christian's views about the future?
2. What is the significance of the biblical picture of divine judgment being carried out by Jesus Christ?
3. What should be the attitude of Christians toward those of other religious faiths?

Epilogue

It is good for an author to express gratitude to all who helped with the book. For a crazily ambitious book like this one—tackling all of Christianity in about 175 pages—the author's debts are immense, ranging from hundreds of other authors read to hundreds of conversations with people in and outside the Church, from a lecture that struck me twenty-five years ago to my wife Lisa, who made a helpful suggestion twenty-five minutes ago. As I name those who read all or part of my manuscript and made it better than it would otherwise have been—Richard Bauckham, Tom Bell, Jason Byassee, Ellen Davis, Robert Jenson, Greg Jones, Jeri Krentz, Peter Krentz, Clint McCann, Walter Moberly, Tish Signet—I am struck by how much each one of them knows about his or her particular field of expertise. Not surprisingly, each one suggested not so much what should be removed from the book, but what should be added. Much has been left out.

For there is always more to say. If some great-grandchild of mine rewrote this book a hundred years from now, I would imagine that two-thirds of the content would not need to be changed (although the form of expression, grammatically and technologically, will seem hopelessly old-timey by then). But plenty will be new, and what is old and secure will play differently in a milieu none of us can begin to anticipate. We continue to hear about new approaches to reading the Bible. Even without new approaches, the Bible has a seemingly inexhaustible multivalence about it. As when we read Shakespeare, listen to Mozart, stand before a Rembrandt, or watch the waves lap the shore, when we read the Bible, something new discloses itself. That something was always there—and such a precious detail! How did I miss it all this time?

A hundred years from now, new chapters of Church history will need to be written, and we know with utter certainty that the ongoing saga will have its share of both the heroic and the embarrassing. As *Saturday Night Live*'s Whitney Brown put it so humorously:

There's a lot we should be able to learn from history. And yet history proves we never do. In fact, the main lesson of history is that we never learn the lessons of history. This makes us look so stupid that few people care to read it. They'd rather not be reminded. Any good history book is mainly just a long list of mistakes, complete with names and dates. It's very embarrassing.[1]

If you have learned anything from this book, I hope it is that embarrassment can be good. The Bible need not be flawless to be God's inspired Word, just as we need not be perfect to be the chosen people of God. For it is precisely our brokenness, our embarrassing inability to fix our mistakes, that flings open the window to let the grace, the power of God into our lives, into the Church and world.

My head spins to contemplate the challenges the next century will face in the field of ethics. The logarithmic explosion of technology will hurtle us toward startlingly complex issues, if not into oblivion. The life of the Church is already gasping for air as we cope with changes in attitudes toward the institutional Church and in notions of what Church looks like. The nontraditional churches seemingly are taking over, with a consumer-oriented, entertainment approach that either threatens Christianity at its very core or offers the Church and people the genuinely hopeful way of moving through this century.

Theologians will raise new questions, so hard they will stagger us. But we may as well get used to it and delight in the adventure. Robert Jenson, from whom I have learned much, suggested that eternal life with God may well be marked, not so much by full knowledge, but by heightened sense of all we do not know.

As knowers of God we will eternally discover that each new revelation presents an infinity of unforeseen questions. . . . God will be more and more unknowable for being so intimately known. And this experience will be precisely the experience of his glory and of our participation in it. Or as Henri de Lubac summed up Eastern patristic teaching: "God . . . would only be found, even in the light of eternal beatitude, by being forever sought."[2]

So, trust the questions. And, like Orpheus's rowers, listen for the song. Marvel at its beauty. And follow.

Notes

Introduction

1. From a sermon preached on the death of George Whitefield in 1770, in *The Standard Sermons of John Wesley,* ed. Edward H. Sugden, 4th ed. (London: Epworth Press, 1956), 522.

2. Simone Weil, *Waiting for God,* trans. Emma Craufurd (New York: Harper Colophon, 1951), 69.

3. Mark Helprin, *Winter's Tale* (New York: Pocket, 1983), 259.

4. Frederick Buechner, *A Room Called Remember* (San Francisco: HarperSan-Francisco, 1984), 11.

Chapter 1: Scripture

1. For a fuller discussion, see Garrett Green, *Imagining God: Theology and the Religious Imagination* (San Francisco: Harper & Row, 1989), 66–74, 105–25.

2. Erich Auerbach, *Mimesis: The Representation of Reality in Western Literature,* trans. Willard R. Trask (Princeton: Princeton University Press, 1953), 15. Of course, Auerbach may be mischaracterizing Homer here.

3. John Updike, *Rabbit Is Rich* (New York: Fawcett Crest, 1981), 226.

4. Allan Bloom, *The Closing of the American Mind* (New York: Simon & Schuster, 1987), 60.

5. Karl Barth, *The Word of God and the Word of Man,* trans. Douglas Horton (New York: Harper & Row, 1957), 143.

6. Francis Schüssler Fiorenza, "The Crisis of Scriptural Authority: Interpretation and Reception," *Interpretation* 44 (1990): 353–68.

7. Charles Marson, *God's Cooperative Society* (New York: Longmans, 1914), 43, 51–52, quoted in Kenneth Leech, *Spirituality and Pastoral Care* (Cambridge: Cowley, 1989), 6f.

8. Quoted and discussed in Nicholas Lash, "Interpretation and Imagination," in *Incarnation and Myth: The Debate Continued,* ed. Michael Goulder (Grand Rapids: Eerdmans, 1979) 20.

9. Stanley Fish, *Is There a Text in This Class? The Authority of Interpretive Communities* (Cambridge: Harvard University Press, 1980), 183.

10. John Calvin, *Commentary on the Book of Psalms* (Edinburgh: Calvin Translation Society, 1845), 1:xxxvii.

179

11. Jim Wallis, *The Soul of Politics: A Practical and Prophetic Vision for Change* (New York: New Press, 1994), 151.

12. Quoted in Eberhard Bethge, *Dietrich Bonhoeffer: A Biography*, rev. Victoria J. Barnett, trans. Edwin Robertson et al. (Minneapolis: Fortress Press, 2000), 204–5. This turning point is highlighted and well discussed in Stephen E. Fowl and L. Gregory Jones, *Reading in Communion: Scripture and Ethics in Christian Life* (Grand Rapids: Eerdmans, 1991), 139–40.

13. Robert Jenson, *Systematic Theology*, vol. 1: *The Triune God* (New York: Oxford University Press, 1997), 173.

14. Søren Kierkegaard, *Journals and Papers*, vol. 3, trans. H. V. Hong and E. H. Hong (Bloomington: Indiana University, 1975), 270, cited by Richard Bauckham, who humbly admits that the mountain of scholarly publication has made "no evident contributions to believing and obedient practice" (*James* [London: Routledge, 1999], 7). Nicholas Lash wryly suggests that "between the New Testament and the ordinary Christian, who seeks so to read these texts as to hear in them the Word of Life, there seem to be set up thickets of expertise, insurmountable barriers of scholarship" ("Performing the Scriptures," in *Theology on the Way to Emmaus* [London: SCM, 1986], 39).

15. Calvin, *Commentary on the Book of Psalms*, (n. 10), xl–xli.

16. St. Athanasius, *On the Incarnation* (Crestwood, NY: St. Vladimir's, 1953), 96. Alasdair MacIntyre has said, "What the reader . . . has to learn about him or herself is that it is only the self as transformed through and by the reading of the texts which will be capable of reading the texts aright" (*Three Rival Versions of Moral Enquiry* [Notre Dame, IN: University of Notre Dame, 1994], 82).

17. Nicholas Lash, thinking of Scripture as a script to be performed, is at least but only half right: "We talk of 'holy' scripture, and for good reason. And yet it is not, in fact, the *script* that is 'holy,' but the people: the company who perform the script" ("Performing the Scriptures" [n.14], 42).

Chapter 2: The Old Testament

1. Dietrich Bonhoeffer, *Letters and Papers from Prison,* ed. Eberhard Bethge (New York: Macmillan, 1971), 156–57. The letter to Bethge, from the Tegel concentration camp, is dated December 5, 1943.

2. Elie Wiesel, *Messengers of God: Biblical Portraits and Legends* (New York: Summit, 1976), 193.

3. David Halberstam, *The Children* (New York: Fawcett Books, 1998), 140.

4. God entered into a relationship with the people, and called it a covenant. In ancient times, a "covenant" was a treaty whereby a weakling king could swear allegiance to a more powerful neighbor, in exchange for protection and benefits; archaeologists have unearthed many such treaties from the Hittites, Elamites, and Assyrians. The Old Testament narrative actually reports three covenants: with Abraham (Gen. 12–17), with Moses at Sinai (Exod. 19–34), and with David and

his lineage (2 Sam. 7). But these covenants were never relics out of the past. Each generation could echo these words: "Not with our ancestors did the LORD make this covenant, but with us, who are all of us here alive today" (Deut. 5:3).

5. The seminal work, which has fueled tremendous controversy, was Norman K. Gottwald, *The Tribes of Yahweh: A Sociology of the Religion of Liberated Israel, 1250–1050 B.C.E.* (Maryknoll, NY: Orbis Books, 1979).

6. Claus Westermann, *Praise and Lament in the Psalms*, trans. Keith R. Crim and Richard N. Soulen (Atlanta: John Knox Press, 1981), 25ff.

7. See the Pulitzer Prize–winning book by Edward J. Larson, *Summer for the Gods: The Scopes Trial and America's Continuing Debate over Science and Religion* (New York: Basic Books, 1997).

8. As recounted in Kitty Ferguson, *The Fire in the Equations: Science, Religion, and the Search for God* (Grand Rapids: Eerdmans, 1994), 21.

9. For this and the broader story of the shattering of the medieval world, see William Manchester, *A World Lit Only by Fire: The Medieval Mind and the Renaissance* (Boston: Little, Brown & Co., 1992), 117; not many historians believe Galileo actually spoke these words.

10. John Polkinghorne, *Serious Talk: Science and Religion in Dialogue* (Valley Forge, PA: Trinity Press Int., 1995), 45; he wisely cites W. H. Vanstone, *Love's Endeavor, Love's Expense* (London: Darton, Longman & Todd, 1977), with its profound exploration of the nature of divine love as it entails vulnerability.

11. Polkinghorne, *Serious Talk*, 84.

12. Alan McGlashan, *The Savage and Beautiful Country* (Boston: Houghton-Mifflin, 1967), 105.

13. Daniel Boorstin, *The Discoverers* (New York: Random House, 1983), 471–72.

14. Not many write better, or criticize faith more stridently, than Richard Dawkins; see his books like *The God Delusion* (New York: Mariner, 2008), which has sold very well but is not as sharp as his earlier and fascinating *The Blind Watchmaker: Why the Evidence of Evolution Reveals a Universe without Design* (New York: Norton, 1996).

15. Francis Crick, *The Astonishing Hypothesis: The Scientific Search for the Soul* (New York: Charles Scribner's Sons, 1994), 3.

16. Loren Eiseley, *The Star Thrower* (San Diego: Harcourt, Brace & Co., 1978), 306.

17. P. Kyle McCarter, *1 Samuel* (Garden City, NY: Doubleday, 1980), 286.

18. Walter Brueggemann summarized a career of great writing on the Old Testament by imagining a courtroom in which all the varied, seemingly dissonant pieces from ancient Israel are presented as testimony, contradictions declared openly, with the debate itself advocating an alternate view of reality, in *Theology of the Old Testament: Testimony, Dispute, Advocacy* (Minneapolis: Fortress Press, 1997). He argues for the relevance of this model in our pluralistic context: "It is possible that the testimony of Israel is to be seen, even in our own time, not as a

dominant meta-narrative that must give order and coherence across the full horizon of social reality, but as a *subversive protest* and as an alternative act of vision that invites criticism and transformation" (713).

19. See Rainer Albertz, *A History of Israelite Religion in the Old Testament Period,* vol. 1, trans. John Bowden (Louisville, KY: Westminster John Knox Press, 1994), 164.

20. Gustavo Gutiérrez, *A Theology of Liberation: History, Politics and Salvation,* ed. and trans. Caridad Inda and John Eagleson (Maryknoll, NY: Orbis Books, 1973), 266.

21. William P. Brown, *Character in Crisis: A Fresh Approach to the Wisdom Literature of the Old Testament* (Grand Rapids: Eerdmans, 1996), 100, concludes that the Wisdom books, especially Job, show that "God does not rule with an iron fist, grinding the wicked into the dust and coercing obedience from earthly subjects. Rather, Yahweh governs with an open hand, sustaining creation in all of its variegated forms, leaving both good and bad characters to weave their existence into the complex network of life." For a full account of God's love and control, and why bad things happen, see my book *The Will of God: Answering the Hard Questions* (Louisville, KY: Westminster John Knox Press, 2009).

22. Gerhard von Rad, *Wisdom in Israel*, trans. James D. Martin (Nashville: Abingdon Press, 1972), 217: "Job stands face to face with a completely new experience of the reality of God, an experience of something incalculable and fearful. . . . And what was really new was that Job involved God, in a quite direct way, much more deeply and more terribly, in the suffering. Job envisages a God who quite personally and with all his powers enters into the suffering and becomes involved in it. That is the only thing that he really knows and, indeed, it nearly drives him out of his mind." My seminary and graduate-school professor of Old Testament, Roland Murphy, pointed to Robert Frost's "Masque of Reason," which poetically imagines a conversation among God, Job, his wife, and Satan, the net result of which is the dismantling of a simplistic doctrine of rewards and punishments. See William Safire's insights linking Job to modern politics: *The First Dissident: The Book of Job in Today's Politics* (New York: Random House, 1992).

23. See the good discussion in Walter Brueggemann, *Finally Comes the Poet: Daring Speech for Proclamation* (Minneapolis: Fortress Press, 1989), 13–41.

24. Anne Tyler, *Saint Maybe* (New York: Alfred A. Knopf, 1991), 122.

25. Martin Luther King Jr. *A Testament of Hope*, ed. James Washington (San Francisco: HarperSanFrancisco, 1986), 277.

Chapter 3: The New Testament

1. N. T. Wright, *The New Testament and the People of God* (Minneapolis: Fortress Press, 1992), 23.

2. Albert Schweitzer, *The Quest of the Historical Jesus*, trans. W. Montgomery (New York: Macmillan, 1968), 4.

3. Ibid., 403.

4. James D. Tabor, *The Jesus Dynasty: The Hidden History of Jesus, His Royal Family, and the Birth of Christianity* (New York: Simon & Schuster, 2006).

5. Carsten Peter Thiede and Matthew D'Ancona, *The Jesus Papyrus* (London: Weidenfeld & Nicolson, 1996).

6. Textual critics sort out differing readings among manuscripts. Some cases are fascinating, rather like detective work. In Luke 10:38–42 we hear Jesus, upbraiding the fastidious Martha, make the startling claim: "One thing is needful." Or so reads the very early Chester Beatty Papyrus. But in manuscripts from the following century, "one thing," *henos,* is suddenly dropped, and inserted in its place is the word *oligōn,* meaning "a few." A few things are needful. Now if *oligōn* looked or sounded like *henos,* we could chalk the change up to a weary copyist, a lapse in attentiveness. But can we explain the shift another way? We cannot interview the copyist, but we may wonder if there was a community of Christians, men separated from the world, devoted to prayer and the Scriptures, and the scribal expert among them scribbled down *oligōn* instead of *henos* as a remedy to laziness. There were meals to be prepared, rocks to be cleared from the garden, sweeping to be done, candles to be filled with oil. When challenged, the men may have unfurled their Gospel scroll and located the moment Jesus upbraided Martha for her labors, reminding her that "one thing" is needful, and that they too were involved in that "one thing," namely, contemplating God. So could the urgent needs of the day have prompted a subtle change, some wise supervisor scratching his head and surmising that "surely Jesus meant for us to get our work done," that indeed "a few" things are in fact needful?

7. See N. T. Wright's assessment in *Who Was Jesus?* (Grand Rapids: Eerdmans, 1992).

8. Ibid.

9. Robert Funk et al., *The Five Gospels: The Search for the Authentic Words of Jesus* (New York: Macmillan, 1993); Robert Funk et al., *The Acts of Jesus: What Did Jesus Really Do?* (San Francisco: HarperSanFrancisco, 1998).

10. Michael Baigent and Richard Leigh, *The Dead Sea Scrolls Deception* (New York: Touchstone, 1993).

11. Marcus Borg, *Jesus in Contemporary Scholarship* (Valley Forge, PA: Trinity Press Int., 1994), 178. The Jesus Seminar's founder, Robert Funk, claims he hopes to "reinvent Christianity" before it wastes away. Less hopefully, Seminar ex-member Burton Mack feels Christianity's "two thousand year run . . . is over." The Seminar's disdain for American fundamentalism is clear. For a thorough assessment, see Mark Allan Powell, *Jesus as a Figure in History: How Modern Historians View the Man from Galilee* (Louisville, KY: Westminster John Knox Press, 1998), 65–82.

12. Joseph J. Ellis, *American Sphinx: The Character of Thomas Jefferson* (New York: Alfred A. Knopf, 1997), 215.

13. In a letter to John Adams; see Ellis, *American Sphinx,* 259.

14. Martin Kähler, *The So-Called Historical Jesus and the Historic, Biblical Christ,* first published in 1892 (Philadelphia: Fortress Press, 1988).

15. Plato, *Phaedo,* 91A in *The Collected Dialogues of Plato,* ed. Edith Hamilton and Huntington Cairns, trans. Hugh Tredennick (Princeton, NJ: Princeton University Press, 1961), 73.

16. Thucydides, *History of the Peloponnesian War* I.22, trans. Rex Warner (New York: Penguin, 1954), 47. The translation of this passage is debated. For a different rendering, see Richard Crawley, *The Landmark Thucydides: A Comprehensive Guide to the Peloponnesian War,* ed. Robert B. Strassler (New York: Free Press, 1996), 15: "It was in all cases difficult to carry them word for word in one's memory, so my habit has been to make the speakers say what was in my opinion demanded of them by the various occasions, of course adhering as closely as possible to the general sense of what they really said."

17. Ben Witherington III, *John's Wisdom: A Commentary on the Fourth Gospel* (Louisville, KY: Westminster John Knox Press, 1995), 6.

18. Richard Bauckham, *Jesus and the Eyewitnesses: The Gospels as Eyewitness Testimony* (Grand Rapids: Eerdmans, 2006).

19. William C. Placher, *Narratives of a Vulnerable God: Christ, Theology, and Scripture* (Louisville, KY: Westminster John Knox Press, 1994), 88. Martin Hengel, *The Four Gospels and the One Gospel of Jesus Christ* (Harrisburg, PA: Trinity Press Int., 2000), 24f., weighs the varying motives behind the repudiation of the *Diatesseron,* still concluding, "So it is all the more a near-miracle that the early church resisted the temptation to replace the four Gospels, which in parts are so different, with a unitary Gospel Harmony. This would have met practical catechetical needs better and done away with [many] problems." On the other side, Hengel notes (p. 11) how strenuously Irenaeus, late in the second century, had to defend the fact that there were *only four* Gospels.

20. John Calvin, *Institutes of the Christian Religion* 3.ii.6, ed. John T. McNeill, trans. Ford Lewis Battles (Philadelphia: Westminster Press, 1960), 548.

21. Quoted and discussed well in Harry Y. Gamble, *Books and Readers in the Early Church: A History of Early Christian Texts* (New Haven, CT: Yale University Press, 1995), 1.

22. For a fuller study, see my *The Beatitudes for Today* (Louisville, KY: Westminster John Knox Press, 2006).

23. James Weldon Johnson, *God's Trombones* (New York: Viking Penguin, 1969), 21–22.

24. For aspects of the following interpretation, see James Breech, *The Silence of Jesus: The Authentic Voice of the Historical Man* (Philadelphia: Fortress Press, 1983), 189–209; Bernard Brandon Scott, *Hear Then the Parable: A Commentary on the Parables of Jesus* (Minneapolis: Fortress Press, 1989), 108–25. Rembrandt's fascinating painting of the father's embrace of the boy returning home is the subject of a thoughtful book by Henri Nouwen, *The Return of the Prodigal Son: A Story of Homecoming* (New York: Image, 1994).

25. Ben Witherington III, *The Jesus Quest: The Third Search for the Jew of Nazareth* (Downers Grove, IL: InterVarsity, 1995), 104: "Clearly Jesus did set aside, or at least saw as no longer applicable in light of the coming dominion of God, the laws about ritual cleanness and uncleanness (cf. Mark 7). It does not follow from this that he rejected all demands for holiness or purity. Rather, I would suggest that Jesus substitutes a more strenuous moral holiness system for one that includes both ritual and moral dimensions."

26. See E. P. Sanders, *Jesus and Judaism* (Philadelphia: Fortress Press, 1985); N. T. Wright, *The New Testament and the People of God* (n. 1).

27. Although the *Mona Lisa* is dated to some time after that of Jesus, the wealth of the city has intrigued scholars such as Richard Batey, who has speculated on the urban, cosmopolitan influences on a young Jesus who might have studied or socialized in Sepphoris: *Jesus and the Forgotten City: New Light on Sepphoris and the Urban World of Jesus* (Grand Rapids: Baker, 1991).

28. Martin Buber, *Moses* (Atlantic Highlands, NJ: Humanities Press, 1946), 75. Contemplating how Israel's history begins in miracle, he writes, "The philosophizing and the religious person both wonder at the phenomenon, but the one neutralizes the wonder in ideal knowledge, while the other abides in wonder; no knowledge, no cognition, can weaken his astonishment. Any causal explanation only deepens the wonder for him."

29. Jürgen Moltmann, *The Way of Jesus Christ: Christology in Messianic Dimensions*, trans. Margaret Kohl (Minneapolis: Fortress Press, 1993), 107, 108f. E. P. Sanders, *The Historical Figure of Jesus* (London: Penguin, 1993), 168, claims that Jesus saw his own miracles as "signs of the beginning of God's final victory over evil."

30. Marcus J. Borg, *Jesus: A New Vision: Spirit, Culture, and the Life of Discipleship* (San Francisco: HarperCollins, 1987), 69.

31. Karl Barth, *Church Dogmatics,* III/2 (Edinburgh: T.&T. Clark, 1960), 600.

32. Andrew Canale, *Understanding the Human Jesus: A Journey in Scripture and Imagination* (New York: Paulist Press, 1985), 34.

33. Hans W. Frei, *The Identity of Jesus Christ: The Hermeneutical Bases of Dogmatic Theology* (Philadelphia: Fortress Press, 1975), 173, noting how the powerless Jesus identifies vicariously with the guilty and thereby brings salvation, writes profoundly, "But neither Nietzsche nor any of us know what it is to be pitied by the strong—the Lord of life himself—whose pity of us, in which he himself becomes weak, is not weakness but his strength which he *perfects* and does not *abandon* in weakness. Such pity, such love, such life remain the secret of a disposition we do not know. Before this incomparable thing we must ultimately fall silent and be grateful."

34. As recounted by Placher, *Narratives of a Vulnerable God* (n. 19), 91.

35. "The Acts of Paul," in *New Testament Apocrypha*, vol. 2, ed. E. Hennecke et al. (Philadelphia: Westminster Press, 1965), 353f.

36. J. Christiaan Beker, *Paul the Apostle: The Triumph of God in Life and Thought*

(Philadelphia: Fortress Press, 1980), 12, argues successfully that Paul is "able to make the gospel a word on target for the particular needs of his churches without either compromising its basic content or reducing it to a petrified conceptuality."

37. C. S. Lewis, *The Four Loves* (New York: Harcourt Brace Jovanovich, 1960), 137–38.

38. Richard Bauckham, *James* (London: Routledge, 1999).

39. Bauckham, *James*, 140.

40. Plato, *Phaedrus* 275e, in *The Collected Dialogues of Plato*, (n. 15), 521.

Chapter 4: Church History

1. Paul Johnson, *A History of Christianity* (New York: Atheneum, 1976), 515f.

2. Rodney Stark, *Cities of God: The Real Story of How Christianity Became an Urban Movement and Conquered Rome* (San Francisco: HarperSanFrancisco, 2006), 67.

3. Quoted and discussed in Ramsay MacMullen, *Christianizing the Roman Empire (A.D. 100–400)* (New Haven, CT: Yale University Press, 1984), 34.

4. Michael Grant, *Gladiators* (London: Penguin, 1967), 101. Grant argues that the Christians, acting formally at the Council of Nicaea, eventually forced the abolition of gladiators' games.

5. Tertullian, "Apology," *Apologetical Works,* Fathers of the Church, vol. 10, trans. Rudolph Arbesmann (New York: Catholic University of America Press, 1950),125.

6. J. Stevenson, ed., *A New Eusebius* (London: SPCK, 1957), 21.

7. Eberhard Bethge, *Dietrich Bonhoeffer: A Biography*, rev. Victoria J. Barnett, trans. Edwin Robinson et al. (Minneapolis: Fortress Press, 2000), 928. Payne Best, a fellow prisoner, spoke of Bonhoeffer's deep joy, how "his soul really shone in the dark desperation of our prison. He was one of the very few men I have ever met to whom his God was real and ever close to him" (920).

8. *Cels.* 8.68, quoted in Robert L. Wilken, *The Christians as the Romans Saw Them* (New Haven, CT: Yale University Press, 1984), 108.

9. Robin Lane Fox, *Pagans and Christians* (New York: Alfred A. Knopf, 1989), 321.

10. G. K. Chesterton, *Saint Thomas Aquinas* (Garden City, NY: Image, 1956), 43.

11. Wendy Farley, *Tragic Vision and Divine Compassion: A Contemporary Theodicy* (Louisville, KY: Westminster John Knox Press, 1990), 126.

12. See the companion book to the BBC series by Malcolm Billings, *The Cross and the Crescent: A History of the Crusades* (New York: Sterling, 1990), 20.

13. A common practice through the centuries, as Jews were alternatively drowned or burned on failure to convert. The memory of Charlemagne inspired the Crusaders; after one battle, he beheaded 4,500 Saxon rebels who tarried briefly over their option to be baptized.

14. Quoted with admiration by Dorothy Day, *The Long Loneliness* (New York: HarperOne, 1981), 150.

15. *Sayings of the Desert Fathers*, trans. Benedicta Ward (London: Mowbray, 1981), 5. Karl Barth, *Church Dogmatics*, IV/2 (Edinburgh, T.&T. Clark, 1958), 13, saw this ascetic withdrawal from society as "a highly responsible and effective protest . . . not least to a worldly church, a specific way of combating it."

16. Henri Nouwen, *¡Gracias!* (New York: Harper & Row, 1983), 174f.

17. Quoted and discussed well in Stephen Neill, *A History of Christian Missions* (New York: Penguin, 1986), 145.

18. Discussed with implications for contemporary theology and practice in Robert McAfee Brown, *Liberation Theology: An Introductory Guide* (Louisville, KY: Westminster John Knox Press, 1993), 39–43.

19. James Wm. McClendon, *Biography as Theology: How Life Stories Can Remake Today's Theology*, 2nd ed. (Philadelphia: Trinity Press Int., 1990), 22. To learn about the lives of the saints, see James C. Howell, *Servants, Misfits and Martyrs: Saints and Their Stories* (Nashville: Upper Room, 2000).

20. G. K. Chesterton, *St. Francis of Assisi* (Garden City, NY: Image, 1957), 117–18.

21. Kenneth L. Woodward, *Making Saints: How the Catholic Church Determines Who Becomes a Saint, Who Doesn't, and Why* (New York: Simon & Schuster, 1990). Controversy surrounds popular candidates like Oscar Romero or Pius XII; Dorothy Day has attracted both advocates for her canonization and adoring followers who are opposed to the whole process.

22. Peter Brown, *The Cult of the Saints: Its Rise and Function in Latin Christianity* (Chicago: University of Chicago Press, 1981), 11.

23. Ibid., 2.

24. Charles Williams, *The Descent of the Dove: A Short History of the Holy Spirit in the Church* (London: Religious Book Club, 1939), 205.

Chapter 5: The Development of Doctrine

1. Karl Barth, *The Theology of John Calvin*, trans. Geoffrey W. Bromiley (Grand Rapids: Eerdmans, 1995), 7.

2. Ramsay MacMullen, *Christianizing the Roman Empire (A.D. 100–400)* (New Haven, CT: Yale University Press, 1984), 19.

3. Karl Barth, *Protestant Theology in the Nineteenth Century: Its Background and History* (Valley Forge, PA: Judson Press, 1973), 17, wrote, "We have to remember the communion of saints, bearing and being borne by each other, asking and being asked, having to take mutual responsibility for and among the sinners gathered together in Christ. We cannot be in the church without taking as much responsibility for the theology of the past as for the theology of the present. Augustine, Thomas Aquinas, Luther, Schleiermacher and all the rest are not

dead but living. They still speak and demand a hearing as living voices, as surely as we know that they and we belong together in the church."

4. James I. Packer, *"Fundamentalism" and the Word of God* (Downers Grove, IL: InterVarsity, 1996), 48. Oliver O'Donovan, contemplating the surprising movements of God's Spirit throughout the long history of the Church, cleverly asked, "What, after all, is tradition other than spontaneity in slow motion?" (*Resurrection and Moral Order: An Outline for Evangelical Ethics*, 2nd ed. [Grand Rapids: Eerdmans, 1994], 141). From the recipient's side, Jürgen Moltmann suggests that "true tradition is always at the same time remembered hope" (*The Coming of God: Christian Eschatology*, trans. Margaret Kohl [Minneapolis: Fortress Press, 1996], 289).

5. Augustine, *Confessions* I.1, ed. and trans. John K. Ryan (Garden City, NY: Image, 1960).

6. Origen, "Letter to Gregory," in Joseph W. Trigg, *Origen* (London: Routledge, 1998), 212.

7. Jean Leclercq, *The Love of Learning and the Desire for God*, trans. Catharine Misrahi (New York: Fordham, 1982), 266.

8. In the Latin edition of 1539, Calvin claims, "My purpose has been so to prepare and instruct those who wish to give themselves to the study of theology that they may have easy access to the reading of the Holy Scriptures, make good progress in the understanding of it, and keep to the good and straight path without stumbling" (quoted with good discussion in François Wendel, *Calvin: The Origins and Development of His Religious Thought*, trans. Philip Mairet [London: Collins, 1963], 146).

9. John Calvin, *Institutes of the Christian Religion* 1.17.11, ed. John T. McNeill, trans. Ford Lewis Battles (Philadelphia: Westminster Press, 1960), and Wendel, *Calvin*, 182.

10. *The Life of Teresa of Jesus*, trans. E. Allison Peers; Garden City, NY: Doubleday, 1960), 71.

11. Eberhard Busch, *Karl Barth: His Life from Letters and Autobiographical Texts*, trans. John Bowden (Philadelphia: Fortress Press, 1976), 489.

12. An interesting introduction to books in nascent Christendom is Harry Gamble, *Books and Readers in the Early Church*. Gamble chalks up the codex's popularity to its use in an early edition of the letters of Paul (58). Hengel (*The Four Gospels and the One Gospel of Jesus Christ* [Harrisburg, PA: Trinity Press Int., 2000], 120) says the codex helped Christians distinguish their worship from that of the synagogue.

13. See Eamon Duffy, *The Stripping of the Altars: Traditional Religion in England, 1400–1580* (New Haven, CT: Yale University Press, 1994). Leo, incidentally, had argued that a fearful volcanic eruption that dumped ash across the Aegean was God's judgment on violators of the commandment to have no graven images.

14. Interestingly, Gutenberg was his mother's name, which he reasonably preferred to his father's, Gensfleisch, which means "goose flesh."

15. Shakespeare, *Merchant of Venice*, I.iii.95. He also said, "There is no error so gross but that some sober brow will bless it with a proper text."

16. Robin Lane Fox, *Pagans and Christians* (New York: Alfred A. Knopf, 1989), 330.

17. Augustine, *De doctrina christiana* II.40.60, in *On Christian Doctrine*, trans. D. W. Robertson Jr. (Indianapolis: Bobbs-Merrill, 1958), 75. Nearly two centuries earlier, in a letter to Gregory Thaumaturgus ("Letter to Gregory," (n. 6), 211), Origen wrote, "I have prayed that you would accept effectively those things from the philosophy of the Greeks that can serve as a general education for Christianity and those things from geometry and astronomy that are useful for the interpretation of the Holy Scriptures. For just as the servants of philosophers say concerning geometry, music, grammar, rhetoric and astronomy that they are adjuncts to philosophy, we say this very thing about philosophy itself with regard to Christianity. And indeed Scripture hints at this principle in Exodus, where, with God himself the person speaking, the children of Israel are told to ask their neighbors and cohabitants for vessels of silver and gold and for clothing (Exodus 11:2 and 12:35). Having in this way despoiled the Egyptians, they may find material among the things they have received for the preparation of divine worship."

18. G. K. Chesterton, *Saint Thomas Aquinas* (Garden City, NY: Image, 1956), 42.

19. Barbara Tuchman, *The March of Folly: From Troy to Vietnam* (New York: Ballantine, 1984), 45f.

20. Friedrich Nietzsche, *The Joyful Wisdom*, no. 125, trans. Thomas Common (New York: Russell & Russell, 1964), 167.

21. Well discussed in Timothy Gorringe, *Karl Barth: Against Hegemony* (Oxford: Oxford University Press, 1999), 129.

22. *On the Trinity* XV.28.51, in *Augustine: Later Works*, trans. John Burnaby (Philadelphia: Westminster Press, 1955), 181.

23. Robert Jenson, *The Triune Identity* (Philadelphia: Fortress Press, 1982), wrote, "The gospel identifies its God thus: God is the one who raised Israel's Jesus from the dead. The whole task of theology can be described as the unpacking of this sentence in various ways."

24. Raymond E. Brown, *An Introduction to New Testament Christology* (New York: Paulist Press, 1994), 143: "The fact that such specifications were not found in the New Testament did not embarrass Athanasius, for he recognized that Arius was raising a question not specifically asked in New Testament times and which therefore could not be answered by quoting the New Testament. The all-important issue for Athanasius was whether the necessary postbiblical specification was loyal to the direction of the New Testament: 'If the expressions are not in so many words in the Scriptures, yet they contain the sense of the Scriptures.'" The quotation in the final sentence is from "Athanasius: Select Writings and Letters," in *Nicene and Post-Nicene Fathers*, Series 2 (Edinburgh: T.&T. Clark, 1981), 4:164. George Lindbeck, *The Nature of Doctrine* (Philadelphia: Westminster Press, 1984), 94, has

inferred the strategies involved: "Three regulative principles at least were obviously at work (at Nicaea and Chalcedon). First, there is the monotheistic principle: there is only one God, the God of Abraham, Isaac, Jacob and Jesus. Second, there is the principle of historical specificity: the stories of Jesus refer to a genuine human being who was born, lived, and died in a particular time and place. Third, there is the principle of what may be infelicitously called Christological maximalism: every possible importance is to be ascribed to Jesus that is not inconsistent with the first rules. This last rule, it may be noted, follows from the central Christian conviction that Jesus Christ is the highest possible clue (though an often dim and ambiguous one to creaturely and sinful eyes) within the space-time world of human experience to God."

25. Ramsay MacMullen, *Voting about God in Early Church Councils* (New Haven, CT: Yale University Press, 2006).

26. Bernhard Lohse, *A Short History of Christian Doctrine,* trans. F. Ernest Stoeffler (Philadelphia: Fortress Press, 1966), 90, wrote: "Perhaps the greatness of Cyril is found precisely in this, however, that in the presence of more profound and speculative questions he limited himself to a repetition of the biblical witness and of the faith of the church."

27. Augustine, *Confessions* (n. 5) VIII.5.10, 188f.

28. Athanasius, "Festal Letter," XIV, in *Nicene and Post-Nicene Fathers*, vol. 4 (Edinburgh: T.&T. Clark, 1981), 543.

29. C. S. Lewis, *The Lion, the Witch and the Wardrobe* (New York: Macmillan, 1950), 159.

30. Robert Jenson, *Systematic Theology*, vol. 1 *The Triune God* (New York: Oxford University Press, 1997), 189.

31. Martin Luther, "Preface to the Latin Writings," in *Luther's Works*, vol. 34, trans. Lewis W. Spitz (Philadelphia: Muhlenburg Press, 1960), 337.

32. Gerhard Forde, *On Being a Theologian of the Cross: Reflections on Luther's Heidelberg Disputation, 1518* (Grand Rapids: Eerdmans, 1997), 62.

33. Luther wrote, "He who does not know Christ does not know God hidden in suffering. Therefore he prefers works to suffering, glory to the cross, strength to weakness, wisdom to folly, and, in general, good to evil." See Forde, *On Being a Theologian*, 82.

34. Gorringe, *Karl Barth*, (n. 21), 31.

35. Robert McAfee Brown, *Spirituality and Liberation: Overcoming the Great Fallacy* (Philadelphia: Westminster Press, 1988), 31.

36. Walter Rauschenbusch, *A Theology for the Social Gospel* (Nashville: Abingdon Press, 1945), 2.

Chapter 6: Theology

1. Joseph Sittler, *Gravity and Grace* (Minneapolis: Augsburg, 1986), 63.

2. Robert Bellah et al., *Habits of the Heart* (New York: Harper & Row, 1985),

221, named the dominant religion in America "Sheilaism," after interviewing Sheila Larson, who said, "I believe in God. I'm not a religious fanatic. I can't remember the last time I went to church. My faith has carried me a long way. It's Sheilaism. Just my own little voice."

3. Maggie Ross, *The Fountain and the Furnace: The Way of Tears and Fire* (New York: Paulist Press, 1987), 80.

4. Arthur Miller, *After the Fall: A Play in Two Acts* (New York: Penguin, 1964), 3.

5. As Hans Frei put it, doctrine is not so much the meaning of the story, but instead the story is the meaning of the doctrine; doctrines draw us back into the Bible's story (*Types of Christian Theology* [New Haven, CT: Yale University Press, 1992], 126).

6. For this analogy I am indebted to David Steinmetz and his paper "Last Things First" in *On Interpretation Studies in Culture, Law and the Sacred* (University of Wisconsin, 2002).

7. Quoted in Robert W. Jenson, *Systematic Theology,* vol. 2. *The Works of God* (New York: Oxford University Press, 1999), 14.

8. Anselm, *Cur Deus Homo,* iii, in *A Scholastic Miscellany: Anselm to Ockham,* trans. Eugene R. Fairweather (New York: Macmillan, 1970), 104. See Jenson, *Systematic Theology*, vol. 1, 49.

9. Daniel W. Hardy and David F. Ford, *Praising and Knowing God* (Philadelphia: Westminster Press, 1985), 1.

10. Quoted and discussed in Rowan Williams, *The Wound of Knowledge* (Cambridge: Cowley, 1990), 78.

11. Dante, *Paradise*, xxxiii, in *The Portable Dante,* trans. Mark Musa (New York: Penguin, 1995), 121ff.

12. Alice Walker, *The Color Purple* (New York: Harcourt Brace Jovanovich, 1982), 167f.

13. As Karl Menninger suggested in his bestselling book *Whatever Became of Sin?* (New York: Hawthorn, 1973).

14. Douglas John Hall, *Professing the Faith: Christian Theology in a North American Context* (Minneapolis: Fortress Press, 1993), 254; his full discussion of these paradigms is superb.

15. Hobbes, *Leviathan* (London: Andrew Crooke, 1651) I.13; see Plato, *Gorgias* 493b.

16. Dante, *Paradise* IV. 124–26, 413.

17. C. S. Lewis, *The Weight of Glory,* ed. Walter Hooper (New York: Macmillan, 1980), 26. Augustine noted that in sin we "desert the best and highest goods, which are you, O Lord our God, and your truth and your law" (*Confessions* [n. 22] II. 5.10, 71).

18. Luther, *Large Catechism,* 2–3. Paul Tillich, from a totally different angle, suggested that faith is our "ultimate concern" and that our god is whatever we are finally passionate about, devoted to. An idol, therefore, is an object of our ultimate

concern that is not itself ultimate. His parade example is patriotism, but the possibilities are endless. Calvin was right when he said the human soul is an endlessly working factory of idols. See Tillich, *The Dynamics of Faith* (New York: Harper & Bros., 1957), 1.

19. From "Strength to Love," in *A Testament of Hope: The Essential Writings and Speeches of Martin Luther King, Jr.*, ed. James Washington (San Francisco: Harper-SanFrancisco, 1986), 508.

20. Martin Buber said that "the lie is the specific evil that the human race has introduced into nature" (*Good and Evil* [New York: Macmillan, 1952], 7).

21. See Augustine, *Confessions* VIII.5.10, trans. John K. Ryan (Garden City, NY: Image, 1960), 188. In *Confessions* II.4.9, 70, he said, "Foul was the evil, and I loved it. I loved my fault itself."

22. Barry Schwartz, *The Battle for Human Nature: Science, Morality and Modern Life* (New York: W. W. Norton, 1986),164.

23. Douglas John Hall, *Lighten Our Darkness: Toward an Indigenous Theology of the Cross* (Philadelphia: Westminster Press, 1976), 101.

24. Ernest Becker, *The Denial of Death* (New York: Free Press, 1973), ix.

25. Fyodor Dostoevsky, *The Brothers Karamazov*, trans. Andrew H. MacAndrew (New York: Bantam, 1970), 295.

26. Jürgen Moltmann, *The Crucified God*, trans. R. A. Wilson and John Bowden (Minneapolis: Fortress Press, 1993), 223. And Thomas Merton, *New Seeds of Contemplation* (New York: New Directions, 1961), 15, says, "Too often the conventional conception of 'God's will' as a sphinx-like and arbitrary force bearing down upon us with implacable hostility, leads men to lose faith in a God they cannot find it possible to love. Such a view of the divine will drive human weakness to despair."

27. Nicholas Berdyaev, *Spirit and Reality* (New York: Scribner's, 1946), 106, wrote, "Evil and suffering exist because freedom exists. Because freedom exists, God himself suffers and is crucified. The divine love and sacrifice are God's answer to the mystery of freedom wherein evil and suffering have their origin. Divine love and sacrifice are likewise freedom."

28. Barbara Brown Taylor, "God's Daring Plan," in *Bread of Angels* (Cambridge, MA: Cowley, 1997), 34f.

29. A point profoundly explored by W. H. Vanstone, *The Stature of Waiting* (London: Darton, Longman & Todd, 1982).

30. Douglas John Hall, *Lighten our Darkness* (n. 24), 119: "The true theology . . . is one that discerns the presence of the omnipotent God, not in manifestations of power and glory, whether in nature or history, but on the contrary in the midst of peril and uncertainty and suffering. In short, he seems altogether absent."

31. Anselm, *Cur Deus Homo*, xviii, in *A Scholastic Miscellany*, (n. 9) 176.

32. Abelard, "Exposition of Romans," in *A Scholastic Miscellany*, (n. 9), 283.

33. The third consideration of the most holy stigmata, in *St. Francis of Assisi: Writings and Early Biographies; English Omnibus of the Sources for the Life of St. Francis*, ed. Marion Habig, trans. Raphael Brown (Chicago: Franciscan Herald

Press, 1973), 1448, discussed more fully in my *Conversations with Saint Francis* (Nashville: Abingdon Press, 2007).

34. Jürgen Moltmann, *The Way of Jesus Christ, Christology in Messianic Dimensions*, trans. Margaret Kohl (Minneapolis: Fortress Press, 1993), 222.

35. Basil, "On the Holy Spirit," 16.38, in *Nicene and Post-Nicene Fathers*, vol. 8, trans. Bloomfield Jackson (Edinburgh: T.&T. Clark, 1905), 23f.

36. *Hildegard of Bingen: Mystical Writings*, ed. Fiona Bowie and Oliver Davies (New York: Crossroad, 1990), 118. For more on the Spirit, see my *The Kiss of God: Twenty-seven Lessons on the Holy Spirit* (Nashville: Abingdon Press, 2004).

Chapter 7: Christian Life and Ethics

1. James Wm. McClendon, *Biography as Theology: How Life Stories Can Remake Today's Theology*, 2nd ed. (Philadelphia: Trinity Press Int., 1990), viii.

2. Walter Lowrie, *A Short Life of Kierkegaard* (Princeton, NJ: Princeton University Press, 1942), 235f.

3. Robertson Davies, *A Mixture of Frailties* (Ontario: Penguin Group, 2006), 228.

4. Modern people resort to "conscience" as an arbiter in ethics, but this is not a biblical concept. Oliver O'Donovan (*Resurrection and Moral Order: An Outline for Evangelical Ethics*, 2nd ed. [Grand Rapids: Eerdmans, 1994], 116) has a thoughtful discussion of what is problematical about conscience. The formation of what we call "conscience" depends on our upbringing and culture, and does not seem in the least to be universally consistent. Aquinas asked whether an errant conscience creates an obligation, or whether an errant conscience constitutes an excuse. The ultimate problem is that conscience is in the self, and relying on the self is counterproductive. "Moral freedom can never be established on a basis of self-sufficiency and independence of the world" (120).

5. Maggie Ross, *The Fountain and the Furnace: The Way of Tears and Fire* (New York: Paulist Press, 1987), 80.

6. Dietrich Bonhoeffer, *Letters and Papers from Prison*, ed. Eberhard Bethge (New York: Macmillan, 1971), 361.

7. Nicholas Lash, "Performing the Scriptures," in *Theology on the Way to Emmaus* (London: SCM, 1986), 42.

8. Samuel Wells, *Improvisation: The Drama of Christian Ethics* (Grand Rapids: Brazos, 2004).

9. *Fioretti* VII, in *Little Flowers, Legends and Lauds,* ed. Otto Karrer, trans. N. Wydenbruck (London: Sheed & Ward, 1947), 183; and "The Life of St. Francis by Thomas of Celano," in *Francis of Assisi: Early Documents*, vol. 1: *The Saint*, ed. Regis J. Armstrong, Wayne Hellmann, and William J. Short (New York: New City, 1999), 283.

10. I have retold these and other stories about Francis in *Conversations with Saint Francis* (Nashville: Abingdon Press, 2008).

11. From Luther's early *Operationes in Psalmos*, cited in relation to the Heidelberg Catechism by Gerhard Forde, *On Being a Theologian of the Cross: Reflections on Luther's Heidelberg Disputation, 1578* (Grand Rapids: Eerdmans, 1997), 64.

12. Ross, *The Fountain and the Furnace*, 71.

13. Aleksandr I. Solzhenitsyn, *The Gulag Archipelago*, trans. Thomas P. Whitney (New York: Harper & Row, 1973), 130. This passage is wisely cited by Joel Marcus in *Mark 9–16*, Anchor Bible 27B (New York: Doubleday, 2009).

14. Natan Sharansky, *Fear No Evil*, trans. Stefani Hoffman (New York: Random House, 1988), 229. The next quotation is from p. 423.

15. Richard Dawkins, *The Selfish Gene*, 2nd ed. (Oxford: Oxford University Press, 1989), v. 2.

16. Thomas Merton, *New Seeds of Contemplation*, (New York: New Directions, 1961), 35.

17. From the first edition of *The Epistle to the Romans*, quoted by Timothy Gorringe in *Karl Barth: Against Hegemony* (Oxford: Clarendon, 1999), 41. Augustine (*Confessions*, ed. and trans. John K. Ryan [Garden City, NY: Image, 1960], III.1.2) put it like this: "There was a hunger hidden in me for the food that nourishes the soul, for you yourself, my God. Yet in that hunger I did not seek the indicated food."

18. Søren Kierkegaard, *Works of Love*, trans. Howard and Edna Hong (New York: Harper & Row, 1962), 34.

19. Dawkins, *The Selfish Gene* (n. 13), 2f., 200f. Aristotle, another outsider to Christianity, taught (*Nicomachean Ethics*, 1095–97) that we must learn to desire the right things, to take pleasure in what is good; the goal is not to satisfy desires, but to reach toward the satisfaction of being good. To him, genuine pleasure requires virtue, and only more paltry, vaporous pleasures are available without virtue—human nature not just given, but achieved.

20. As suggested and cleverly analyzed in M. Douglas Meeks, *God the Economist: The Doctrine of God and Political Economy* (Minneapolis: Fortress Press, 1989), 20ff.

21. Richard Foster, *Celebration of Discipline: The Path to Spiritual Growth*, rev. ed. (San Francisco: Harper & Row, 1988), 56.

22. Dietrich Bonhoeffer, *Psalms: The Prayer Book of the Bible*, trans. James H. Burtness (Minneapolis: Augsburg Publishing House, 1970), 9–10; the next two quotations are from 11 and 14f.

23. An eloquent book on the wonder of the Sabbath is Christopher D. Ringwald, *A Day Apart* (New York: Oxford University, 2007).

24. Thomas Merton, *Spiritual Direction and Meditation* (Wheathampstead, U.K.: Anthony Clarke, 1975), 85.

25. Henri Nouwen, *The Return of the Prodigal Son: A Story of Homecoming* (new York: Image, 1994), 85f.

26. Probingly discussed by L. Gregory Jones, *Embodying Forgiveness: A Theological Analysis* (Grand Rapids: Eerdmans, 1995).

27. In an interview with Robert Coles, *Dorothy Day: A Radical Devotion* (Reading, MA: Addison-Wesley, 1987), 28.

28. Mother Teresa, *My Life for the Poor,* ed. José Luis González-Balado and Janet N. Playfoot (San Francisco: Harper & Row, 1985), 15–16.

29. Robert McAfee Brown, *Gustavo Gutiérrez* (Atlanta: John Knox Press, 1980), 29.

30. *Luther's Works* (Philadelphia: Muhlenberg Press, 1960), vol. 3, 81f.

31. Quoted with shrewd discussion by Alasdair MacIntyre in his Gifford Lectures at Edinburgh, *Three Rival Versions of Moral Enquiry* (Notre Dame, IN: University of Notre Dame, 1994), 35.

32. Jim Wallis, *The Soul of Politics: Beyond 'Religious Right' and 'Secular Left'* (New York: Harvest, 1995).

33. Alasdair MacIntyre, *After Virtue: A Study in Moral Theory,* 2nd ed. (Notre Dame, IN: University of Notre Dame Press, 1984), 69. For a provocative, insightful analysis of "rights" and American culture, see Mary Ann Glendon, *Rights Talk: The Impoverishment of Political Discourse* (New York: Free Press, 1991).

34. Stanley Hauerwas, *A Community of Character: Toward a Constructive Christian Social Ethic* (Notre Dame, IN: University of Notre Dame Press, 1981), 195, writes, "What the young properly demand is an account of life and the initiation into a community that makes intelligible why their interest in sex should be subordinated to other interests. What they, and we, demand is the lure of an adventure that captures the imagination sufficiently that conquest means more than the sexual possession of another."

35. Anne Sebba, *Mother Teresa: Beyond the Image* (New York: Doubleday, 1997), 100f.

36. Alfred North Whitehead, *Process and Reality* (New York: Macmillan, 1929), 520.

37. James Washington, ed., *A Testament of Hope: The Essential Writings and Speeches of Martin Luther King, Jr.* (San Francisco: HarperSanFrancisco, 1986), 225.

Chapter 8: The Church

1. Thomas Merton, *New Seeds of Contemplation,* (New York: New Directions, 1961), 142.

2. Lorraine Hansberry, *A Raisin in the Sun* (New York: Random House, 1959), 36.

3. Avery Dulles, *Models of the Church* (New York: Doubleday, 1987).

4. H. Richard Niebuhr, *Christ and Culture* (New York: Harper & Bros., 1951).

5. Chiara Frugoni notes what was novel about Francis: "It was not that the church did not help the needy and distressed in his time. But it had never put itself in question as a privileged structure. It had never departed from its certainties or its established positions. By the conditions in which they lived, their culture, the

guarantee of a solid well-being, the clergy maintained between themselves and the host of the disinherited a clear frontier which could not be crossed" (*Francis of Assisi: A Life* [New York: Continuum, 1999], 46).

6. Frederick Buechner, *The Clown in the Belfry* (San Francisco: Harper, 1992), 158.

7. W. H. Vanstone, *Love's Endeavour, Love's Expense: The Response of Being to the Love of God* (London: Darton, Longman & Todd, 1977), 109.

8. Stanislao Loffreda, *Recovering Capharnaum*, 2nd ed. (Jerusalem: Franciscan Printing Press, 1993).

9. Jerome Murphy-O'Connor, *St. Paul's Corinth: Texts and Archaeology* (Collegeville, MN: Liturgical Press, 1983), 163–68.

10. Jürgen Moltmann, *The Source of Life: The Holy Spirit and the Theology of Life*, trans. Margaret Kohl (Minneapolis: Fortress Press, 1997), 109.

11. Cicero and Livy had used this image, usually to rein in rebellious forces, urging malcontents to accept their lot. For Paul the "body" image is more hopeful. See Dale Martin, *The Corinthian Body* (New Haven, CT: Yale University Press, 1995).

12. C. S. Lewis, "Membership," in *The Weight of Glory*, ed. Walter Hooper (New York: Macmillan, 1980), 110.

13. Anne Frank, *The Diary of a Young Girl*, trans. B. M. Mooyaart-Doubleday (New York: Bantam, 1967), 3.

14. Well discussed in Paul J. Wadell, *Friendship and the Moral Life* (Notre Dame, IN: University of Notre Dame Press, 1989).

15. John Wesley, "The Rules of the United Societies," in *John Wesley*, ed. Albert C. Outler (New York: Oxford University Press, 1964), 178.

16. Søren Kierkegaard, *Works of Love*, trans. Howard and Edna Hong (New York: Harper & Row, 1962), 113.

17. "On the Councils and the Church," in *Luther's Works*, vol. 41 (Concordia & Fortress, 1955), 148–68, excerpted with accompanying essays in *Marks of the Body of Christ*, ed. Carl E. Braaten and Robert W. Jenson (Grand Rapids: Eerdmans, 1999).

18. As put so wonderfully by Robert Jenson, "Catechesis for Our Time," in *Marks of the Body of Christ*, 138.

19. Jean Vanier suggests that "the Church has two sorts . . . those who know how to conserve those traditions come down to us. . . . But there must also be those who have primarily at their heart the salvation of their fellows and are always trying to find new ways to make the message more living. . . . And in the designs of Jesus these two groups will always make each other suffer" (quoted in Kathryn Spink, *Jean Vanier and L'Arche: A Communion of Love* [New York: Crossroad, 1991], 28).

20. T. S. Eliot, "Choruses from *The Rock*," VI, lines 17ff.

21. O'Donovan, *Resurrection and Moral Order: An Outline for Evangelical Ethics*, 2nd ed. (Grand Rapids: Eerdmans, 1994), 171.

22. Amos Wilder, "Electric Chimes or Rams' Horns," in *Grace Confounding* (Philadelphia: Fortress Press, 1972), 13.

23. Clarissa Stuart Davidson, *God's Man: The Story of Pastor Niemoeller* (New York: Ives Washburn, 1959), 59.

24. Calvin, *Institutes,* 4.1.9, ed. John T. McNeill, trans. Ford Lewis Battles (Philadelphia: Westminster Press), 1023.

25. "The Holy and Blessed Sacrament of Baptism," in *Luther's Works,* vol. 35, (Philadelphia: Muhlenburg Press, 1960), 34–36.

26. Søren Kierkegaard, *Attack Upon "Christendom"*, trans. Walter Lowrie (Princeton, NJ: Princeton University Press, 1968), 205. Kierkegaard was just as biting in his satire on the second sacrament: "It is a tradesman. And preferably a tradesman ought to have the religion which prevails in the land. So two or four times a year this man puts on his best clothes and goes to communion. Up comes a priest who jumps up when he sees a 'blue banknote.' Thereupon the priest celebrates the Holy Communion, from which the tradesman, or rather both tradesmen (the priest and the honest citizen), return home to their customary way of life, only that one of them (the priest) cannot be said to return home to his customary way of life, for in fact he had never left it, but rather had been functioning as a tradesman. And this is what one dares to offer to God under the name of the Sacrament of the Lord's Supper. . . . It was at the Last Supper that Christ met for the last time before His death with His disciples, who also were consecrated to death or to the possibility of death if they truly followed Him. . . . And now the solemnity is this: to live before and after in complete worldliness—and then a ceremony. However, for good reasons the priests take care not to enlighten people about . . . the obligation it imposes. Their whole business is based upon living off of the fact that others are sacrificed, their Christianity is, to receive sacrifices. If it were proposed to them that they themselves should be sacrificed, they would regard it as a strange and unchristian demand, conflicting violently with the wholesome doctrine of the New Testament, which they would prove with such colossal learning that the span of life of no individual man would suffice for studying all this through" (206f.).

27. Jürgen Moltmann, *The Church in the Power of the Spirit*, trans. Margaret Kohl (Minneapolis: Fortress Press, 1993), 245.

28. These words are the theme of my book *Yours Are the Hands of Christ: The Practice of Faith* (Nashville: Upper Room Books, 1999). The last chapter concludes with this prayer from Lancelot Andrewes:

> Lord Jesus, I give you my hands to do your work.
> I give you my feet to go your way.
> I give you my eyes to see as you do.
> I give you my tongue to speak your words.
> I give you my mind that you may think in me.
> I give you my spirit that you may pray in me.
> Above all, I give you my heart that you may love in me, your Father, and
>   all humankind.

I give you my whole self that you may grow in me,

So that it is you, Lord Jesus,

Who live and work and pray in me.

Evelyn Underhill, *The Ways of the Spirit* (New York: Crossroad, 1990), 101.

29. Chesterton, *St. Francis of Assisi* (Garden City, NY: Image, 1957), 47.

30. Karl Barth, *The Epistle to the Romans*, trans. Edwyn C. Hoskyns (London: Oxford University Press, 1968), 407.

31. Oscar Romero, *The Violence of Love*, trans. James R. Brockman (Farmington, PA: Plough, 1998), 29–30.

32. Jim Wallis, *The Soul of Politics: A Practical and Prophetic Vision for Change* (New York: New Press, 1994), xvii.

33. While division within Christendom is evil, a certain indication that Christians clearly don't have their act together, there is a more hopeful "spin" many may wish to place on the hodgepodge of denominations, including those who say they aren't denominations. Division may be used by God to function as a surprisingly beautiful expression of what it means to be the body of Christ. Usually we apply the image of "the body" to a congregation, but perhaps this metaphor can help us celebrate the curious fact of divergent denominations. Pentecostals are not like the Presbyterians, and AMEs are not like the Catholics—but yet they are very much alike, and they certainly need each other. All denominations strive with resolute energy to follow Christ. Each one has a different angle on the multifaceted orb that is the kingdom of God. The Baptists know the centrality of the Bible. The Quakers embrace the need for silence. Methodists try to engage social issues. The Catholics embody the rich tradition of the faith and the need for saints. The nondenominational denominations creatively reach people wary of the encrustations of churchiness. Mennonites are humble, Presbyterians use their brains, and the AME Zions can outsing us all. We have a choice. We can choose rancor, passing judgment on one another, trumpeting our superiority, suspiciously eyeing those who think differently. Or we can decide we are part of a bigger body, with our own peculiar contribution to make to the whole. Surely God calls us to be a body, going in every way conceivable after our real competition, which is never another church, but rather that many-headed monster of cynicism, hollowness, violence, greed, hedonism, selfishness, disbelief. Yes, it's embarrassing that we have black churches and white churches, wealthy churches and poor churches, great big churches and little tiny churches. But our dream is that in our crazed variations we will be able to counter the discomfort of those who are a little hesitant by saying, "There is a place for you." Surely God calls us to stay at the table together and learn from each other. To be the body of Christ in this way requires humility. No gang of mere mortals has it all figured out, and they won't next year either. But we need not water down what we believe or seek the lowest common denominator. To stay at the table requires, and enables, tenacity. Each one of us is on to something important. We mainliners who are stiffly fixed in our pews need a little liberation from the Pentecostals, so that we too can show a little emo-

tion and move, if only a little bit. The evangelicals want to save souls, while some of the more liberal groups want to administer medicine and food. Surely both are needed. Independent congregations can teach us all to take initiative, while connectional churches with bishops and even a pope can expand our vision and help us realize we are part of something bigger, that we in fact have in common the only thing that really matters.

34. Quoted with admiration by Dorothy Day, *The Long Loneliness* (New York: HarperOne, 1981), 150.

35. Barth, *The Epistle to the Romans* (n. 30), 375, 416.

36. Karl Barth, *Dogmatics in Outline*, trans. G. T. Thomson (New York: Harper & Row, 1959), 144–45.

37. Augustine, *Retractiones*, II.18 (44).

Chapter 9: Eschatology

1. Jean Daniélou, *The Lord of History: Reflections on the Inner Meaning of History*, trans. Nigel Abercrombie (London: Longmans, 1958), 352.

2. Douglas John Hall, *Confessing the Faith* (Minneapolis: Fortress Press, 1996), 476, wrote that "eschatology is not about what people naturally think of when they hear a term like 'last things'; it is about everything. . . . Eschatology is not 'a doctrine' among doctrines, but a dimension of every other doctrinal area. Without this dimension they all—theology, Christology, anthropology, ecclesiology, and the rest—become flat and one-dimensional: they do not live."

3. J. Stevenson, ed., *A New Eusebius* (London: SPCK, 1957), 21.

4. Guy Gaucher, *The Story of a Life: St. Thérèse of Lisieux* (San Francisco: HarperSanFrancisco, 1987), 146; the next quotation is from p. 197.

5. Christopher Lasch, *The True and Only Heaven: Progress and Its Critics* (New York: W. W. Norton, 1991), 81. Henri Nouwen, *Here and Now* (New York: Crossroad, 1994), 33, wrote: "While optimism makes us live as if someday soon things will go better for us, hope frees us from the need to predict the future and allows us to live in the present, with the deep trust that God will never leave us alone but will fulfill the deepest desires of our heart. When I trust deeply that today God is truly with me and holds me safe in a divine embrace, guiding every one of my steps, I can let go of my anxious need to know how tomorrow will look, or what will happen next month or next year. I can be fully where I am and pay attention to the many signs of God's love within and around me."

6. James Brockman, *Romero: A Life* (Maryknoll, NY: Orbis Books, 1989), 234, 248.

7. Reinhold Niebuhr, *The Irony of American History* (New York: Charles Scribner's Sons, 1952), 63; Jürgen Moltmann, *Theology of Hope* (New York: Harper & Row, 1967), 32.

8. Ida Friederike Görres, *The Hidden Face: A Study of St. Thérèse of Lisieux*, trans. Richard and Clara Winston (New York: Pantheon, 1959), 308f. Battling the

anguish of tuberculosis, she wrote, "My heaven is to smile at this God I adore when
he is hiding and testing my love" (Gaucher, *Story of a Life* [n. 4], 163).

9. Annie Dillard, *Pilgrim at Tinker Creek* (New York: Harper & Row, 1974),
178.

10. J. Christiaan Beker, *Paul the Apostle: The Triumph of God in Life and Thought*
(Philadelphia: Fortress Press, 1980), 155.

11. Moltmann, *Theology of Hope* (n. 7), 144f.

12. Norman Cohn, *The Pursuit of the Millennium*, rev. ed. (New York: Oxford
University Press, 1970), 52 et passim.

13. When Revelation reveals the name of the evil leader as 666, the author is
inviting readers to assess names of candidates to see who fits. The wicked one in
question surely is the slain emperor Nero. His throat was slit (either by exasperated senators or by his own hand) on June 9 of the year 68—but rumors began to
circulate that he was not really dead, that he was hiding in Parthia, that he was
planning an invasion to devastate the Mediterranean world. The historians Taci-
tus and Suetonius tell us about pretenders who emerged, claiming to be Nero
revived. One was a slave from Pontus, a crazed musician like Nero himself. As it
turns out, Nero's name, as the Jews would have known it, was QSR NRWN (Caesar Nero), and the numerical value of QSR NRWN is exactly 666. Additional support for this reading comes from the fact that when the Bible was first rendered
into Latin, the translators altered the number to 616, since the last N was dropped
in Latin. John was writing to people who very much feared the Nero rumor, that
the kind of vicious persecution begun during his brutal reign was about to be
revived. Revelation's message was that, yes, there would be trouble; there would
always be Nero-type figures around (like Emperor Domitan, as they were discov-
ering) who would claim to be divine and would demand worship, and persecution
would follow. But God is not mocked; God is in control, and bogus powers like
Nero and Domitian would eventually be undone, and Christians would live eternally with God.

14. John Henry Newman, "Waiting for Christ," in *Parochial and Plain Sermons*,
vol. 6 (San Francisco: Ignatius, 1987), 1326.

15. Robertson Davies, *Fifth Business* (New York: Penguin, 1970), 46.

16. Dietrich Bonhoeffer, *The Cost of Discipleship*, trans. R. H. Fuller, rev. ed.
(New York: Macmillan, 1959), 47.

17. Karl Heim, *The Transformation of the Scientific World View* (New York:
Harper & Bros., 1953), 21.

18. Jürgen Moltmann, *The Coming of God: Christian Eschatology*, trans. Margaret Kohl (Minneapolis: Fortress Press, 1996), 250f.

19. This construct is typically associated with John Calvin, and yet a majority
of theologians since Augustine have agreed. Calvin called this decree "horrible,"
although many argue that the Latin *horribile* has the connotation of awesome.

20. Karl Barth, *Church Dogmatics* (Edinburgh: T.&T. Clark, 1960), II/2, 162f,
319, 749.

21. C. S. Lewis, *The Weight of Glory*, ed. Walter Hooper (New York: Macmillan, 1980), 18.

22. Hans Urs von Balthasar, *Dare We Hope "That All Men Be Saved"?* trans. David Kipp and Lothar Krauth (San Francisco: Ignatius, 1988), 35.

23. Origen, *Peri Archon* I.6.1.

24. Thomas Merton, *New Seeds of Contemplation* (New York: New Directions, 1961), 65.

25. Von Balthasar, *Dare We Hope* (n. 22), 53f, n. 10.

26. C. S. Lewis, *The Great Divorce* (New York Macmillan, 1946), 124.

27. Ibid., 60, 69, 72. Later he writes, "Every shutting up of the creature within the dungeon of its own mind—is, in the end, Hell."

28. Augustine, *City of God* XXI.17.

29. Calvin, *Institutes* 3.24, ed. John T. McNeill, trans. Ford Lewis Battles (Philadelphia: Westminster Press, 1960).

30. Origen, *On First Principles* I.6.1, trans. G. W. Butterworth (New York: Harper & Row, 1966), 52.

31. George A. Lindbeck, *The Nature of Doctrine: Religion and Theology in a Postliberal Age* (Philadelphia: Westminster Press, 1984), 54.

32. *Lumen gentium* 16, in *The Documents of Vatican II*, ed. Walter M. Abbott (New York: America Press, 1966), 35.

33. As told in Elie Wiesel, *All Rivers Run to the Sea: Memoirs* (New York: Knopf, 1995), 354f.

Epilogue

1. A. Whitney Brown, *The Big Picture: An American Commentary* (New York: HarperPerennial, 1991), 12.

2. Jenson, *Systematic Theology*, vol. 2, *The Works of God* (New York: Oxford University Press, 1999), 346.

Index